"An outstanding achievement, this book describes the practice of ethnographic fieldwork from a 'pedagogy of exemplification' perspective. Showcased are the contrasting constraints and opportunities of strikingly different field sites. From competitive boxing, preschooling, and senior activism, to migratory encampments, juvenile detention, and imprisonment, the reader comes to understand the many things it can mean *in situ* for the working ethnographer to discover and document social worlds."

Malin Åkerström, *Professor Emeritus, Department of Sociology, Lund University, Sweden*

"This volume demonstrates how fieldwork is crafted in site-specific settings. In this sense, ethnography cannot be reduced to a set of techniques or to overblown theories. Written by a distinguished set of authors, I can think of no better introduction to ethnography for novices, while seasoned ethnographers will find much to enjoy."

David Silverman, *Professor Emeritus, Department of Sociology, Goldsmiths' College, University of London, UK*

"Amir B. Marvasti and Jaber F. Gubrium, two highly accomplished and respected ethnographers, have assembled an edited collection that describes the ontology and practices of a mature craft of ethnographic fieldwork. Chapters demonstrate the importance of site-specificity, imagined subjectivity, and procedural tolerance regardless of whether the focus is youth detention centers in Sweden, migrant camps in Sierra Leone, prisons in India, or Montessori pre-schools in the United States. The book does an important service by moving beyond the typical, unworkable recipe-like renditions of the craft."

Donileen R. Loseke, *Professor Emeritus, University of South Florida, USA*

CRAFTING ETHNOGRAPHIC FIELDWORK

Through a series of case studies, this book provides an understanding of the practice of ethnographic fieldwork in a variety of contexts, from everyday settings to formal institutions. Demonstrating that ethnography is best viewed as a series of site-specific challenges, it showcases ethnographic fieldwork as ongoing analytic engagement with concrete social worlds. From engagements with boxing and nightlife to preschooling and migratory encampments, portrayed is a process that is anything but a set of pre-packaged challenges and hurdles of simple-minded procedural tropes such as entrée, rapport, and departure. Instead, ethnography emerges as what it has been from its beginnings: a rough-and-ready analytic matter of seeking understanding in unrecognized and diverse fields of interaction. *Crafting Ethnographic Fieldwork* will appeal to scholars and students across the social sciences with interests in the practice of participant observation and related questions of research methodology.

Amir B. Marvasti is Professor of Sociology at Penn State Altoona, USA. He is the author of *Qualitative Research in Sociology* and the co-editor of *Researching Social Problems, The Sage Handbook of Interview Research* and *Doing Qualitative Research: A Comprehensive Guide.*

Jaber F. Gubrium is Professor Emeritus of Sociology at the University of Missouri, USA. He is the co-author of *Constructing the Life Course* and the co-editor of *Postmodern Interviewing, Aging and Everyday Life* and *Qualitative Research Practice.*

Routledge Advances in Research Methods

Silences, Neglected Feelings, and Blind-Spots in Research Practice
Kathy Davis, Janice Irvine

Social Causation and Biographical Research
Philosophical, Theoretical and Methodological Arguments
Giorgos Tsiolis, Michalis Christodoulou

Participatory Case Study Work
Approaches, Authenticity and Application in Ageing Studies
Sion Williams, John Keady

Behind the Scenes in Social Research
How Practical and Personal Matters Affect a Project
Herbert J. Rubin

Crafting Ethnographic Fieldwork
Sites, Selves, and Social Worlds
Edited by Amir B. Marvasti and Jaber F. Gubrium

CRAFTING ETHNOGRAPHIC FIELDWORK

Sites, Selves, and Social Worlds

Edited by Amir B. Marvasti and Jaber F. Gubrium

LONDON AND NEW YORK

Designed cover image: © Getty Images

First published 2023
by Routledge
4 Park Square, Milton Park, Abingdon, Oxon OX14 4RN

and by Routledge
605 Third Avenue, New York, NY 10158

Routledge is an imprint of the Taylor & Francis Group, an informa business

British Library Cataloguing-in-Publication Data
A catalogue record for this book is available from the British Library

Library of Congress Cataloging-in-Publication Data
Names: Marvasti, Amir B., 1966– editor. | Gubrium, Jaber F., editor.
Title: Crafting ethnographic fieldwork: sites, selves, and social worlds / edited by Amir B. Marvasti and Jaber F. Gubrium.
Description: Milton Park, Abingdon, Oxon; New York, NY: Routledge, 2023. | Series: Routledge advances in research methods | Includes bibliographical references and index.
Identifiers: LCCN 2022051027 (print) | LCCN 2022051028 (ebook) | ISBN 9781032217802 (hardback) | ISBN 9781032230009 (paperback) | ISBN 9781003275121 (ebook)
Subjects: LCSH: Sociology—Research. | Ethnology—Research. | Sociology—Fieldwork. | Ethnology—Fieldwork.
Classification: LCC HM571.C73 2023 (print) | LCC HM571 (ebook) | DDC 301/.072—dc23/eng/20221101
LC record available at https://lccn.loc.gov/2022051027
LC ebook record available at https://lccn.loc.gov/2022051028

ISBN: 978-1-032-21780-2 (hbk)
ISBN: 978-1-032-23000-9 (pbk)
ISBN: 978-1-003-27512-1 (ebk)

DOI: 10.4324/9781003275121

Typeset in Times New Roman
by Apex CoVantage, LLC

In memory of Monteith College Professors Sally Whelan Cassidy and Paule Verdet, educational visionaries of everyday life, its sites, selves, and social worlds.

CONTENTS

ABOUT THE EDITORS

Amir B. Marvasti is Professor of Sociology at Penn State Altoona, USA. His research focuses on identity management in everyday encounters and institutional settings. Using a symbolic interactionist framework, he approaches culture, discourse, and social institutions as interrelated and ongoing practices that collectively shape the self in a social context. His empirical research in this area examines how people (e.g., the homeless) present themselves to others, particularly when required to explain their backgrounds and intentions; and how their self-presentations are related to whether they are helped or accepted by others. Extending his interest in identity management to the subfield of the sociology of emotions, his current research looks at how people narrate their emotions in ways that reinforce gender stereotypes.

Jaber F. Gubrium is Emeritus Professor of Sociology at University of Missouri, USA. The working premise of his research program is that no system of social rules is robust enough to understand its everyday application. Areas of study informed by this are aging and the life course, health and illness, human service organizations, constructions of family, institutional selves, and narrative analysis. Applying a critical constructionism, the goal is to make visible the assemblages of meaning that rationalization erases. Centered on the comparative ethnography of human service settings, he continues to explore and document novelty and pattern in troubles/problems reflexivity within the framework of what Erving Goffman called the "interaction order" and in tandem with a concertedly local brand of Michel Foucault's concept of "discursive practice." Gubrium is also founding and former editor of the *Journal of Aging Studies*.

CONTRIBUTORS

Mahuya Bandyopadhyay is Professor of Sociology at the Indian Institute of Technology, Delhi, India. She is a social anthropologist studying varied manifestations and experiences of the carceral mesh in contemporary urban society. A critical focus on anthropological ways of knowing and the use of ethnographic methods is central to her work. She is currently working on a collaborative research project on prison architecture in India with colleagues from the Department of Design.

Hilde Fiva Buzungu is a social anthropologist with a PhD in social work and social policy. Her research interests are focused on communication in public service provision, language discordance, minoritized languages, and linguistic domination and subordination. In her research, she works primarily with participant observation and qualitative interviews.

Shannon K. Carter is Professor and Associate Chair of Sociology at the University of Central Florida, USA. Her research examines inequalities in reproductive health, illustrating reproductive injustices impacting minoritized groups, and stigmatized practices like breastmilk sharing and breastfeeding in public. Her work is published in journals including Gender & Society, Sociology of Health & Illness, and Sociology of Race & Ethnicity. She is author of *Sharing Milk: Intimacy, Materiality*, and *Bio-Communities of Practice* with Beatriz Reyes-Foster.

Gary Alan Fine is Professor of Sociology at Northwestern University, USA. He received his PhD in social psychology from Harvard University and has received fellowships from the Guggenheim Foundation, the Russell Sage Foundation, the Rockefeller Foundation, the Center for Advanced Study in the Behavioral Sciences, and the Institute for Advanced Study at Princeton. His current research has four distinct streams. He is interested in understanding difficult reputations and problematic collective memories of figures such as Joseph McCarthy, Charles Lindbergh, Warren Harding, and Benedict Arnold.

James A. Holstein is Emeritus Professor of Sociology at Marquette University, USA. His research and teaching interests include social problems, deviance and social control, and research methods. He has published over three dozen books on diverse topics including social problems, mental health and illness, family, the life course, the self, and qualitative research methods.

Hsiao-Chuan Hsia is Professor at the Graduate Institute for Social Transformation Studies, Shih Hsin University, Taipei. She initiated the Chinese programs for marriage migrants in 1995, leading to the establishment of the TransAsia Sisters Association of Taiwan, spearheading the movement for marriage migrants' rights and welfare in Taiwan. She is an active officer of various regional and international organizations, including Asia Pacific Mission for Migrants, Alliance of Marriage Migrants Organizations for Rights and Empowerment, and International Migrants Alliance.

Andrew M. Jefferson is Senior Researcher at DIGNITY—Danish Institute against Torture, Denmark. His research focuses on ethnographies of prisons and prison reform processes in the global south and has featured a range of collaborations with activist organizations engaged in torture prevention, human rights work, and prison reform. He has a long-standing interest in the relationship between confinement and subjectivity and the intersections of knowledge and power.

Tarja Pösö is Professor of Social Work at Tampere University, Finland. She has studied child protection with a variety of interests, methods, and theoretical standpoints for many years and published her work in Finnish and English. The current projects focus on assessment and decision-making of childhood troubles and the selection of "clients" for different organizational paths.

Brittany Presson is a doctoral candidate at the University of Missouri in Columbia, USA, and an instructor at Virginia Tech in Blacksburg, Virginia, USA. Her research focuses on everyday life, identity construction, meaning-making, and qualitative methodology. Research topics include Gold Star Mothers, gold star families, and non-suicidal self-injurers. She has previous publications in the *Journal of Deviant Behavior*, *Researching Social Problems* (book chapter) and *Advances in Autoethnography and Narrative Inquiry* (book chapter).

John C. Pruit is Assistant Professor of Sociology at Stephen F. Austin State University, USA. His research program analyzes talk and interaction in education contexts. In Between Teaching and Caring in the Preschool (2019), Pruit considered preschool teachers' identity work in relation to early childhood education. He has published in journals such as *Journal of Contemporary Ethnography*, *Studies* *in Symbolic Interaction*, and *International Review of Qualitative Research*. His current project is on the college student experience.

Alex Stewart-Psaltis is Senior Lecturer at the School of Sport Science and Physical Activity, University of Bedfordshire, England. Having conducted a 5-year ethnographic study of amateur and professional boxers in England, his central research interests now lie in the examination of cultural and social aspects of the sporting experience. His academic interests and teaching competencies are in the following related areas: the socialization process into and through sport, embodiment and identity formation, sport violence, sporting subcultures, and sport development for change. In a previous life, Alex spent this time split between boxing competitively as an amateur and briefly a professional boxer and backpacking and working his way around the globe.

Beatriz Reyes-Foster is Associate Professor of Anthropology at the University of Central Florida, USA. Her research examines the intersections of health, medicine, and society, particularly the production of health disparities and social inequality. Her foci include mental health, reproduction, coloniality, and gender. She is author of over 20 peer-reviewed academic articles and 2 books, P*sychiatric Encounters: Madness and Modernity in Yucatan, Mexico*, and *Sharing Milk: Intimacy, Materiality, and Bio-Communities of Practice* (with Shannon K. Carter).

James M. Thomas is Associate Professor of Sociology at the University of Mississippi, Broadly, USA. His scholarship centers racism as a socio-historically contingent phenomenon, global in its force, and rooted in the dynamic nexus between ideology and practice. To date, he is author or co-author of 4 book-length monographs and over 20 peer-reviewed journal articles, book chapters, and invited essays on the causes and consequences of race and racism in America and abroad. His scholarship is wide-ranging in its coverage: from comparative and historical analyses of racial formations and racism in Western Europe and in the United States; to theorizing the complex interplay between race, citizenship, and affect along the US–Mexico border; to critical investigations of diversity, equity, and inclusion initiatives on college campuses. He is also co-editor of *Sociology of Race and Ethnicity*, the journal of the American Sociological Association's Section on Racial and Ethnic Minorities.

David Wästerfors is Professor of Sociology at the Department of Sociology, Lund University, Sweden. His research is often focused on interactions, institutions, emotions, and social control. He has completed three projects with ethnographic data from Swedish detention homes (on conflicts, schooling, and violence). At the moment he is working on two other projects, one on accessibility for people with disabilities in urban and digital settings, and another one on people's digital discussions around crime cases.

INTRODUCTION

Contours of the Craft

Jaber F. Gubrium

Culture and society are big concepts, too big to capture increasingly complex, contradictory, and chaotic, even evanescent, forms of everyday life. Exactly the point of departure for ethnographic fieldwork, which is all about the discovery and documentation of social worlds. Delimited and fleeting as social worlds can be, the knowledge captured by the ethnographers in this book is particularistic and sited, realized through field encounters and interaction, which some would ignore as trivial or view as threats to more generalized portrayal. Conversely, intimate in detail, grounded in the everyday, and rendered transparent, knowledge of social worlds can be enormously enlightening.

Centered on ethnographic positioning and related understandings, the book presents first-person accounts of the crafting of fieldwork. Researchers taking a crafting approach to ethnographic fieldwork typically expand everyday identities remit to include identities of place and of living conditions, along with identities of people (cf. Atkinson, 2015; Gubrium & Holstein, 1997; Holstein & Gubrium, 2000; Puddephat et al., 2009; Smith, 1987). The focus is on social worlds discovered in contrasting field sites, from the mundane such as nightlife to the formally organized such as detention centers and prisons. The theme is fieldwork that discovers the grounded realities of social worlds is a practical endeavor, neither led by theoretical abstraction nor filtered through transcendent research steps such as the familiar procedural trope of entrée, trust, rapport, and departure. Rather, site by site, chapters show how the knowledge captured is a complex and varied artifact of situationally conditioned conceptual and methodological practices.

Site-Specificity

The fieldwork in view derives from research conducted by a range of international scholars, from the seasoned to the newly emerging. All have participated in and

DOI: 10.4324/9781003275121-1

observed *in situ* the varied forms of interaction under consideration, presenting their work biographically as a craft engages practice. Numerous introductory textbooks, handbooks, and edited volumes cover field ethics and procedures mostly and sometimes the analysis of ethnographic research results but few if any marry theory and method to practice in the manner presented. Most are how-to books, the specific location, and analytic thereness of ethnography faded into a background of applicable technologies.

As ethnographic conceptualization and method unfold reflexively in field researchers' participant observation, questions of social organization form on two reflexive fronts. One is analytic, ongoing in site-mediated conceptualization, which can be variously naturalistic or constructionist in orientation. The other front is procedural, integral to, and extending beyond the varied *in situ* challenges of ethnographic presence. The aim is to showcase these related fronts, correcting recipe-like formulations bereft of local strategic sensibilities.

The idea of site-specificity is showcased throughout the book, the implication being that no system of analytic rules is robust enough to understand any rule's everyday application. This includes methodological rules, which upon application need to be adapted to site-specific particulars. Collectively, as of necessity, the contributors feature novelty as much as pattern in ethnographic practice and discovery. While they do not advocate a radical abandonment of procedural sensibility, they caution against universalizing tendencies and cookie-cutter applications of concepts and methods.

Imagined Subjectivity

The ethnographies presented in this book are autobiographical in tone, offering engaging stories, or what Margaret Mead (1928), referred to in her introduction *Coming of Age in Samoa* as "good tales." The style of writing adopted bears resemblance to autoethnography but is not a complete imitation of the genre, which itself has evolved. Earlier, references to the concept defined it in a limited way. Writing in 1979, David Hayano suggested the concept referred to instances where "the researchers possess the qualities of often permanent self-identification with a group and full internal membership, as recognized both by themselves and the people of whom they are a part" (p. 100). Recently, the concept has been broadened and applied in a vibrant and reflexive turn (Ellis et al., 2010; Anderson, 2006). Feminists and other researchers on the margins have found the approach useful for hearing and documenting voices that were otherwise suppressed or unheard and for telling their own stories (see Rose, 1996; Smith, 2005).

While autoethnographic in a general sense, rather than focusing on fieldworkers' inner lives the chapters tilt toward empirical out-thereness. The authors present their personal and internal trials and tribulations as pathways, barriers, or resources for grasping the empirical realities of the field rather than an end in themselves. This is in keeping with Carolyn Ellis, T. C. Adams, and Arthur Bochner's general definition of autoethnography as a means to an end, or as the analysis of "personal experience in order to understand cultural experience" (2010, paragraph 1). References to personal characteristics in this book are about their impact on the practice of ethnographic research. As one of the contributors, Tarja Pösö, puts it, "My age—or myself—is not, however, the key issue here but rather the [field] relations it enabled" (see Chapter 5).

Another way to capture the significance of the personal in the book is through the notion of imagined subjectivities. This concept has been discussed in other contexts. For example, Alison Chand (2014) distinguishes the "imagined" and "real" subjectivities of male civilian workers in Scotland during World War II. Despite not being directly involved in the war, some of these men "asserted masculinity by associating their work with the activities of the armed forces" (p. 236). This type of "imagined masculinity" is contrasted with the "real" subjectivity of men who focused on immediate everyday experiences and thus saw themselves as "breadwinners" and "earning a living wage" (p. 236).

Interest in the concept is grounded in the tradition of symbolic interaction. Imagined subjectivities are akin to Charles H. Cooley's (1902) notion of "the looking glass self" or George H. Mead's (1934) self-reflexive "me." Importing the concept into ethnographic research practice serves as an analytic device for better understanding the everyday work of ethnographic research. As the chapters show, the researchers enter the field with images of who their participants are and what role they themselves would occupy in the field. However, the imagined is constantly adapted to the everyday realities of the site, often resulting in reformulations of how the site is viewed and the researcher's place in it. Ethnographic practice involves the continuous comparison of the observed subject with the imagined subject and then textually representing the provisional observations. The practice of doing ethnographic fieldwork is simultaneously a reflexive matter of hypothetically and continually imagining, testing, and exploring the empirical terrain of the social worlds in question. Seen in this light, ethnographers are constantly asking: Who are these subjects we are observing and what is it like to experience life as they do in the circumstances under consideration? What are the contours of experience in being there—in that site—thinking, feeling, and doing as participants go about their lives?

As both participants and observers, ethnographers imagine the answers as much by being there themselves as by formulating empirical questions. The process is filled with imagination—grounded images—constructed in relation to the concrete activities and conditions they observe, experience themselves, or possibly could experience should circumstances permit. Imagined subjectivities are a byproduct of the ongoing and located work of understanding, of placing ourselves in the shoes of the selves and lives in view. The contributors in the book showcase themselves confronting, both conceptually and empirically, the circumstantial field they observed and worked through in developing ethnographic understanding. To put it another way, as argued in David Wästerfor's chapter, ethnographers employ "personalization techniques" or mental exercises as a way of sensitizing themselves to what is going on in the field.

Procedural Tolerance

The idea of "site-specificity" is related to the broader concept of "research reflexivity" (Whitaker & Atkinson, 2021), which applies to all sites of social science methodology, including interviewing (see Gubrium & Holstein, 2002). As Whitaker and Atkinson note, reflexivity is "a pervasive and generic issue in all research and in the social sciences most importantly" (p. 2). They elaborate that there are many types of reflexivity, such as "disciplinary," "methodological," "textual," and "positional" (pp. 2–3), each emphasizing a different facet of research complexity. At the broadest level, "methodological reflexivity" implies that:

> methods create the possibility of research, framing *what* is to be studied, *how* it is to be studied, what will count as a plausible outcome of the research, and *how* it will be evaluated. Issues of method are, therefore, productive in the creation of knowledge, as well as implicitly constraining what knowledge is thinkable.
>
> *(pp. 38–39)*

Adopting an everyday approach, this book highlights the reflexive relationship between ethnographic sitedness and ethnographic research practice. The chapters showcase sites as significant *a priori* and continuing challenges to methodological sensibilities. As indicated by the range of sites considered, the contributors were contacted based on how dissimilar their sites were from each other. Andrew M. Jefferson's chapter, for example, deals with the conduct of fieldwork in "sites" that are situationally tentative, while Mahuya Bandyopadhyay's centers on sites of stable confinement. The questions addressed are similar: How did they navigate the now classic tropes of entry-trust-rapport-departure and degrees of participant observation from "complete participant" to "complete observer" (Adler & Adler, 1987)? Rather than approaching associated procedures as checklists of items that are neatly resolvable and then set aside for the duration, the contributors discuss the ongoing and reflexive practice of crafting their fieldwork in relation to proverbial tropes within specific sites of inquiry. Ethnographic research practices and tropes are constantly adapted in relation to the contingencies of procedure's everyday immediacies.

Relatedly, there is the matter of research ethics. Research ethics are an integral and indispensable part of the ethnographic craft. However, while the general principles can be established in advance, the everyday particulars of research ethics (do's and don'ts, as it were) unfold in specific research sites. The apparent contrast between the "anticipatory" and "unfolding" nature of research ethics has engendered a good deal of discussion and controversy. Critics of the anticipatory model, which is largely informed by bioethics, have argued that its application is incompatible with the emergent contingencies of fieldwork. For example, Sara Delamont and Paul Atkinson note, "Anticipatory consent, individualized participation and predetermined research designs are all repugnant to the conventions and practice of ethnographic fieldwork" (2018, p. 10). Similarly, Martin Hammersley points out that

> the image of the research process built into the rationale for ethical regulation neglects the unavoidable role of relatively autonomous, situated decision-making by researchers: right action cannot be produced by some process of pseudo-calculation; guidelines can only be guidelines not algorithmic rules that govern behavior.
>
> *(2009, p. 215)*

The experiences of the contributors in the field reflect some of these concerns, showing that "research ethics itself [can be viewed] as a socially constituted and situated field" (Ryen, 2011, p. 416; see also Miller-Day 2012). Each ethnography discussed in this book presents its own site-specific challenges. While adhering to the general principles of research ethics, the contributors also had to adapt to site-specific concerns, ranging from their physical safety (as in Mahuya Bandyopadhyay's ethnography of a women's prison) to their emotional well-being (as in David Wästerfors's mental anguish about confinement in a juvenile detention center), to a sense of moral obligation to create positive social change (as in Hsiao-Chuan Hsia's mobilization of "migrant brides" and Reyes-Foster and Carter's attempts to normalize breastfeeding).

Removed from practice, research ethics become routinized, if not ethereal, reducing everyday complexities to orderly but contrived constructs of what they were beforehand. Though artificial, the constructs are elegantly consumable and memorable for a variety of educational and organizational purposes. In contrast, once viewed as foundational matters of human relationships and everyday practice, principles are subject to continual navigation. For example, at a nursing home, the ethnographer can have reasonable rapport with both a resident and his or her children. But as the latter's relationship deteriorates, it may leave the researcher with the need to choose sides, as it were. Thusly, rapport is called into question, requiring reengagement with a predefined "trope." As Brittany Presson's chapter shows, the everyday vicissitudes of rapport challenge the linear conceptualization of this type of relationship-building practice.

Given this diverse ethnographic landscape and the related methodological reflexivity, questioning the logic and practicality of universalized rules, this volume calls for the procedural tolerance of craft to lead the way toward understanding. Methods should be subservient to the novelties of the field, rather than the reverse. Procedural tolerance stands in sharp contrast to methods regimens, which are more pertinent to quantitative data collection and analysis. Site-specific variations in the application of procedures in quantitative circles are something to be "controlled" and "standardized." In contrast, for the purpose of ethnographic research, procedural tolerance provides for emergent "analytic inspiration" (Gubrium & Holstein, 2014).

The chapters in the book offer what can be termed a "pedagogy of exemplification" based on a pragmatist approach that seeks ethnographic insight in proximity to its groundings. Seemingly old-fashioned, the intent is to teach by example. Significant is the growing realization that the conduct of ethnographic fieldwork is mediated by the choice and organization of increasingly diverse research sites, calling for concerted attention to site-specificity. How one secures entry, gains trust, and establishes rapport, and the process of departure are far from matters of goal-attainment, but rather operate and continually unfold in the everyday interactions of distinct field sites, which are now more complex, varied, and fleeting than ever.

Sites and Social Worlds

An important premise of the chapters is that sites are not containers of a fixed set of social interactions and roles but in some degree are always in the making, reflecting and refracting multiple, sometimes competing social worlds. To illustrate this point, consider the following personal reflections on my ethnographic research in a nursing home.

> When I look back at my own ethnographic fieldwork starting in the 1970s, which led to the publication of *Living and Dying at Murray Manor* (Gubrium, 1975), the first ethnography of a nursing home, it is clear in retrospect, although not fully evident at the time conceptually, that the nursing home was rent with contradictory social worlds. If I had been as savvy then as I am now (pardon the plaudits), I might have even documented the narratively-bounded contradictory discourses even within the staff's world of meetings, which I tended to treat as a whole and in opposition to the world of bed-and-body work (aides) and of passing time (residents) on the floors.
>
> I won't go into the many evanescent social worlds that cropped up in my organizational fieldwork. One though was exemplary and usually presented itself across the board toward the end of meetings. I'm still amazed at how deeply performative these were, with the most devoted "care-providing" staff members phenomenologically shifting into different persona, suddenly contributing to "how to put things" and "thinking about the patient census." It was so regular that I amusedly looked forward to when that world-shift would occur, usually flagged by certain phrases such as "wait a bit," "let's think again carefully about this," and "I was wondering." It wasn't hypocrisy, which requires a communicatively-consistent universe. Rather, it flagged the border for the time being of a different social world with its own talk and moral horizons, oriented to organizational consequences rather than institutionalized responsibilities. If anyone (rarely) objected to such ostensible *non sequiturs*, the usual response was something akin to "We're not talking about that now, Harry!." Voila, a semantic social world marked as readily as dogs do fire hydrants—natural and incidental.
>
> Somewhere I described worlds as doing something (grief, excellence, shame, schooling vs nurturing, whatever) together with words/interaction.

(It might have been titled "doing things with words."). Some worlds are tiny and located within or following larger ones, such is that which emerges at the end of a meeting, say, when someone asks, "Ok, how do we want to put that?" This subsequent world is different, often more highly consequential, than the previous one. Other worlds are larger in being peopled with more variegated issues and conditions, such as described in the chapter of *Murray Manor* titled "Top Staff and its World" and the chapter titled "Passing Time." (Chapter contributor Gary Alan Fine is very good at documenting that form of social world; "tiny publics" he's called them.) The same or different individuals can people alternative social worlds, implicating contrasting roles and moral horizons as much as personal characteristics.

Sites and Social Interaction

Site-specificity also has important implications for the ethnographic study of social interaction. Sites, interactions, and social worlds are closely linked concepts, both empirically and analytically reflexive in practice. While they occur together and relate reflexively, they need to be defined distinctly because each varies to a degree in its own rights. Sites vary along structural lines, some being very relaxed, say, such as the proverbial family home, while others such as the detention home being rigid and regimented. The same is true for differences in interaction, from complex to simple, peaceful to aggressive. Social worlds in turn are informed by both sites and interaction. Empirically, for example, when a child says to his or her parents that, "This isn't school, Dad!," he or she is using the social world concept rhetorically to manage or challenge particular strings of social interaction. As such, a leading question of fieldwork in this regard is how the members and ethnographers manage their roles and relations/interactions in sites of contrasting social worlds, which is focal in John C. Pruit's chapter in this book.

To illustrate this point regarding contrasting social worlds evinced in site-specific social interaction, consider the following everyday vignette. It presents a conversation I had while getting a haircut during the time of COVID, in which I (Jay) could be a hypothetical ethnographer who, together with my barber Mason[1]—mid-haircutting—evoke contrasting social worlds in the ordinary give-and-take of the exchange. The site, a barber shop, and the encounter, commonplace chatting, illustrate both their reflexivity and relative independence in practice. Varied sites—schooling, households, workplaces—momentarily mix, their commonplace independence shattered, in the uneasy flux of the referred interaction of an encounter.

Jay: "Well, Nelson, how are things at home with the covid thing and school closing, making it necessary for some parents to home school, right?"

Mason: "No kidding. As you might guess, it ain't a picnic. The kids don't like when I get them to sit down at the desks we bought and do their homework."

Jay: "Yeah, I know what you mean. They think of you as . . ."

Mason: "I'm Dad! That's what they say. Yeah, sure, I am but trying to be teacher. They giggle when I tell them to get to work. Kids think it's funny."

Jay: "Sounds like home's a different world than school."

Mason: "Sure is and I'm just not up to doing it. Wife has an easier time. She doesn't work and she's, well, home to them. [She] can do that better."

Jay: "The problem I suppose is made worse because you even have to deal with the setup, buying desks and that. Don't you wish you had a principal you could send the kids to when they act up?" (Both laugh.)

Mason: Hell, Jay, I have to be the principal and the teacher and Dad, and that don't work when you wanna do the school thing.

Parts and Chapters

This book's substantive chapters fall into three parts. The chapters of Part I, titled "Sites," features the overarching theme of the book. In its first chapter, contributor Alex Stewart-Psaltis, whose early career is situated in the sport of boxing, now considers how the boxing ring can be the ethnographic venue sustaining the viable participant observation of an insider. Deconstructing the notion of "insider ethnography," Stewart-Psaltis charts the development and transformation of his relationship with the research site over a 5-year period. In his words, the chapter chronicles "the ongoing requirement to manage and re-negotiate my boxer/researcher identity as I moved between the disparate social worlds of pugilism and academia" (see Chapter 1). In the chapter following that, contributor David Wästerfors explores how ethnography is carried out in the confined spaces of youth detention centers in Sweden. Wästerfors is particularly interested in the degree to which the researcher can rightfully claim to be experiencing the same social world as the members of the field. In doing so, he carefully analyzes his own experiences of being at once "caged within the institution" and still "enjoying the privilege of freedom" (see Chapter 2). In the third chapter, contributor Mahuya Bandyopadhyay showcases the disorderly nature of some field sites. She takes readers into the world of an Indian prison, which she describes as "chaotic," governed by unpredictable rules that "create contexts of violence, subjugation, and denial" (see Chapter 3). She skillfully delineates her own membership role at this site and how it facilitated and impeded her observations. In the final chapter of Part I, contributor Andrew M. Jefferson provides a vivid portrayal of life at two migrant camps in Sierra Leone. Jefferson's comparative analysis of the two sites points to the need for an acute awareness of "a sense-making strategy in social life, the work it does and can be made to do, and the contradictions it illuminates" (see Chapter 4). Taken together, the site-specific contrasts and related challenges to ethnographic fieldwork are legion in Part I, hardly reducible to a checklist of entry, rapport, trust, and departure.

The chapters of Part II, titled "Selves," features facets of the reflexive relationship between sites and ethnographers' selves. Starting off, contributor Tarja Pösö offers an intimate look at the role the ethnographer's age and related lived research experience plays in shaping the ethnographic analysis of institutional care for young people in Finland. Revisiting the same site over time as well as looking back, Pösö discusses how her perspective, or what she "saw" in the field, changed as she aged and assumed different roles, from being a "big sister" to "a mother" and from being "a PhD student to an associate professor in social work" (see Chapter 5). Alternatively in the chapter following, contributor Gary Alan Fine invites readers to consider the "opportunities of age." Fine analyzes the site-specific implications of the ethnographer's personal characteristics based on his research in a political advocacy organization for senior citizens. As Fine explains, though his age and status as a senior citizen may have opened some doors, it did not necessarily translate into better rapport at this site: "While my relationship with the members was as an equal, gaining easy camaraderie, the staff were more skeptical of my role as my age did not overwhelm the reality that I was an outsider to the movement" (see Chapter 6). In the next chapter, contributor Brittany Presson's discusses "the challenges of researching social worlds that are saturated by heavy and shifting emotional expression" (see Chapter 7). Her fieldwork is based on attending events, conventions, and associated interviews involving the Gold Star Mother's Organization. The organization is comprised of mothers who have lost a child who was serving in active-duty military service. Through detailed analysis of her own site-specific emotion work, Presson demonstrates that fieldwork needs to contend with fleeting membership; a craft that must navigate the "shifting codes" of changing social worlds involving continual "vetting" in practice and recurrent rapport-building. In the final chapter of Part II, Hsiao-Chuan Hsia's ethnography shows how her commitment to praxis required restructuring her research site to create a space for research participants to "talk back" (see Chapter 8), along with interrogating her own imagined subjectivity and motivations to help.

The chapters of Part III of the book, titled "Social Worlds," shifts attention to the complex substances of ethnographic discovery. This begins with a chapter by contributor John C. Pruit describing ethnographic results of his fieldwork in a Montessori preschool. Pruit asks: "What is it like to work ethnographically at the crossroads of social worlds?" (see Chapter 9). The conflicting social worlds in Pruit's research are formal "schooling" and "nurturance." As he writes, "One is fueled by the everyday roles and rules of learning, the other by the everyday roles and rules of caring" (see Chapter 9). Pruit demonstrates how he adapted to these competing social worlds in the course of his fieldwork. In a parallel vein in the chapter following Pruit's, contributor James M. Thomas discusses how the ethnographer recognizes and negotiates the contrasting, at times conflicting, interests of social worlds. Emphasizing the "going concerns" of members and the ethnographer, Thomas offers an interesting comparison of "a study of urban nightlife and a study of a public university's planning and implementation of its diversity initiative" (see Chapter 10). The contrast provides a detailed example of how ethnographers unravel and adapt to the diverse contingencies of site-specificity. The next chapter by contributors Beatriz Reyes-Foster and Shannon K. Carter offers "a feminist ethnographic approach to studying breastfeeding communities" (see Chapter 11). They expand the notion of sitedness to include an entire community. Drawing on autoethnography, Reyes-Foster and Carter explore the meaning and practice of ethnographic research for women who are bodily, emotionally, and politically involved in their participant observations, notably, sites and membership at once fluid and permeable, the social worlds of motherhood, homelife, research, and activism crossing over diverse settings. In the last chapter of Part III, based on her ethnographic study of Norwegian social welfare offices, contributor Hilde Fiva Buzungu showcases the challenges and lessons of how ethnographers and members convey the meaning of their social worlds specifically in the context of "language discordant interaction" (see Chapter 12), extending the complex challenges of ethnographic discovery.

The book closes with a separate reflective chapter by James A. Holstein titled "Afterword: Elaborating Contours of the Craft." Fittingly, it emphasizes the analytic inspiration that cuts across the contours of sitedness, ethnographic selves, and the discovery and documentation of social worlds. It is sited analytic inspiration, Holstein argues, that makes visible and gives shape to the social worlds that come into view.

Note

1 All names provided are pseudonyms.

References

Adler, P. A., & Adler, P. (1987). *Membership roles in the field*. Sage.

Atkinson, P. (2015). *For ethnography*. Sage.

Anderson, L. (2006). Analytic autoethnography. *Journal of Contemporary Ethnography*, *35*(4), 373–395.

Chand, A. (2014). Conflicting masculinities? Men in reserved occupations in Clyde side 1939–45. *Journal of Scottish Historical Studies*, *34*(2), 218–236. https://doi.org/10.3366/jshs.2014.0121

Cooley, C. H. (1902). The looking glass self. In *Human nature and social order* (pp. 179–185). Scribner's.

Delamont, S., & Atkinson, P. (2018). The ethics of ethnography. In R. Iphofen & M. Tolich (Eds.), *The Sage handbook of qualitative research ethics* (pp. 119–132). Sage. https://dx.doi.org/10.4135/9781526435446.n8

Ellis, C., Adams, T. E., & Bochner, A. P. (2010). Autoethnography: An overview [40 paragraphs]. *Forum Qualitative Sozialforschung/Forum: Qualitative Social Research*, *12*(1), Art. 10. http://nbn-resolving.de/urn:nbn:de:0114-fqs1101108

Gubrium, J. F. (1975). *Living and dying at Murray Manor*. University Press of Virginia.
Gubrium, J. F., & Holstein, J. A. (1997). *The new language of qualitative method*. Oxford University Press.
Gubrium, J. F., & Holstein, J. A. (Eds.). (2002). *Handbook of interview research*. Sage.
Gubrium, J. F., & Holstein, J. A. (2014). Analytic inspiration in ethnographic fieldwork. In U. Flick (Ed.), *Sage handbook of qualitative data analysis* (pp. 35–48). Sage Publications.
Hammersley, M. (2009). Against the ethicists: On the evils of ethical regulation. *International Journal of Social Research Methodology*, *12*(3), 211–225. https://doi-org.ezaccess.libraries.psu.edu/10.1080/13645570802170288
Hayano, D. M. (1979). Auto-ethnography: Paradigms, problems, and prospects. *Human Organization*, *38*(1), 99–104. www.jstor.org/stable/44125560
Holstein, J. A. & Gubrium, J. F. (2000). *The self we live by: Narrative identity in a post-modern world*. Oxford University Press.
Mead, G. H. (1934). *Mind, self, and society*. University of Chicago Press.
Puddephat, A. J., Shaffir, W., & Kleinknecht, S. W. (Eds.). (2009). *Ethnographies revisited: Craftinbt theory in the field*. Routledge.
Mead, M. (1928). *Coming of age in Samoa*. HarperCollins.
Miller-Day, M. (2012). Toward conciliation: Institutional review board practices and qualitative interview research. In J. F. Gubrium, J. A. Holstein, A. B. Marvasti & K. D. McKinney (Eds.), *The Sage handbook of interview research: The complexity of the craft* (pp. 495–507). Sage.
Rose, N. (1996). *Inventing our selves*. Cambridge University Press.
Ryen, A. (2011). Ethics and qualitative research. In D. Silverman (Ed.), *Qualitative research* (3rd ed., pp. 416–438). Sage.
Smith, D. (1987). *The everyday world as problematic*. University of Toronto Press.
Smith, D. E. (2005). *Institutional ethnography: A sociology for people*. Alta Mira Press.
Whitaker, E. M., & Atkinson, P. (2021). *Reflexivity in social research*. Palgrave Macmillan.

PART I

Sites

1

INSIDER ETHNOGRAPHY IN PROFESSIONAL BOXING

Alex Stewart-Psaltis

In this chapter, I discuss my experiences researching, as a doctoral student and ethnographic insider, cohorts of professional boxers located in and around London, England, over a 5-year period. It echoes John Van Maanen's (2011, p. xvi) sentiment that "appreciation and understanding of ethnography comes like a mist that creeps slowly over us while in the library and lingers with us while in the field." I chart the process of carrying out fieldwork as an embodied researcher within a cultural setting—the boxing gymnasium—I was intimately familiar with, and the reflexive challenges involved in getting to understand and ultimately harness, in epistemologically productive ways, my "insider" know-how. My discussion seeks to evoke something of the necessarily introspective, perpetually messy, and emotionally draining requirement to manage and re-negotiate my boxer/researcher identity as I moved between the disparate social worlds of pugilism and academia. This barely conscious subplot of identity transformation, by way of ethnographic process, contributed to my (re)interpretations of the culturally situated insider knowledge I was able to access.

Researching the "Fight Game"

The broadly defined aim of my research was to critically evaluate the patterns of meaning through which boxing practitioners constructed worldviews and values and the limits and possibilities of their identification with, and experiences of, boxing. This investigation in the context English society is complex, as since the late nineteenth-century boxing in England has been socially organized into two independently governed, ideologically distinctive, and spatially segregated codes (Shipley, 1989). As such, although both versions of boxing are closely related, each has its own unique social world and athletic character. To put it in practitioner

DOI: 10.4324/9781003275121-3

parlance, amateur boxing is a "sport" and professional boxing is a "business"; amateur boxers are "athletes": while professional boxers are "prizefighters." That said, the long-standing popular cultural appeal of professional boxing as a spectator sport ensures that the two codes are symbolically and socially intertwined—very close cousins rather than anonymous neighbors. Most professional boxers have been socialized through, or "farmed" from (Sugden, 1996), the amateur system and have taken a rite-of-passage or "crossed-over"—metaphorically and pragmatically—into the professional boxing universe. A direct descendant of eighteenth- and nineteenth-century bare-knuckle pugilism (Gorn, 1986), "pro" boxing is in its present-day guise is practiced in gymnasiums inconspicuously located within the post-industrial landscapes of Britain's major metropolises and surrounding urban conurbations. Much as Shipley (1989) tells us, "prize fighting at the highest level had been elitist within the working-class, a sub-culture within a culture" (p. 90), the occupational day-to-day norms and practices through which professional boxing practitioners experience, learn, understand, and communicate their athletic craft remains somewhat hidden from society at large (including most amateur boxers).

I sought to gain access to the "pro" subculture by calling upon my "insider" boxing credentials to emulate the journey of most other amateur boxers who have "crossed-over." Prior to the commencement of what might be called site crossover ethnography, I had been a schoolboy, youth, and senior amateur boxer and attained "open class" status at senior level of competition.[1] I was thus able to gain a professional boxer's license[2] administered by the British Boxing Board of Control (BBBC). In doing so, I was "officially" granted insider access to the "real" world of professional boxing in England. As a professional boxing insider, I then set out to collect a mixed bag of qualitative data among cohorts of professional boxing practitioners based in gymnasiums located in and around London and surrounding urban conurbations. By way of introduction to my ethnographic experience, the following narrative description adapted from fieldnotes seeks to evoke something of the occupational day-to-day norms and practices through which professional boxing practitioners experience, learn, understand, and communicate their athletic craft, as experienced from my insider standpoint. within one of the research sites of inquiry.

Accessing "The Real Thing"

> I arrive at the Chorley Street Community Center (a pseudonym), an old Victorian building situated in the corner of a residential street only a few minutes from my home.[3] Bypassing the mum and toddler group occupying the main hall, I make my way to the back end of the building. As I approach the sturdy wooden door pointed out to me, I can faintly hear the rhythm of a dance track and the all-familiar noise of a buzzer sound. Upon prising the heavy wooden door open, the vibrancy of the "pro" lifeworld of boxing engulfs my senses . . .
>
> I enter a cramped space almost entirely filled by a boxing ring and an assortment of punch bags and speed balls lining the periphery. The walls are

decorated with dozens of fight posters and yellowing newspaper clippings and photographs depicting past ring exploits of boxers from current and previous generations. Assortments of boxing gloves, skipping ropes, used bandages, protective headguards and discarded sports kits, are strewn on wooden benches along the perimeters. The air is filled with the aroma of liniment oil and a faint odor of stale sweat. Immediately to my right is a tall Black boxer stripped to the waist and assiduously studying his own muscular reflection in a mirror while shadowboxing. Letting out loud rhythmical grunts to accompany a stream of punches, he looks up as I enter and jubilantly acknowledges my presence, "*All right mate!*" He then shouts over to the only other person in the room, "*I'm starting to get the feel again Terry . . . I'm really buzzing . . . LOVING IT!*"

"Coach-Terry," an amiable looking man in his seventies who nonetheless appears remarkably fit and healthy, is at the far corner of the room untangling a bundle of skipping ropes. He looks up and peers at me behind a set of thick-rimmed glasses. I walk over to him and ask if it's OK to have a "shake-out." He tells me "*Not a problem*" remarking that he knows who I am having read reports of my fights in *The Boxing News*.[4] He asks, "*You're with Coach-Don, aren't you?*" I respond that I am dissatisfied with the level of sparring at my amateur boxing club and consequently on the look-out for a "pro" training environment to learn from. Nodding in agreement, Coach-Terry confirms, "*Yes, you must have decent sparring in the pro game.*" He continues, "*as long as I'm not stepping on any toes . . . no problem, you're welcome to train with us. There's Micky* (pointing at the boxer shadowboxing) *who's coming back after a bit of a lay-off due to injury. He's unbeaten in twenty and is looking for titles. There's Delroy who's a novice and should be here soon and we have one or two other guys due back so you can mix in with them nicely. They're all a bit bigger than you, but we don't go silly here. We had Tommy* (surname) *up until his last one last month. That's right, he got knocked-out badly by a guy he shouldn't have . . . a nasty knock-out* (shaking his head in dismay) . . . *and I advised him to call it a day. He's a family man and he doesn't need the money . . . he's on six figures running the family building firm so what's the point? And there's* (surname of renowned elite level boxer—"Champ") *who I'm training for a World title shot in Vegas coming up in a couple of months. You won't see much of him . . . he's mostly training during the day. When he's down here, I will be concentrating on him so be aware of that . . . but you're welcome to train here.*"

I proceeded to have a workout and later that week stepped into the ring for six-rounds of sparring with Mickey and Delroy. The tempo was energetic as we swapped punches with measured intent in a bid to fathom each other's styles out. As both men were of weight classifications substantially heavier than my own, the body-mass to core-strength disparity meant that I found our exchanges physically draining. To compensate, I concentrated on utilizing my speed of punch and fleet-footed evasive movement to good effect. During those initial rounds, a tacit understanding was established between us. I traded my speed and mobility for Mickey's tactical guile and Del's rugged strength in a quest to mutually benefit from the problems our respective abilities set each other. I left Chorley Street gymnasium feeling physically drained, although content at establishing a learning curve that would not have been possible among my amateur club-mates. I was eager to return the following week . . .

Entering the gymnasium, I lock eye contact with a man I'm familiar with having seen many of his fights on television. "Champ" is sitting on a stool facing Coach-Terry who is assiduously applying strips of tape and bandages to his proteges fists. I also notice three middle-aged men, all wearing suits standing by the ring apron attentively observing proceedings. Looking up from his duties, Coach-Terry nods at me an instructs, "*Get ready Alex and jump in the ring*." Noticing that Mickey and Delroy are also meditatively applying their own bandages, a wave of adrenaline surges through me. Instinctively, I internalize my focus to steel my resolve . . .

Having retreated to a corner of the room to get changed into my sports gear, I notice Champ intently self-engrossed in the rhythms played-out on his personal stereo shadowboxing in the ring. Another wave of adrenalin surges through me as I "wrap" my hands in bandages and strips of elastic tape, apply Vaseline to my face, don a pair of 16 oz boxing gloves and jump through the ring ropes. Coach-Terry beckons me over to him, ties the laces of my gloves and fastens my head-guard securely. He does the same for Champ. I pace the ring exhaling deep breaths through my nose while brushing past my "spar mate." I sense the scrutiny of those outside the ropes and simultaneously feel the physical presence of the World-class performer I'm sharing intimate space with. He appears very powerful; a thick-set upper body and strong although slimly tapered legs that seemed to belie his "fighting-weight" of 63.5 kgs, a weight classification that appears near impossible for a man of his body frame to attain. Despite Champ wearing a full-face headguard leaving only a thin strip for his vision, I catch sight of his heavily scarred eyebrows. Of course, I too have acquired my own scar tissue from the six stitches inserted from my previous professional contest only a few months ago.[5] Purposively snorting deeply inhaled breaths through my nose, I seek to channel my resolve into an energy that will ensure no further additions to that tally. Coach-Terry stands on the ring apron and stopwatch in hand instructs, "*TIME . . . take it away fellas!*"

We both skip to the center of the ring and forcefully tap each other's gloved fists a "friendly" gesture acknowledging our intent to honor the unspoken boundary differentiating "sparring" from "fighting." Seeking to explore the proceedings about to unfold, I venture a "polite" jab. It is effortlessly dismissed and a powerful response, in the form of a right-cross, slams into my jaw, knocking my head back and forcing me to veer into the ring ropes. I hear a voice from the periphery of the ring remarking, "*Good shot son!*" I seek to regain my composure by rhythmically back-peddling along the perimeter of the ring. Champ effortlessly "holds" the center of the ring strategically asserting his dominance. More punches with "intent" are fired at me although I manage to steel myself to their power and counter with a series of scoring punches of my own. Their accuracy does nothing to alleviate the wave of measured aggression coming my way, however, and once again I am forced to stand my ground and "trade" punches with every ounce of strength at my disposal . . . "*T-I-M-E!*" We both pace the ring for the one-minute rest period. Coach-Terry applies Vaseline to our faces and offers mouthfuls of water of which we spit into a bucket. He then glances at his stopwatch and instructs the next three-minute round of sparring to commence.

Steeling my focus, I turn to face Champ and we once again exchange a "friendly" tap of gloved fists. I am instantly confronted with a stream of powerful punches. Slotting into a more fluent rhythm, I manage to slip his jab and "bring him on" to my countering jab and utilizing "quick feet" move laterally "out of reach." As I seek to establish to that all-important "hand-eye-time-distance" coordination to be able to control the tempo of punches delivered and received between us, my counter is met by Champ's own countering-counter and a powerful right-hand punch, once again, slams into my jaw, jolting my body and "sparking" my consciousness. The same unrecognizable voice punctuates my concentration with unwelcome (to me) commentary advising, "*Great shot, now double up . . . down stairs then up . . . use your feints*" . . . I retaliate with a series of powerful punches with both fists; Champ immediately reciprocates and we "bang" at each other center ring propelling Coach-Terry to instruct, "*EASY, EASY!.. (softening tone), you're having a war both of you! Keep it respectable . . . come on let's go!*" We both take a step back to resume proceedings. Another booming jab whistles past my ear and I offer a counter with as much force as I can muster. Champ reciprocates and continues applying a surging will-power translated into physical and psychological intensity as the salvo for unremitting aggression makes me fight just to stay there, stay on my feet and punch back . . . TIME!

I manage to complete two more rounds at much the same tempo. Midway through the fourth-round, I feel the strength of my punches steadily subsiding as I struggle to fill my over-worked lungs with labored gulps of oxygen. As I become increasingly fatigued, all I can offer is the willpower to absorb the "punishment" levelled at me by the heavier, stronger and more experienced Champ without folding altogether. Sensing my resistance has waned, Coach-Terry pulls me out at the end of the fourth round and Mickey takes my place for two more rounds of "work." As I exit the ring, Champ quips through his gum-shield, "*How do you like the real thing?*" I smile at him defiantly and exhausted remove the boxing gloves and bandages from my hands, undertake a few stretching exercises and replenish my body with carbohydrate liquid while watching the remainder of the sparring. With every part of my body twitching from the exertion, and nursing a sore head and neck from the whiplash effect of Champ's punches, I inform Coach-Terry I will be back in two days' time. Before I manage to finish my sentence, Champ beckons Coach-Terry over, who responds immediately.

Embodying Cultural "Truths"

The previous narrative offers the semblance of my insider initiation into the real world of professional boxing. My position at the beginning of the research journey was to assume my prior socialization and athletic competence in boxing would afford me a kind of insider phenomenological and cultural privilege that would enable relatively unproblematic access to "pro" social world norms and practices. My expectation at that time was to harness my insider know-how to culturally blend in as a bona fide member of the professional boxing milieus studied and create nearly instant and legitimate rapport. By being able to fully partake in the everyday gymnasium goings-on, experiencing firsthand the frontstage rituals of boxing competition and being privy to, and on occasion the subject of, backstage dealings, negotiations, and expectations, I expected to make ethnographic sense of the field from a more nuanced and intuitive insider perception that, in turn, would credibly add to existing discourse. In doing so, I also assumed it would be unproblematic to maintain a credible insider presence for the duration of the research.

Like others (Sherif, 2001; Sands, 2002; Labaree, 2002; Chavez, 2008), my insiderness was certainly advantageous in establishing a presence in the field quickly and intimately because of my athletic know-how and the perceived or real closeness of my social identity to the members of the research sites. As such, my insider competence as the boxer provided multiple levels of insight into human behavior and the linguistic, cognitive and emotional conventions enacted by professional boxing practitioners and the practical happenings of the field necessary for data collection, interpretation, and representation (Chavez, 2008). My ability to immerse myself socially and bodily as a real member of the pro community of practitioners, and by submitting to the dictates of boxing tradition, allowed me to experience firsthand the "structure of feeling" (Williams, 1963) through which pro boxing is collectively and passionately understood as highly skilled craftwork with entrepreneurial potential, sustained by way of bravado.

During the first 2 years of this insider research agenda, I was able to experience firsthand a myriad of insider realities known among professional boxing practitioners as *living the life*, including the tranquility of early morning runs in still "sleeping" urban neighborhoods; the exhilaration of feeling one's body *tune-in* when arriving at peak fitness prior to a scheduled *fight-night* and following moths of monastic dedication to rigorous training regimes and dietary restrictions; the collective effervescence and sensuous intoxication of a *buzzy* gymnasium full of fellow boxers toiling hard; "good" days when bodily and psychologically *tuning-in* to execute combination punches with precision and *snap* under the watchful tutelage of coach-elders; "bad" days *at the office* when energy levels are low and the desire to *push-on* lackluster; the camaraderie, humor, and mutual apprehension among boxers sharing changing rooms pre-fight juxtaposed by the solitude and emotional turmoil of contemplating a contest to become real in the days and hours before the event; the presence and duty of care received from significant others emotionally embroiled in a boxers welfare; the exhilaration and public acclaim when being declared *the winner* and the despair and social awkwardness accompanying a "loss"; getting paid for my efforts and manifold other *fight game* practices and relations. As such, I could readily identify and empathize with the "sensorial and emotional pedagogy" (Wacquant, 2004, p. 15) of "real" boxing as a participant sport geared toward self-discipline, craftsmanship, "honorary" respect for others as for self, self-denial and differed gratification, the glorification of an autonomously "heroic" masculinity manifesting as an adventurous risk-orientated spirit (Sugden, 1996; Wacquant, 2004; Woodward, 2007). Likewise, as a practitioner yet also a fan of professional boxing, I held a reverence laced with curiosity for the pantheon of legendary boxing champions from England and overseas who had forged (to me) heroic destinies.

So, my initial foray into boxing-related literature was somewhat dismissive. For instance, when contemplating Joyce Carol Oates's (1987) observation that, "Impoverished people prostitute themselves in ways available to them, and boxing offers an opportunity for men to make a living of a kind" (p. 34), I shook my head in disbelief at the comparison of boxing with prostitution—"What is she on? How can anyone not declare boxing the one sport that all other sports aspire to be?" Equally, I stubbornly rejected the dominant discourse that boxing was somehow an affliction of societies divided by privilege and oppression, wealth, and poverty (Sugden, 1996; Wacquant, 2004; Woodward, 2008). Intellectually, I was formatively drawn to a Weberian interpretative agenda and its empathetic stance toward the subjective orientations people offer for their actions—verstehen (Giulianotti, 2005). Moreover, a theoretical stance that emphasized the power of human agency validated my suspicions, held at that time, of the dominant discourse which relied on economic determinism to interpret the need to engage in a sport as inherently "barbaric" professional boxing (Sammons, 1989). That said, having accessed the insider reality of professional boxing narrated earlier, my thoughts noted having shared the ring with Champ reveal an inner turmoil, a nagging intuition, that this *"just doesn't feel right,"* a feeling that never really left me for the duration of the research. Under the heading "Thoughts on Retirement?" I noted the following "headnotes" in my reflective diary:

> Has the time come to let go? I still enjoy the training and I feel that I'm getting better . . . I'll miss the intensity . . . in some ways I need boxing . . . is it time to think long term however . . . employment and health? Part of me says it's time to walk away.
>
> I'm occupying the role of (cheap) sparring partner . . . but this is surely not what it's about . . . or is it? Have I been consigned to the role of gymnasium "sparring partner," or worse, had I become the "punch bag"?
>
> Should I just persevere? Is this what should be done to improve? Not too much wear and tear (yet). Do I need the scar tissue or brain damage? Can I trust the intentions, or abilities, of those around me . . . ?
>
> Am I essentially being exploited or "prostituted" in line with the literature . . . or am I just making excuses? Am I bottling it?

With the benefit of hindsight, I can see that my feelings of unease toward the insider reality I had accessed manifest the more "hidden" insider layers of boxing reality that, like many of the boxers I had cast my insider analytical gaze upon, revealed somewhat veiled yet ever-present impulses toward vulnerability and value conflict. This embodied tension essentially confronted the aspects of my insider boxer identity that were necessarily self-centered and defined through the viscerally fueled tunnel vision of "real" boxing competition. Over the ensuing period of 18 or so months, although retaining my professional boxing license, I lost much of my appetite for the "sacrificial" (Wacquant, 2004) training regimens required of professional boxers to be able to compete in the squared ring. In what felt at that time as "paralysis by analysis," my motivation to train with the verve and dedication I had cultivated over many years steadily declined. Over a relatively condensed timespan, the symbolism through which I enchanted my identity as the boxer was dulled and in a *burned-out* manner I, albeit reluctantly and self-consciously, retreated from pursuing the real thing; my days as a fully fledged competitive boxer had started to peter out.[6]

"Becoming" Ethnographic

As time wore on, I (as the boxer) became increasingly disgruntled and was compelled to more fully acknowledge my nagging and ever-present intuition that "*this just doesn't feel right.*" Increasingly, I entertained doubt when estimating the intentions of those around me while questioning cultural truths and moral codes of boxing per se. For instance, when on early morning runs in the guise of "the professional boxer," I processed the critical perspectives encountered from the field and the literature as I listened to the music playing on my personal stereo. The fledgling *pro* met the neophyte "academic" in this sense, in a bid to analytically make sense of professional boxing as a lived socially constructed experience: How do Champ and Coach-Terry understand this or that value orientation, relationship, or practice? Do I feel differently? How am I perceived by the gym membership? As a "journeyman," "prospect," or perhaps a *dreamer who's got no chance*? Is boxing really the "exploitation of the disadvantaged" as Sugden (1996) likes to think? Should I trust this mob? Am I simply inventing academic absurdities and thinking too much?

I found this to be an uncomfortable period in which the seeds for developing a critical attitude toward the cultural "truths" informing my own and other boxers' interpretative logic took form. With hindsight, I can see that as I steadily succumbed to the demands of PhD scholarship, I was experiencing my self-in-transition, torn between two strikingly differing, even oppositional, lifeworld systems; the physical expressivity, social effervescence, and practical consciousness of boxing; and, by way of contrast, the prevailing academic lifeworld stream of consciousness demanding verbal and written acuity, accompanied with inevitably contemplative, sedentary, and, by definition, solitary library-based musings. Albeit, at that time, I was floundering into a kind of apathetic rendition of my previous boxer-self, this process of identity and consciousness transformation can be understood as ethnographically "becoming" culturally sensitized to the patterns of the social world engulfing us, which have profound implications on how we create order and meaning to our lives (Ballantine & Roberts, 2010. This ongoing process of "awakening" to the research task at hand I formatively attribute to my "identity-in-transformation" crisis I experienced while seeking to maintain and re-negotiate an insider ethnographic presence as a member of the research sites explored. Of equal significance was my improving academic literacy. From here, I offer some examples of how my imagined, embodied, and shifting perceptions of being an insider to the research sites frequented merged with my comprehension of the literature to shape my cultural (re)interpretations. Two ethnographic texts, in particular, allowed me to incrementally comprehend how my evolving and shifting situatedness in relation to the field of inquiry.

Re-defining a Sense of Identity, Place, and Culture

Upon commencing this research journey as a novice academic, I was instantly drawn to and identified with John Sugden's (1996) and Loic Wacquant's (2004) excellent ethnographies of boxing. Fascinated by their detailed and sophisticated analysis of the culture of boxing and the sports place and role in society, their ethnographically grounded genre of scholarship spoke to me in a way that much other academic analysis and prose failed to do. Nonetheless, my initial interpretations of either author's work shifted over time because of my improving capacity to comprehend the contextualized vision of their discussions more clearly in sociological and methodological terms. Significantly, by reflecting upon and critiquing both authors' positioning as inquirers within their respective research settings, I was better able to reflexively unpack and complicate my own evolving situatedness as a researcher.

Initially, while reflecting on Sugden's writing I harbored considerable ambivalence, if not a measure of disdain, toward his essentially deterministic understanding of boxing as a cultural practice of the dispossessed and powerless in society. Noting that Sugden paid homage to the early Chicago School of ethnographers analysis of, "subterranean aspects of social life which . . . either border on or are the very center of that area of social life designated as deviant by the guardians of social order" (p. 201), I felt aggrieved at his insistence that his own research of boxing in the United States, Northern Ireland, and Cuba was comparable to previous studies of deviant subcultures, ranging from drug users, delinquent gangs, and football hooligans and other social misfits. More poignantly, I felt Sugden succumbed to a stereotypical and rather crude view of the boxer as being a poverty-stricken rough whose worldview and life opportunities were limited by the structural determinism of a life eked out at the basement end society. I questioned the extent Sugden was able to formulate accurate understandings of boxing as a social practice and athletic experience from his (to me) peripheral presence among the boxing practitioners studied as "odd-job man" (Sugden, 1996, p. 2).[7] The following extract guided my initial thought processes:

> Vic is a six-foot two-inch White heavyweight with the head of a bulldog, supported by a massive neck and sloping shoulders. (Vic's eyes lit up the first night that I came to the gym—because of my size he assumed that Mack had brought me down to spar with him). I had every intention of being a fully-fledged participant observer and "doing a bit" when I first went into the club. However, once I saw Vic and realized what was on his mind I reached for the broom and water bottle, *rationalizing* that the role of part-time janitor/corner man would be sufficient for my research purposes.
>
> *(Sugden, 1996, p. 74 emphasis added)*

My initial comprehension of Sugden's rationale of the risks inherent in sharing the ring with Vic was, to say the least, rather dismissive. Albeit it was perfectly understandable that having never boxed before he was wary of the potential risks inherent, I estimated that his refusal to experience boxing for "real" was at the expense of communicating, negotiating, and therefore truly understanding boxing as a lived cultural experience. Moreover, I felt that he pre-judged and evaluated the possibilities of boxing, and even, the capacities of boxers as human beings.

Nonetheless, having returned to Sugden's thesis multiple times over the duration of fieldwork and during analytical periods of writing and re-writing, my standpoint changed somewhat. It became increasingly apparent that Sugden's series of case studies captured the lived meanings of the boxers researched with admirable ethnographic detail, interpretative richness, and theoretical sophistication. Following my readings of Sugden over the course of my research, I was incrementally *forced* to acknowledge that it would be folly to not consider the structural impositions of poverty surrounding the vast majority of boxing gymnasiums in England, and the web of micro- and macro-power relations underpinning boxing practitioners' social practices and cultural understandings.

Reflecting upon my insider situatedness as the boxer, the following commentary penned by Hargreaves (1986, p. 101) round about the same time as I started boxing as a schoolboy, offers a degree of causality to the structural arrangements through which boxing became my chosen sport:

> The dislocated working-class with a preponderance of semi- and unskilled manual workers, the unemployed and the unemployable, and an increasing proportion of people in ethnic minorities, has a relative low involvement in the more organized, institutionalized forms of sporting activity, due to the relative weakness of the social network, the low accessibility and availability of alternatives and inability or willingness to comply with middle-class norms.

My social standing since arrival in the United Kingdom could explain the attractions boxing held for me in the following way: A dual-national immigrant from a one-parent female-headed household hailing from a "rough" council estate was always likely to be attracted to the low-cost, individualistic, and assertively masculine sporting outlet of boxing. From this standpoint, having adopted the social profile of the (half)-immigrant since my arrival in England, the appeal of boxing was a means for me to construct an assertive sense of individuality in an alien and at times hostile environment. Reciprocally, it can be inferred that the (at that time) male-dominated social world of boxing provided a paternalistically nurturing environment lacking at home. In this way, through displaying a degree of talent and the necessary fortitude to apply myself during training and, crucially, accrue success during what is perhaps the prototypical individualists' sport accessible within the urban, working-class landscapes of British society, I was encouraged to yearn for, and prove, a very pronounced masculine self-worth. Whatever structural and agential dimensions are apparent, one insider ethnographic process I experienced caused me to re-evaluate the possibility that I may, in part, subconsciously embody an aptitude akin to the folksy analogy of "the hungry fighter."

During the data collection period of my study, I revisited the neighborhood where I spent formative years in the United Kingdom growing up from a 10-year-old boy into a 15-year-old youth (and schoolboy boxer). As I walked by my old home, primary school, boxing gymnasium, and other landmarks by this time vague in my memory, I noted the mix of (relative) poverty and material decay of the part of the estate where my family once lived. This certainly was "rough" England and I felt anger at the structural determinism imposed on those eking out daily life at the bottom of the social pile. As far as my attraction to boxing is concerned, I found myself contemplating if my desire to compete in a combat sport and thereafter conquer, or tolerate even, my fear of fighting and the inner determination that resulted on the most part in success was in consequence to my early socialization into this "rough" social environment since emigrating to England. On the other hand, abiding memories of school, playing football on the common, the opportunity to practice many other more "civilized" sports, hanging out with my friends, and attending youth club discos and such like were invariably care-free and I cannot recall, in my young consciousness, any overriding concern with the pressures of life. Even when my family moved to an idyllic village on the outskirts of town, I still chose to jog the three miles to and from the boxing gymnasium and willfully persisted with my sport of choice. Upon reflection, however, I was propelled more to fully acknowledge the sense of ambivalence toward my experience of boxing in schoolboy and youth tournaments staged in working-men's clubs, community halls, leisure centers, and nightclubs throughout the East Midlands during the Thatcher years. Whether this was due to the qualms generated by pre-contest nerves at the uncertain outcome of a boxing "bout," the possibility of public and painful humiliation etched in the back of my mind, the ambience emanating from elements in the audience who pints of beer in hand sought to be entertained by "*a good scrap with plenty of shots getting in*" I can't be clear. Although confined as somehow peripheral and somewhat less animated memories of my past boxing experiences, those thoughts and feelings were there, however. If and to what extent similar thoughts were shared among other boxers and in which incarnations is a question that begs to be considered.

Loic Wacquant's (2004) ethnography was equally significant in shaping and defining this research. His series of articles and published book, *Body and Soul: notebook of an apprentice boxer* (2004), is also mindful of the deprived social environment through which the informants of his study inferred logic to the value of their chosen sport.[8] However, his intent on focusing on the reasons why boxers *persisted* with, as opposed to logically assuming they were *pushed* into, boxing afforded a worldview that, to degrees, I instantaneously and willfully identified with. Wacquant's theorization of boxing, although producing countless empirical similarities to Sugden's analysis of US boxers, differed in as much as he incorporated a phenomenological frame of analysis to understand "how boxing makes sense as soon as one takes pains to get close enough to it to grasp it with *one's body*" (2004, p. 7 original emphasis). Wacquant achieved this by learning how to box alongside, and sparring with, professional boxers on a regular basis.[9] Through his observant participant research role, Wacquant was able to access, elucidate, and theoretically examine the visceral and practical logic that was felt and sensed by boxing practitioners, as much as verbally transmitted. Nonetheless, far from relying on how boxing was kinetically experienced by boxers from "the inside,"

Wacquant applied his phenomenological comprehension of boxing as a way of rethinking how culture and the self can be tied to analysis of wider structures of power and domination. As he observes, professional boxer's passion-laden attachment to boxing is a skewed and malicious one as there is no escaping the "barbaricness" (Wacquant, 1995, p. 520) of their athletic craft. Wacquant's thinking considerably served to inform my own understandings of boxing.

As an embodied, situated, and subjective boxing insider, I was forced to acknowledge the extent matters of my own and other boxers' taste, and meaning orientations were divergent despite our shared understandings of, and passion, for boxing. Although my insider pedigree gave me access to interact with other professional boxers with easy rapport (for instance, discussing common opponents or exchanging news of acquaintances and general boxing gossip), and shared bodily experience (training, sparring, and intimate knowledge of fighting), there were many unforeseen and rather "hidden" power-laden cultural dimensions defining our identities that I was unfamiliar with and was, at times rather awkwardly, compelled to negotiate.

This realization more fully took hold when I accessed pockets of professional boxing in London. Moreover, this geographical shift of focus demanded a broader scope of consideration be applied to the alien (to me) "cultural materialism" (Hughson et al., 2005) through which boxing signified meaning and value.[10] For instance, Robson (2000, p. 40) demonstrates how specific and historically situated structures of feeling and patterns of culture give rise to very distinctive modes of masculinity characteristic of the Southeast London habitus.[11] Accordingly, the economic opportunity afforded a young man in his late teens or early twenties to box at a venue located within London, and watched by his grandfather, father, and other family members who had also competed at the same venue their generations since, as well as work colleagues, friends, and other locals, for instance, may take on a signifying quality remarkably different from my own and others socialized externally to this cultural-specific vantage. Equally, it quickly became apparent that my insider presence as a relative cultural outsider within the London gymnasiums, marginalized my potential worth to the gatekeepers of social worlds that danced to the tune of commercial transaction accrued by way of "spectacular," and thus highly intensive and often brutal, athletic competition (see Sugden, 1996; Wacquant, 2004; Beamish & Ritchie, 2006). In terms of forging an identity among the professional milieus of boxing I had accessed, it was difficult to penetrate the bonds defining the relations between boxers, coaches, and managers unless being drawn into the value system of commodity exchange—namely my physical capital in exchange for the coach's expertise (or pugilistic capital) and the manager's business acumen (or social capital) in a bid to mutually accumulate economic gain. Moreover, by having from the outset traded my insider identity to gain access into the world of professional boxing in London, I felt that to maintain my insider presence I was expected to reciprocate by engaging the "real" professional boxers' stock in trade—serious sparring, and even more serious fighting. It was usual for coaches residing as gatekeepers of the *pro* universe, after initially showing a level of interest, to consign my identity as a rather peripheral, although accepted, member of the gymnasium social orders.[12] In short, my evident resistance at *being serious* (or fully *real*) effectively marginalized my presence in the London gymnasiums frequented. It was here that my rather reticent insider identity both stimulated access to and interpretation of rich insider data, yet simultaneously, undermined my quest to forge a more intimately familiar ethnographic presence. Nonetheless, the process of (re)negotiating my perpetually evolving "status" among "friendly" or "antagonistic," "trusted" or "duplicitous," "respected" or "inferiorized," "friendly" or "arrogant" (or whatever else) boxing practitioners enabled me, over time, to situate my own insider intuition and interactions in parallel with my more analytically minded and academically informed agenda.

Insider Know-How Situated

As is well noted, access to research settings and their cultures is not limited to the moment of entry into a social world; it is an ongoing process that needs to be managed and negotiated during social interactions with participants (Chavez, 2008; Hammersley & Atkinson, 2019). Accordingly, the distinctiveness of the different sites at which knowledge is produced and the embodied, situated, and subjective presence of the researcher carrying out analysis, are reflexively interconnected and interdependent (Mauthner & Doucet, 2003; Greene, 2014). Furthermore, following Woodward (2008, p. 577), "The suggestion that all knowledge is situated provides a route into reflection upon the position (situatedness) of the researcher as well as that of the subjects of the research" (Woodward, 2008 p. 577).

Hence, if I had what Bourdieu (1984) has called the "cultural competence" (p. 2) to interact with other boxing practitioners from an associational insider vantage of knowing, I was nevertheless propelled to interrogate how the layers of reflexivity informing my boxing "truths," or at least my perception of them at given moments in time and through space, impinged upon the production of knowledge. It is here that my Anglo-Greek heritage and early socialization having been born and raised in Athens for the first 10 years of my life, in comfortable economic circumstances, offsets, and destabilizes "shared" cultural affiliations with British markers of social identity based around class, gender, and ethnicity. Where I sensed a "disparity of sensibility" from other boxing practitioners during the period of data gathering, this served to raise further issues and perspectives to be interrogated.

Over time, it became possible to problematize and theme the many taken-for-granted "insider" everyday routines of practice and social interaction through which I/other boxing practitioners inferred logic and value orientations. While "living the same life" as other boxing practitioners, deepening analytical issues emerged gradually revealing cultural and power-laden dimensions that lay hidden beyond my subjective understandings of what boxing is and is not, as both "the boxer" and social actor of multiple identities more generally. It is also worth pointing out that for a significant period of this research it was far more alien for me to sit through a departmental meeting at university than it was to participate in a 2-hour workout in a professional boxing gymnasium. Nonetheless, as my familiarity with the working culture of higher education evolved, I consequently acquired, and perhaps unconsciously embodied, an "academic professional" identity. As has been discussed earlier, in many ways "boxing" and "academia" are contrary social worlds with in many ways contradictory cultural logics. Much like Hobbs (1988) before me, therefore, I avoided remaining a boxing "native" by going "academic." Thus, albeit always a reflexive and messy process, my imagined, embodied, and shifting perceptions of being familiar with, and stranger to, the research sites accessed merged with my comprehension of the literature to shape my cultural (re)interpretations. The tension and identity-in-crisis experienced was not a problem that needed resolving; rather it became a productive force I had to learn to confront.

Notes

1 Senior amateur boxers are classed as "Novice," "Intermediate," and "Open" in accordance with the number of bouts competed in and level of success attained. Open-class boxers must have won regional, area, and/or national level tournaments and are therefore eligible to compete on the "elite" international stage.
2 This is a rather innocuous-looking brown passport that nonetheless granted me license to legally kill, or be killed, while engaging in athletic competition.
3 The previous week I had more than once walked past this same building in my attempts to locate this somewhat "hidden" professional boxing microcosm patronized by one of the most accomplished British professional boxers of the present era. Having initially located these premises, the sight of toddlers playing with dolls or sleeping in creches made me double track assuming I have entered the wrong building. It was only after asking passers-by on the street outside as to the whereabouts of a boxing gymnasium nearby, when I was redirected to the same space I had emerged from.
4 The Boxing News is the trade paper of the British boxing fraternity and has been in circulation since 1909. It is religiously purchased every Friday by practitioners and boxing aficionados alike.
5 In addition to the cut received during my second professional contest, my winning debut was marred by a broken left hand I sustained when landing repeated jabs on my shorter opponent's forehead.
6 Boxing practitioners compare the process leading toward retirement from competitive boxing to the withdrawal a heroin addict is subjected to (Wacquant, 2004)—the disorientating uncertainty of this experience cannot be over-emphasized.
7 Sugden adopted this persona in his ethnography of a boxing gymnasium in Hartford, US (see Sugden, 1996).
8 His detailed analysis of a boxing gymnasium situated in the Black ghetto of South Chicago explicitly documents the deprived, crime-ridden, and stiflingly limiting circumstances experienced daily by the near exclusively African-American group of boxers he trained alongside (see pp. 17–31).
9 As a finale to his research, Wacquant boxed in the preliminary stages of the Chicago Golden Gloves, a state-sponsored competition for amateur boxers.
10 As much literature indicates the structural characteristics contributing to inner city realities in London's vast conurbations bare a strong resonance with previous ethnographies of boxing located at the heart of ghettos situated elsewhere in the world (see Harrison, 1983; Hobbs, 1988; Sugden, 1996; Robson, 2000; Wacquant, 2004).

11 Robson (2000) argues that specific modes of class-based masculinity inform the stylized presentation and on occasions actions of some of the most notorious football hooligans in Britain, South East London's Millwall fans.
12 It was usual for Coaches to refer to me a "keep fitter" or, at best, "ex pro".

References

Ballantine, J. A., & Roberts, K. A. (2010). *Our social world: Introduction to sociology* (3rd ed.). Sage.

Beamish, R., & Ritchie, I. (2006). *Fastest, highest, strongest: A critique of high-performance sport*. Routledge.

Bourdieu, P. (1984). *Distinction: A social critique of the judgement of taste*. Routledge.

Chavez, C. (2008). Conceptualizing from the inside: Advantages, complications, and demands on insider positionality. *The Qualitative Report, 13*(3), 474–494.

Giulianotti, R. (2005). *Sport: A critical sociology*. Polity.

Gorn, E. J. (1986). *The manly art: The lives and times of the great bare-knuckle champions*. Robson Books.

Greene, M. J. (2014). On the inside looking in: Methodological insights and challenges in conducting qualitative insider research. *The Qualitative Report, 19*(29), 1–13.

Hammersley, M., & Atkinson, P. (2019). *Ethnography: Principles in practice* (4th ed.). Routledge.

Hargreaves, J. (1986). *Sport, power and culture*. Polity/Blackwell.

Harrison, P. (1983). *Inside The Inner City: Life Under the Cutting Edge*. Pelican Books.

Hobbs, D. (1988). *Doing the business: Entrepreneurship, the working-class, and detectives in the east end of London*. University Press.

Hughson, J., Inglis, D., & Free, M. (2005). *The uses of sport: A critical study*. Routledge.

Labaree, R. V. (2002). The risk of "going observationalist": Negotiating the hidden dilemmas of being an insider participant observer. *Qualitative Research, 2*(1), 97–122.

Mauthner, N. S., & Doucet, A. (2003). Reflexive accounts and accounts of reflexivity in qualitative data analysis. *Sociology, 37*(3), 413–431.

Oates, J. (1987). *On boxing*. Harper Collins.

Robson, G. (2000). *"No one likes Us, we don't care" the myth and reality of Millwall Fandom*. Berg.

Sammons, J. (1989). *Beyond the ring: The role of boxing in American society*. University of Illinois Press.

Sands, R. (2002). *Sport ethnography*. Human Kinetics.

Sherif, B. (2001). The ambiguity of boundaries in the fieldwork experience: Establishing rapport and negotiating insider/outsider status. *Qualitative Inquiry, 7*(4), 437–447.

Shipley, S. (1989). Boxing. In T. Mason (Ed.), *Sport in Britain: A social history*. Cambridge University Press.

Sugden, J. (1996). *Boxing and society: An international analysis*. Manchester University Press.

Van Maanen, J. (2011). *Tales of the field: On writing ethnography* (2nd ed.). University of Chicago Press.

Wacquant, L. (1995). The pugilistic point of view: How boxers think and feel about their trade. *Theory and Society, 24*, 489–535.

Wacquant, L. (2004). *Body and soul: Notebooks of an apprentice boxer*. Oxford University Press.

Williams, R. (1963). *Culture and society 1780–1950*. Penguin.

Woodward, K. (2007). *Boxing, masculinity and identity*. Routledge.

Woodward, K. (2008). Hanging out and hanging about: Insider/outsider research in the sport of boxing. *Ethnography, 9*, 536–560.

2

GETTING AT THE EXPERIENCE OF CONFINEMENT IN DETENTION

David Wästerfors

A site-specific feature of youth detention homes—and any other rigidly controlled or prisonlike institution—is the fact that the inmates cannot just leave. They might escape, and there are ways to be transferred, enjoy an excursion, and get permission for home visits, but typically residents are supposed to stay within their institution during all their days and nights. As a visitor engaged in ethnographic research of residential youth care, I have been eager to not only describe this feature but also be aware of the difficulties, since few of my own conditions resemble those of the inmates. The "participant" aspect of participant observation has, to say the least, been quite limited in this respect. I have, of course, always been able to just leave.

In this chapter, I will identify several ways I have tried to come closer to the everyday experience of confinement, including (a) getting bored, (b) tasting "light paranoia," and (c) fiddling with my "identity kit" (Goffman 1961, 1990, p. 20) inside detention homes. By this I mean experiences of having nothing to do and longing to get out, experiences of being controlled, watched, and filmed by the staff, and my handling of my private belongings in a setting where the positions of items are carefully watched and regulated. I argue that these and similar approaches can help ethnographers gain insights into what institutional confinement means, while personally enjoying the privilege of freedom. Confinement can be looked upon as a site, practice, and state of mind, and it is typically challenging to investigate ethnographically (Jefferson, 2014).

I will concentrate on my data from a project on schoolwork inside youth detention homes. Some personal experiences during this project made me extra-sensitive to the confinement aspect, since they included some days where I actually lived within an institution and did not return home to sleep. Due to practical circumstances, it was hard for me to investigate a particular institution by commuting

DOI: 10.4324/9781003275121-4

back and forth as I usually did (sleeping at home, at a relative's place, or at a hostel), and an opportunity to stay overnight at the institution turned up. By paying attention to how I articulated some of these "all-day experiences" in my fieldnotes, I will try to show how my sensitivity toward the confinement aspect emerged and encourage other fieldworkers to work in equivalent ways, if possible. The sociologist Erving Goffman (1961, 1990, pp. 67–68) analyzed this aspect in various ways in his famous study *Asylums*, for instance, when he remarked that there is a strong feeling in the so-called total institutions that time spent in the establishment is time wasted or destroyed; "it is time that must be written off; it is something that must be 'done' or 'marked' or 'put in' or 'pulled'" (cf. Gubrium, 1975, 1997, pp. 158–159, on "passing time" in nursing home, and Jefferson, 2014; p. 58, on confinement as temporal). "As a result, the inmate tends to feel that for the duration of his required stay . . . he has been totally exiled from living."

A sharpened attention to confinement (possibly originating in personal experiences) might help us read notes and listen to recordings from a certain angle, so that the closed, inward-looking, and surveilled atmosphere of such sites can come forth in the data. We may get closer to "glimpses of confining practices" (Jefferson, 2014, p. 49) and what they do to people. At the end of this chapter, I will describe how I made use of this knowledge during a project on violent events inside detention homes, in which confinement played a crucial role.

Inside the Detention Homes for Young People With Criminal Experiences

There are 23 "special approved homes" (*särskilda ungdomshem*) in Sweden, admitting around 1,100 young people each year. These young people are mostly between 15 and 17 years of age, and municipalities have chosen these homes (and paid for them) from the menu of social services offered to young people with extensive psychosocial problems and criminal experiences. Most of the young people are placed here under the *Care of Young Persons Act* (the LVU law) but some are placed under the *Secure Youth Care Act* (LSU), which means that they are convicted of crimes and the special approved homes execute the penalty. Basically, all inmates are confined against their will because of criminality or other "socially destructive behaviour," an amorphous label that can encompass a range of acts and circumstances, including crime, extensive truancy, and drug use (Enell et al., 2018).

These young people are often deemed "the worst." Many had lived in other and more open treatment institutions, or with foster families, and endured many hardships when growing up. The detention homes are typically situated in the countryside and within the same buildings as the "reformatories" of the twentieth century. The usual arrangement is a so-called cottage system, with a central building surrounded by wards spread out in cottages or separate houses or villas (Platt, 1969, 1977). A visitor meets fences, locked gates and bars, as well as locked doors, surveillance cameras, and alarm systems, which give a prisonlike impression. But there are also workshops, garages, sports centers, school buildings, and spacious parks with nice walks that moderate this impression. The setting is similar to not only a prison in many respects but also reminiscent of boarding schools or campsites, and it is sometimes surrounded by scenic nature. The staff consists of treatment assistants in each ward as well as teachers, administrators, psychologists, and nurses. With the exception of treatment assistants, whose work stretches into the night, all other workers have day shifts. The average institution has a spacious parking lot with a good deal of traffic, which includes all the deliveries to the site. The clients, however, mostly stay put, on average for about 5 months for those placed under the LVU, and for 6–12 months for most of those placed under the LSU.

The special approved homes occupy a particular place in the discourse on treatment and rehabilitation in Swedish youth care. At times they are almost forgotten since they are discreetly situated outside the cities and only admit a small proportion of the country's troublesome youth. At other times, they are the subject of media scandals (Enell et al., 2018). Cases of maltreatment and violence inside these homes regularly gain much attention, especially when they involve the staff's right to isolate inmates. Isolation (in Swedish euphemistically referred to as *avskiljning* or "separation") means that a disobedient and "wild" youth can be removed from others and placed in a separate room to calm down. When young people themselves describe the experience of isolations, their stories can be rather appalling (Wästerfors, 2019). Some years ago (in 2018), the time limit for isolations was cut from a maximum of 24 hours to a maximum of 4 hours, in an effort to strengthen the young people's rights and appease the critics. Still, the debate on the welfare of these young people is far from over, and wards may be closed down because of maltreatment if it is discovered by the Health and Social Care Inspectorate.

I have conducted fieldwork at six special approved homes since 2006 during three research projects[1] and, with the help of research collaborators and students, collected data from additional sites. The first project was about conflict and conflict management, the second was about schoolwork and the lessons inside these institutions, and the third was about interactions involving both young people and staff that escalate into physical violence. My main sources of data were interviews and fieldnotes, especially when I studied everyday conflict management and schoolwork. Violence is rare, but it is talked about a lot. It erupts rather spontaneously and is thus hard to capture "live," or as it happens. Nonetheless, it generates a lot of attention and narratives. In contrast, lessons or instructional activities are planned and quite easy to follow and record. For the most part, the same goes for quarrels, disputes, and other relatively low-intense conflicts. The social life is compact at these sites, and with that comes a range of disagreements and negotiations.

During my stays, I found it both enjoyable and difficult to capture what Emerson et al. (1995, pp. 66–107) call "scenes on the page"—observed actions and dialogue belonging to social life within these institutions—regarding anything from how certain fights come to be defined as playful rather than serious and how everyday concerns are embedded into disputes, to issues of social ties, loneliness, and seclusion (Wästerfors, 2011, 2012, 2016). I stayed within the frame of my interests as not only stated in the project proposals but also refined it a bit. For instance, I tried to pinpoint how young people accomplish "home" in a heavily controlled environment characterized by surveillance and tight scheduling (Wästerfors, 2013). To make a provisional (and relatively pleasant) home out of an austere institution can be a matter of sustaining a personal touch in one's room, one's clothes and style, or of finding spaces and time to be left alone, unreached by the staff gaze. It is about accomplishing relative privacy and integrity.

The naked setting in general, with empty tables, often empty walls, just a few plants and bare corridors, is for security. Loose items might be used in fights, riots, and suicide attempts. In the staff areas, however, the impression is very different. Pens and papers, binders, calendars and coffee mugs, desk lamps, and personal belongings—a lot of stuff is allowed to be left on tables and desks—give the impression of things going on, of engagement. Staff also make their space cozy.

A typical day in a special approved home consists of a few school lessons or treatment sessions in various programs, interspersed with meals and breaks. A typical evening consists of watching TV or playing console games, hanging around in the ward living room, perhaps chatting with staff or playing table tennis. The sofa and armchairs are central to this leisure part of the day, whereas the desk and chairs inside schoolrooms and school buildings are central to "work" and study. All inmates are offered schooling, though the homes have been criticized for not always prioritizing it and instead focusing on treatment. Treatment, on the other hand, has been criticized for being empty, just "watching TV with adults" and "doing time." The sense that "I don't get any real treatment" is quite common among the young people I have met. The National Board of Institutional Care, which runs these homes, argues the opposite. On its homepage it lists a range of rehabilitative programs—for instance, *Aggression Replacement Training* and *Cognitive Behavioural Therapy*—along with promises that they are evidence-based and are employed in the homes. There is a striking incongruity between the official discourse and everyday life inside detention homes. Whereas the official image of these institutions is action and task-oriented—it is about saving young people at risk—inside, a slow and routinized mood dominates.

Getting Bored

It is not that nothing happens inside these detention homes, it just feels like time moves slowly (cf. Torbenfeldt Bengtsson, 2012, p. 537). A single day feels long. Even a temporary visitor soon gets acquainted with the premises and the people, and becomes resigned: "this is how this place is," "I won't get outside today." An institution can be quite large, and the area it covers quite varied, but a given ward is not. The young people spend most of their time inside their ward, and when they go to other locations for programs, school, and meals, they go to the same places over and over again.

When I review my fieldnotes from a single day during my school project, for instance, I can find a range of observed activities, relations, and quite animated events, but—eventually—I come to notes about the monotony and boredom. I seem to have been occupied with people's talk and performance during the day, but in the evening and at night I found reasons to note the stillness and its emotional landscape. I will illustrate this paradoxical combination—of action and boredom, to use Torbenfeldt Bengtsson's (2012) dichotomy in her study of confined youth—by retelling a couple of passages from a single day.

A Lively Setting . . .

During breakfast that day, I took notes on a conversation between a treatment assistant, two teachers, the caretaker and myself, regarding a new inmate: a young man who had committed a robbery and was rumored to have hidden away millions of Swedish crowns. I asked how they know such things, and the treatment assistant said it was just things "you hear." We also discussed the caretaker's position at the detention home, and the fact that he sometimes had good relations with the residents. One boy even complained when the caretaker went on vacation, one of the teachers said, since he could not understand why he had to go. Staff had to say, "we need to follow the law [on vacations]" to comfort the boy, who missed the caretaker tremendously. All laughed and enjoyed this story. The point was the caretaker's rehabilitative role at the detention home was unexpected, since it was officially assigned to the treatment assistants.

I also took notes on my efforts to interview young people, and the fact that I didn't succeed until the afternoon, when I interviewed three right away. I went over to another ward and asked some guys if they wanted to be interviewed, and almost got one, here called Oscar, interested. But then he regretted it, and "looked down." The guys were watching TV, and it felt like the fact that I asked them to be interviewed all at once made them uncomfortable in some way. When I talked with Marika, one of the teachers, about this, she said that probably one of them, Felipe, was "governing" the others. She indicated an internal hierarchy that would account for their lack of interest.

That afternoon, I also went and sat in the teachers' room, listening to how they discussed Dave, one of the inmates. One teacher said she had "found a diagnosis that fits him" and read out the symptoms from a screen. The other teacher said "yes," and "uhum," confirming her idea and the symptoms. Later, I listened to parts of a talk between these two teachers and a newly recruited substitute and noted that the teachers were "elated" as the recruitment meant they could go on vacation "in peace and quiet" and not leave too much difficult stuff for a third teacher to handle alone. They were particularly happy that the substitute had some previous work experience, and that she happened to be present this particular day when one of the inmates "had an outburst." I also witnessed this outburst: a guy hit a window, yelling, and I had noted that the newly recruited substitute hardly seemed to react at all. She just responded very calmly, and I know this is the preferred way among staff in general. The two teachers said that this means that the substitute now "knows what this job is about."

. . . *But Still Boring*

So, on the one hand, these multifaceted and varied notes on how staff described the young people, how they dramatized their job and accounted for their knowledge, and how teasing and funny poses by the young people could entertain a whole ward after the dinner. And, on the other hand, this note, from late at night the same day:

> The boredom—what to do with all time? It is no coincidence that detention homes are filled with TVs, computer games, board games. Everywhere these sofas, games. The deck of cards at the ward, the well-filled shelves with board games . . . the nice armchairs, etc. I'm surprised how quickly I get bored, a bit depressed even, start calling home, start ruminating, "What am I really doing?" (with this fieldwork). I start playing solitaire on the laptop, I haven't done that in years. I switch channel after channel in a way I only do when I'm ill or when I was a student. I have a lot of time left, despite having done my interviews and interesting observations today . . . There's an impulse to go into a vegetative state with a lot of TV. I watch a complete commemoration show for an artist I don't even care about, without being interested at all, since (ironically stated) it is relatively interesting . . . (compared to the detention home boredom). I also ruminate about the project a bit, well not really the project but this practice of sociologizing things in life. I also think about all these resources, what it takes to keep an institution like this going (the staff, the premises, all furniture, etc.) and how little time seems to be devoted directly to changing the young people, who must be fooling around pretty much just like me this evening and night.

Even at the end of an ethnographically productive day (fieldnotes taken, interviews done), I observe my boredom and associate it directly with the setting. The available activities (TV, computer games, board games) are noted as institutional means to address this boredom in the detention home, as if it is natural to feel bored here, and as if staff and the whole institution even expect it. I also start to note my own behavior, finding it odd and out of character (playing solitaire, watching TV shows I usually do not care about, etc.), and criticize myself for lapsing into meaningless things. An ocean of time makes me "ruminate" about the essence of my work, as well as the essence of the institution. I start to question its *raison d'être*. What is the point of these specially approved homes if the young people feel like I feel, and if so little energy is mobilized to improve their lives? I question sociology's *raison d'être*. What is the meaning of all these studies?

My point is not to encourage self-absorbed or melancholic writing but to underline how fieldnotes like these can articulate a glimpse of experienced confinement. I felt stuck at the detention home and, to express this, I drew on a sort of drifting writing style, in which I wander between my own and the inmates' situation, combining and juxtaposing them (linking their TV watching to my own, their gaming with my own, etc.). I also wander between myself and the institution. The experienced lack of meaning seemed to expand from my personal emotions into the setting (and my work there) as well as the other way around. Bored, I start to let go of the disciplined (and externally more descriptive) writing style I had used during the day. My style turned less consistent. I don't seem to really care what I write in the notes, as if I have quit working and just write whatever I feel. I don't think I ever imagined I would cite these notes directly.

Fieldnotes like these not only are site-specific, grounded in the institution and its atmosphere, but also feed back into it. They sensitized me toward certain aspects and thereby contributed to constructing it along certain lines in my fieldwork, in both my perception and my interactions. I could more easily pay attention to boredom and a sense of meaninglessness in the wards, and how this was managed. I could become more alert to the institutional members' signs and invocations of confinement.

Some of the scenes retold from that day—such as the teachers' discussions of diagnoses and a newcomer's crimes, as well as their conversation about the recruited substitute and an inmate's outburst—might actually be quite dependent on the closed environment and are better understood if confinement is taken into account. Staff express a sort of "ownership" over the young people by continuously describing and typifying them, and the young people find ways (and reasons) to destabilize the staff they constantly see around them, if just temporarily. Risk-taking action, as Torbenfeldt Bengtsson (2012, p. 528) notes, can be a way to deal with experiences of boredom in confinement, creating a momentary feeling of freedom and power. The social world in place is organized and transpires reflexively in relation to the sited conditions of production.

Tasting "Light Paranoia"

A related aspect is the surveillance which makes a detention home a place of tension and control. When you enter the buildings, you have to identify yourself. Doors are locked and the staff have the keys. They control the cameras and the institutional alert system. The staff also control the office area in each ward, which is situated in the middle, with big windows facing the living room and corridors. Together with the screens from the surveillance cameras, this creates a sort of panopticon. They aim to watch all, through windows and cameras, and they possess the overview. They write running case reports on each inmate, which can be read by all the staff (Wästerfors & Åkerström, 2015), and they have many meetings and conferences discussing them. Over the years I worked on these three projects, many have said to me that control and security at these institutions have increased, step by step. At one institution, for instance, fences were complemented with barbed wire on top, and more cameras were installed.

As a visiting ethnographer it can be wise to not identify too closely (or too often) with the staff, so I was careful to spend a lot of time in the young people's areas, such as the living room, the kitchen, and the corridors. When I followed lessons, I similarly tried to stay close to the young people's desks and computers. I followed their work, helped out sometimes, and we had breaks together, drinking coffee, eating biscuits, and chatting. Quite early, I mentioned the cameras in my notes, but only in passing. This is from the day I arrived at the institution I described earlier:

> The young people watch TV, move around in the corridors, I introduce myself to them. They are filmed by cameras; I can see the screens (with the live surveillance shown) at the office where the staff hang around. I ask an inmate where the camera is, and he points to one.

The cameras meant that I easily ended up feeling a bit surveilled, too. Of course, a researcher is not zoomed in as much as the inmates, but still the self-awareness was there. There have been cases of staff smuggling in drugs and mobile phones, and the young people's social contacts with the outside are carefully regulated. Staff can be fired if they misbehave, for instance, if they over-react in conflict management, and a visiting researcher is, of course, also supposed to behave. At the same time, many occasions are relaxed and "loose" at these detention homes. When joking together after dinner, the interactions are far from rigid or contained and this is true also when playing TV games on a Saturday afternoon, or when playfighting briefly in the workshop (Wästerfors, 2016). The constant surveillance blends into the background and is only pointed out now and then, such as in anecdotes and insinuations. This is from a lesson:

> Victor (one of the inmates) wants to go directly for lunch, but it's not time yet. He grabs a chair, raises it slowly in the air in a sort of elaborate way, showing that this is just for fun, and aims it at Pete (a staff member) who sits by the table. He treats the chair like a weapon against Pete, but again, just for fun. "You can tell time," Pete says, and smiles. "It's two minutes left." Victor says to me and Pete that it is too damned bad there are cameras here, they will just rewind the film and see all that has happened. He jokingly implies that this is the only thing that stops him from hitting Pete with the chair. Pete quickly responds—also jokingly—that cameras won't help him (Pete), implying that Victor will hit him even if filmed, if he wants to, and adds that he won't hit back anyhow.

Cameras are integrated into this setting, treated as natural parts, and can be joked about or pointed at, like many other components of the setting, as long as it makes sense in the ongoing interaction. It seems telling for this setting that cameras do make sense in the situation depicted earlier, where violence is joked about. Mostly, though, cameras are seen but unnoticed, and not invoked in interaction.

Noting Surveillance—and Intellectualizing It

In the separate apartment within the institution where I stayed (used for visiting family members and as a training apartment in the later stages of rehabilitation), there were also cameras. This is the site of my personally heightened sensitivity in relation to them. As I moved between the rooms, I was unsure whether they were turned on—but it didn't really matter. I started to feel surveilled anyway. As I went from the sofa to the kitchenette to make myself yet another cup of tea, I started to look at my own behavior "from above." Do my movements make sense? Did I go back and forth one time too many? I tried to shake off this thought, reprimanding myself for being paranoid, but I could not get rid of the feeling of behaving oddly in the eyes of an anonymous watcher. I could not relax and longed for company. I later arranged to sleep in another part of the buildings, in a small room without cameras, and with staff members nearby. This is a note from my time of "light paranoia," before I moved:

> There are cameras in "my" apartment, too, influencing my movements, undoubtedly. I turn more self-conscious and start thinking things like, "Am I really going to make another errand to the kitchenette?" "Does it look weird?" ([The cameras] impose as sort of extra demand for accountability onto everyday actions, it appears to me.)

That night in the rehabilitation apartment was not pleasant. My fieldnote just touches upon the feelings I had, which were probably a bit too embarrassing to write down, or perhaps just too messy. To feel watched by—a most likely imagined—institutional Big Brother after a day of observations and interviews in a fairly new place was not what I wanted. I felt out of place as it was, and the thought that staff could see me watching TV and walking around and perhaps have a laugh at, say, me not finding the right stuff in the kitchenette, was not a nice one. I think the last part of the previously cited fieldnote—the sentence in brackets—is illustrative in this respect. Yes, cameras may well impose an extra demand to account for one's actions—an "extra demand for *accountability*"—but thinking back on my situation and what I felt, I now realize that this was an intellectual note, a sort of theoretical flight. It did not pinpoint the feeling of paranoia but explained it, as if the term "accountability" would help me feel better, there and then.

I think this note—along with the experience itself—was a helpful one in the long term. I got a slight sense of how surveillance can be integrated into a feeling of not being oneself at a detention home, not being able to relax even when backstage, and I got a reminder of the amount of energy that must be devoted to processing local surveillance by those being surveilled. Whereas staff logged out after their shifts, those staying at the detention home—the young inmates—did not. They never logged out, and my brief "participation" in this predicament was educational.

I tried to log out myself. I used an intellectual term in my note-takings and thereby tried to underline the difference between me and the setting: I'm here, but still, I'm not.

Fiddling With an Identity Kit

"Identity kit" is Erving Goffman's (1961, 1990, p. 20) concept. He writes that inmates in total institutions are stripped of their identity kit when taken in. They have to hand over their private clothes, get dressed as patients, and they also have to hand over their private belongings (the ones used "for the management of his personal front," Goffman, 1969, 1990, p. 20). From that point on, asking and begging for this or that private item is a significant part of their days. Site-specifics can temper this. The situation in contemporary Swedish detention homes is not as extreme as Goffman envisioned. Inmates wear their own clothes, and individual styles are allowed: make-up and jewelry, caps and hats, private belongings in one's room, music and posters, private letters and shopping excursions, etc. Still staff regulate what to keep, and unannounced strip searches occur, as well as room inspections. I once had my camera stolen by some inmates (see the story in Wästerfors, 2013; I got the camera back but lost the memory card), so there are reasons to keep an eye on one's belongings. Stories about theft and losses are common, and Goffman's principal observation of the institution's effort to dismantle a previous identity and manufacture a new one is still valid. The young people's identity kits are delimited and constrained, inspected and watched, and nobody would argue that their styles on display inside the wards are identical to those outside.

For example, the site-specifics of entry to the institution are ethnographically pertinent. As with boredom and surveillance, private belongings are telling when it comes to confinement. My way of handling the items I brought in was far from identical to the young inmates' ways, but I noticed some parallels.

First, when entering a ward, one may go through either the main entrance used by the inmates and staff (as the staff must open the door) or the entrances leading directly to the staff rooms, which are used only by staff. From the staff rooms, one may enter the rest of the ward via the office area with its surveillance screens and windows looking onto corridors and the living room. This means that if I enter through the main entrance, there is no backstage in which I can prepare myself and put away personal belongings. I have to knock on the door to the office and ask about leaving my jacket, my mobile phone, my bag, etc. Entering via the staff rooms is in many ways more convenient, but ethnographically it associates me with the staff. I then behave like a staff member or, to be precise, a staff member who is not accompanying inmates. If I use the main entrance, I come closer to the inmates, but I also find myself in a sort of identificatory limbo. The young people can walk straight to their rooms and put their belongings there. I have to knock and ask if I can unload my things in the office, or—as I have sometimes done—just leave my jacket on the sofa in the living room and keep my bag with me. I enjoy the relative privacy of neither the staff nor the inmates.

I never settled into a clear routine. One time I did this, another time that. Often, I kept my bag with my voice recorder, some extra batteries, some pens, and extra notebooks (and some books to read, in case of free time), but then I agonized over where I put it, in case somebody took something from it or staff started an inspection. Maybe I had mistakenly brought something forbidden or regulated, like painkillers or the allergy pills which I usually keep in my bag. Sometimes staff said, "Would you like to keep some stuff in here?," or "You can hang your jacket in my locker." But sometimes they were too occupied to notice or simply assumed that I would deal with my things the way I wanted. As I moved around, walking to and from the school building together with the young people, or to and from the dining hall (some meals, though, were eaten inside the ward), I faced a new round of knocks on doors and requests for my stuff (put inside the staff areas), in case I did not have them close to me already.

All this resulted in quite complicated maneuvers with my belongings. I had to constantly watch them and keep them in mind, even though they were few in number and hardly valuable, at least not in terms of money. My notebook and the recordings, though, were highly valuable for my research, and quite sensitive. If somebody were to take my recordings, they could start listening to what people had told me in confidential interviews, and the notebook contained similarly sensitive materials. The notebook, however, was the least of my problems. I usually had it in my hand or close by on a table or desk, and I made it a habit not to hide what I wrote from the young people. After an initial spark of interest, they soon stopped paying attention. My notes were too dull and commonplace for them, just line after line on what was happening right in front of their eyes, with prosaic jottings about things they knew all too well. There was juicy stuff, too, but embedded into a tapestry of mundane text, mostly not even readable because of my handwriting. Still, I wanted to keep the notes close to me, even though I didn't treat them as secret, since my work and my writings depended on them. So my attention was always directed at exactly where I had put them—they defined my identity.

My fiddling with my stuff is far from identical to how inmates did it, nor is it the same as the staff variant. But, as I gradually learned to watch and take care of my belongings as soon as I got inside a ward, I became attuned to what confinement can mean materially. This aspect of site-specificity crept close to my body and the things I usually wear and carry. There is no other place where I think about my belongings and handle them so carefully and consciously as I did inside these detention homes. In a way, the items were also imprisoned.

Conclusion

In this chapter, I have discussed some ways to get at the experience of confinement in institutions with the help of my ethnographic data from youth detention homes in Sweden and my research role in this setting. The young people cannot leave without permission, whereas the visiting researcher can, so the conditions can be seen as relatively difficult for the researcher when it comes to gaining personal knowledge about how it feels to be confined and what adaptations and tactics it may entail.

However, there are some possible solutions. By paying close attention to one's own sense of relative and temporary confinement—in my case evident in my sense of boredom, surveillance, and identity kit management—fieldworkers can sharpen their attention also to the situation of institutional members. In my subsequent studies of violent events in detention homes, many of the experiences narrated by young people and staff revolved around a feeling of being pushed into a corner or being stuck in a tiny spot. "I always get mad when somebody grabs me," a 16-year-old boy said when talking about an incident. When staff did exactly this and diminished his elbow room even more—which was already small—he almost exploded. "So I pushed him away," he said, referring to his protest, "and I asked them to just be, you know, move a bit, back off, so that I can breathe." By defending his space and making sure he had some room to relax, the feeling of being pushed into a corner subsided. "Then, after that, I calmed down pretty soon." Even though this boy talked about a particular tense situation—not one that occurs every day in a detention home—I started to consider that he was, in fact, pushed into a corner interactionally and culturally, simply by experiencing confinement. This is not a legitimate excuse for behaving violently, but it might be a key to understanding it socially. I started to look more systematically for narratives of similar social pressures—tightened control, diminished elbow room, too closely delivered corrections or what Black (2011, Chapter 2) calls "overintimacy"—and I started to analyze the institutional members' preventive advice in terms of giving the other space (Wästerfors, 2019).

Diminished elbow room was what I experienced during the days I exemplified earlier, although in a downplayed and temporary way. I tried out a drifting writing style in my fieldnotes—wandering between myself and the institution—and at times I let go of the more disciplined depictions and allowed myself to just write what I felt. But I also made use of intellectual flight and distance markers in my note-takings, as if keeping the pressure from the institutional regime at arm's length, and could only retrospectively—when reviewing the notes again—trace my emotions between the lines.

I think my experiences of fieldwork in these settings may help us further understand the significance of site-specificity and how it both conditions and stimulate concrete fieldwork. To attain local knowledge, as well as manage it in social interaction, is to strengthen the ethnographers' personal sense of what is specific at a site, and to cultivate a responsive research role. This means that ethnographers cannot rely merely on procedural principles or lists of general criteria. They need to try out and tailor their material-generating sensitivities in situ and in close interaction with field members, and in so doing pay close attention to which features these sensitivities come to speak of.

To get at the experience of confinement within my projects, the ethnographic method could not be specified before fieldwork. Rather, the fieldwork—as it played out—specified the method.

Note

1 All projects have been reviewed by the Swedish Ethics Review Board. All names have been fictionalized and some details replaced in the data presented in this chapter to protect the informants' identities.

References

Black, D. (2011). *Moral time*. Oxford University Press.

Emerson, R. M., Fretz, R. I., & Shaw, L. L. (1995). *Writing ethnographic fieldnotes*. University of Chicago Press.

Enell, S., Gruber, S., & Vogel, A. M. (Eds.). (2018). *Kontrollerade unga. Tvångspraktiker på institution*. Studentlitteratur.

Goffman, E. (1961, 1990). *Asylums. Essays on the social situation of mental patients and other inmates*. Anchor Books.

Gubrium, J. F. (1975, 1997). *Living and dying at Murray Manor*. University Press of Virginia.

Jefferson, A. M. (2014). Conceptualizing confinement: Prisons and poverty in Sierra Leone. *Criminology & Criminal Justice*, *14*(1), 44–60.

Platt, A. M. (1969, 1977). *The child savers. The invention of delinquency*. Rutgers University Press.

Torbenfeldt Bengtsson Tea. (2012). Boredom and action—experiences from youth confinement. *Journal of Contemporary Ethnography*, *41*(5), 526–553.

Wästerfors, D. (2011). Disputes and going concerns in an institution for 'troublesome' boys. *Journal of Contemporary Ethnography*, *40*(1), 39–70.

Wästerfors, D. (2012). Analyzing social ties in total institutions. *Qualitative Sociology Review*, *VIII*(2), 12–27.

Wästerfors, D. (2013). Fragments of home in youth care institutions. In M. Kusenbach & K. E. Paulsen (Eds.), *Home. International perspectives on culture, identity, and belonging*. Peter Lang Publishing Group.

Wästerfors, D. (2016). Playfights as trouble and respite. *Journal of Contemporary Ethnography*, *45*(2), 168–197.

Wästerfors, D. (2019). *Vanskligt och kort. Om våldshändelser bland unga på institution*. Studentlitteratur.

Wästerfors, D., & Åkerström, M. (2015). Case history discourse. A rhetoric of troublesome youngsters and faceless treatment. *European Journal of Social Work*, *19*(6), 871–886.

3

WORKING AGAINST SOCIAL ORDER IN DOCUMENTING IMPRISONMENT

Mahuya Bandyopadhyay

Following the so-called writing culture debate in social research, ethnography took a fierce self-reflexive turn presenting the entanglements of power, privilege, marginality, grounded categories of understanding, and long-standing theoretical ideas (Clifford & George, 1986). In this spirit, resisting totalized and integrating concepts such as "culture" and "society," this chapter argues for a critical perspective on the ordering of complex, paradoxical, and irreconcilable processes of the "social order" in prison (cf. Abu-Lughod, 1996). The fundamental question of what constitutes the social in prison shines a light on how to retrieve it, make it intelligible, and theorize around it.

Probing this question leads to explorations beyond the domain of "order," which is fundamental to a prison, and ultimately to what I will refer to as "chaotic." This enables us to reconsider our relationship to fieldwork and ethnography in social research. The discussion is divided into three parts. In the first part, I present some of the chaotic practices of prison life as a way of articulating the problems and strategies of recording the imponderabilia of everyday prison life. In the second section, I trace a somewhat haphazard, resistant, and critical genealogy of the question of sociality and order in the social sciences, showing the connections between these ideas and my field experience. Finally, I reflect on how prison sociality may be discovered, known, and represented by focusing on the embodied, sensory experience of prison life.

Ethnographic Context and Fieldwork

I draw on reflections on my fieldwork in the late 1990s in two large central prisons in India over 2 years. Provincial and local, rather than federal, laws govern the prison system in India, and there is some variation between how different provinces manage their prisons and prison populations. How prison reform projects

DOI: 10.4324/9781003275121-5

are imagined and implemented too is different in the states and in different prisons within a province. Gaining access to prisons was not easy, and in my case, it was enabled only through informal channels of family friends and connections with political leaders. The lack of any formal policies and institutionalized provisions for research on prisons made access difficult. On the other hand, the lack of institutionalized processes of ethics review and human subject protocols implied that the university placed relatively fewer constraints on such research. The ethics review and human subject protocols were not built into university bureaucratic practices as they are now. Ethical issues and our training to deal with them were largely the domain of supervisor–scholar relations and were often worked out through the regular, formal, and informal conversations that scholars had to engage in as part of the requirements of the doctoral program.

I began my fieldwork with the framework of "quasi-ethnography" (Bandyopadhyay, 2015; Fairbrother, 1977; Moczydlowski, 1992), with self-consciousness about the drawbacks of my doctoral project, as I would never really be able to participate fully in the lives of those I was studying. I would not be able to observe at all hours over a long time. My access to the field was fractured due to the breaks between the periods of the permission granted to me. It was also fractured because of the constant surveillance of me, the prisoners, and the organization of the prison. The prison housed both male and female prisoners. I had relatively unhindered access to the female ward of the prison. The enclosure for the women prisoners was in one corner of the prison compound. At the far end of this enclosure, there was a dilapidated structure with small rooms intended as cells for one or two prisoners. One of the rooms on the first floor of this building was a schoolroom for the children of prisoners and for adult prisoners who wanted to get basic literacy. I would be accompanied to the enclosure by a female warder and was allowed to sit in the schoolroom. I held more formal interviews with male prisoners in the main office of the prison, which was located at the entrance to the prison compound. On some days, the Prison Welfare Officer would take me to his office inside one of the male wards of the prison. Over time, my interactions with the prisoners moved outside the prison. I connected with prisoners who were released, prisoners going on their court dates and with friends and families of some prisoners.

What does it mean to engage in ethnographic fieldwork when only a speck of the prison fieldwork experience is tuned to established practices of ethnography? The hierarchization of ethnographic sites and fields, practices and concerns regarding the valid questions, concepts, and themes of study that guide and frame ethnography is not productive for ethnography and the ethnographic method. As essential signposts of its technique and practice, ethnography has tended to draw from a (Bronislaw) Malinowskian conception of "imponderabilia of daily life," a (Clifford) Geertz (1973) notion of "thick description," and William Foote Whyte's (1955) cultural dialogues and absorption in street corner gang life. Over time, a hierarchy of venues and behaviors has emerged (Gupta & Ferguson, 1997) based on the capacity to duplicate the practice of immersing oneself in the lives of the people being studied, as well as geographic, cultural, and social isolation from the fieldworker's social sphere, and a rigorous separation from home and the ethnographic field.

Because ethnography in prisons does not satisfy these criteria, it has been reduced to the status of quasi-ethnography. While conducting fieldwork, I realized that many ethnographic techniques needed to be repurposed to align with ethnography's methodological prescriptions. For example, I found that practicing subversions with inmates was a tactic for overcoming access constraints and minimizing the limitations on establishing solidarities. Prison ethnography might thereby nurture ethnographic and methodological sensibilities that would otherwise be elusive in the typically free, open, and inviting ethnographic environments of villages, small towns, and neighborhoods. This may help rethink how ethnographic research may be undertaken in these relatively free settings, largely anchored to rapport-building, immersion, and a participative, helpful orientation (Drake et al., 2015).

Everyday Chaos and Its Limits

I focus on some constituent practices of prison life to understand interruptions in the everyday and the boundaries of chaos. Chaos is defined in this context as the unpredictable, disorderly experience of prison life. It implies a close connection of systems so that minor alterations in one part of daily life might have significant and often severe ramifications in the other domains. I outline three activities: *gunti*, or head count of inmates; *diet dhora*, or eating; and *mulaqat*, or scheduled encounters between convicts and family members. These organizational practices were critical in establishing a temporal rhythm in daily life, monitoring body movement within the prison's many locations, and managing all forms of physical activity. As a male warder pointed out:

> What work do they (prisoners) have? Giving gunti, eating, bathing, cleaning, and sleeping. Some inmates work like cooking, cleaning the wards, sewing, and working in the offices, but most inmates must be kept busy with just gunti and eating and sleeping. That is their work.

These practices have the potency to encourage and forge bodily changes in individuals who encounter them. The routines prompt changes in temporal patterns and the resetting of the body clock. These transformations occur when prisoners spend sufficient time in prison and transition from fearful, unsure, and subservient inmates to confident, subversive, and fierce navigators.

The practice of gunti or regular head count of prisoners is a defining aspect of prison administration and a core practice to instate discipline and order in everyday prison life. Matching the physical head count of prisoners with the figures available with the main office cross-checking with the number of prisoners who are out on bail, court dates, or recent releases forms part of the practice of gunti.

This task was divided according to the wards and cells, with the convict warders[1] of each ward being responsible for doing the physical count and informing the warders who would, in turn, inform the deputy jailors and other prison staff in the main office. The protocols of this practice are rigid and streamlined, yet it appears in the prison everyday as a forceful, disruptive event. Gunti was the responsibility of convict helpers or mate pahara and the writer (the convict who helps the prison warders manage prisoners and keep records). They would bark orders and yell at all prisoners to get them to be in their respective cells, wards, and designated places within the ward. After this, the mate pahara or convict in charge of the ward would do a physical count, shouting at anyone who happened to move or not be in her place. If the count did not match the stipulated number, more shouting ensued. Small arguments inevitably broke out as blame was apportioned to some inmate for the error in gunti. Then the physical count had to be redone again until it was right. The convict helpers in the "female ward" were tense and nervous about getting it wrong. A minor error would mean complete recounting, leading to a general state of agitation in the wards. Not being in the designated space at the time of gunti not taking full responsibility for being counted were seen as severe infractions. Sending prisoners off on their court dates was also an everyday task that needed care and involvement of the staff, convict warders, and prisoners. I have argued that prisoners tended to present these everyday activities as "work" and reclaimed a sense of control and agency over imposed activities designed to structure their daily life in prison. These everyday practices were meant to ensure that the fundamental task of securing prisoners within a particular space, putting controls on physical mobility and enforcing participation in specific everyday tasks, was being followed. Through this, the routinized, homogenized order became an everyday reality. The noisy observations around the task of gunti involved the liberal exchange of abuses, arguments and conflicted interactions, display of power by warders and convict helpers, and a general sense of anxiety till the gunti was settled.

Similarly, all convicts were required to follow diet dhora, or eating at predetermined times. The food was distributed by a mate pahara, a convict assistant who sat in the female ward compound's center. All the convicts would come to her with their tin plates and bowls to collect their food. I have also termed diet dhora as a disorderly activity (Bandyopadhyay, 2010). As people crowded around to get their meal, disputes and scrambling for space were inevitable. Although the prison authorities intended diet dhora to be an ordering everyday practice, it became a hotbed of unanticipated interactions. Accusations of unethical distribution and grievances against the convict assistant in charge of food distribution were frequent. Throughout my fieldwork, the convict assistant was an angry woman who would not allow such complaints. She was continually retaliating, hurling abuses, which added to the activity and allocated space's hostile atmosphere. Warders frequently chose to ignore animosity, disputes, and confrontations. They would argue that "we do not wish to intervene in every minor altercation. We simply allow them to do so till they come to blows and fistfights." Occasionally, this antagonism manifested itself exaggeratedly in the form of slaps and beatings among convicts, followed by the forced involvement of warders. Punishments would be meted out. The situation would be peaceful only following a full-fledged conflict involving multiple prisoners and warders, even if the conflict began as a minor argument over food proportions or turn-taking for food collection.

The mulaqat or interview, prisoners' encounters with family and life beyond prison walls, and the outsider's glimpse into the inmate world inside prison walls were all but a chaotic interlude (Moran, 2013). While some mulaqat rooms have been updated, most remain the traditional chambers where convicts must meet their family members across a wire mesh. There will always be more individuals to meet than there is time or room. There were no glass enclosures or telephones in most prisons to facilitate communication. The mulaqat chambers and the practice of family visits are critical spaces in shaping convicts' perceptions of prison space and time. These interludes serve as a reminder of the liberties available outside of prison. While they allow for a rights-based approach to the management of the prison population, the design of the space and the mulaqat's constituent elements contribute a sense of disorder, arbitrariness, and unpredictability. Mulaqat is also a discretionary privilege that can be granted or revoked. Some prisoners can use their privilege within the system or even pay bribes to get permission for out-of-turn mulaqat, private meetings, or longer meetings. All of this contributes to the mulaqat's perception of disorder.

Two themes emerge here: a culture of lenience and chaotic daily life within an ordered, total institution. A culture of lenience implies a laxity in the application of prison rules and a differential experience of incarceration for different groups of prisoners. Such lenience, I have argued, emerged from the fusion of functions, when convict prisoners are enlisted to help the warders in everyday management and administration of the prison. Continuous limitations and monitoring on time, place, and the body are imposed by the fusion of functions. A few convicts are chosen to do the daily tasks of counting, feeding, and securing inmates, blurring the distinction between controller and controlled. Inmates undertaking these tasks receive formal and informal incentives. The practice of mixing tasks results in power entanglements, as warders and prison authorities no longer exercise sole authority. This approach supports informal prison hierarchies based on the crimes inmates are accused of or convicted for, their social class outside prison, access to money and other resources, and relationships formed within prison walls. These power and privilege entanglements and interconnected duties generate daily instability and foster a permissive prison culture, allowing some convicts to endure extreme cruelty and punishment while others enjoy relative freedom and privileges.

Introducing flexibility and lenience in the application and practice of prison rules leads to chaos in everyday prison life. The paradoxical and incompatible parts of chaos further enable a reflective assessment of repression in Indian prisons. Repression and violence do not always emerge from the rigidities of discipline and order, as is widely assumed. Rather, the chaos of daily life leads to the unpredictability of norms, arbitrariness in enforcing rules, and the disproportionate exercise of rights, privileges, punishments, and rewards. These contribute to the production of environments conducive to violence, enslavement, and denial. What kind of methods might we use while doing ethnographic fieldwork in prisons to uncover these repressions in these chaotic encounters, which often render close observation, reflexivity, and analysis difficult? What are the consequences of acknowledging this chaos for the craft of ethnography?

The Imponderabilia of Objects, Spaces, and Bodies

In practices of incarceration, the imprisoned body is not free. Nor is the body of the fieldworker who enters the prison and spends time there trying to make sense of prison life. In this section, I show that unraveling the embodied experience of incarceration through the imbricated relations between bodies, spaces, and daily objects is central to understanding prison sociality. The restrained, unfree body and simultaneously the agentic, resistant deployment of the prisoner's body in creating emergent forms of everyday are crucial in everyday prison life.

Between three and five o'clock, every afternoon, I made my way down from my imprisoned space, the schoolroom at the far end of the female ward, where I was instructed to sit and conduct my interviews with women prisoners. Female prisoners would be sent up to the schoolroom to speak to me. I spent a lot of time with the schoolteacher, the children, and the odd prisoner eager to learn to read and write. Just at the entrance to this building, there was the sewing room and a few cells on the first floor. Women gathered around the entrance to this building around 3 in the afternoon every day, sitting, talking, and laughing. Sensing this to be an opportunity to speak to prisoners informally, I began hanging out here. I would carefully position myself at the door of the building, from where I would be visible to the women who sat around but not fully visible to the warders who were at a distance. If anyone came up to the group, I could easily retreat into the dark interiors of the building or run up the stairs to my designated spot—the schoolroom. So began my furtive, subversive hanging out with prisoners in the female ward. This was the closest I could get to participant observation and an immersive prison experience for a few hours every day. On most days, I spent the last 2 hours of my prison day in this space, chatting, observing, and being observed.

I learned a great deal about how the women prisoners saw themselves. I realized that the women prisoners did not want to come too close to me, as they did not want me to be repulsed by their body odor. On a typical day, as I sat talking and listening, one of the young, gregarious women prisoners, Bina,[2] came and sat next to me and spoke with her hand on my arm. Bina was loud, dramatic, and often the center of many "scenes" in the female ward. Reshma was quick to scold her. "Sit apart from Didi,"[3] she said, "you stink." I was equally quick to retort that she did not stink, and it was alright. I was embarrassed. It was as if I had uttered those words. Bina took it well, only because it came from her best friend, Reshma. She moved ever so slightly, respecting Reshma's command and retaining her sense of proximity to me. Gaye porish na—don't fall on my body—was a common refrain for Bina and among women prisoners generally. They would use it for women they thought were always too close physically. It was also an expression used to signal an unwanted relationship—falling all over someone, even though the person was not interested in a friendship or interaction. The proximity of physical bodies, body odors, and perceptions around the bodies of women prisoners—my initial discussions on love and intimacy were anchored to these aspects. For many women, their intimate relationships outside were crucial, for either survival or imprisonment. The body and perceptions around the prisoners' bodies are imbricated with the culture of intimacy in the female ward. Often, women prisoners spoke not of their own lives and intimacies but of others.

I use this world of "gossip" to discuss the cultures of closeness in the prison's female quarters. The manner in which the women convicts conducted themselves, dressed, and utilized their bodies to communicate their gender and sexual identities was crucial to this gossip. I shall use Renu didi, a female guard in her mid-thirties, as an example. She was a tall, sturdy woman with a commanding demeanor. On one occasion, when she accompanied me from the prison's main entrance to the female ward, which was located in a corner, we encountered a male prisoner near the hospital ward. He was an undertrial prisoner in a highly publicized case. Renu didi exchanged glances with him as we passed and remarked, "*o amar bon, sister*" (literally, she is my sister, sister). As we approached the female ward's entrance, I asked what was going on, and she said, "*jail e shob hoy didi, bujhe nao. Tomay porey bolbo ek din*" (Everything occurs in jail, didi, you must understand. I will tell you another time). The warder's remark alluded to sexual ties within the jail and payment for sexual interactions. However, the guard feigned not to have divulged any information, and I appeared not to have grasped anything. I did not write about this experience. Nonetheless, I felt a profound sensation of unease and an unexplained threat. I felt the same way when I walked through the prison to reach the female ward. As I traversed the enormous male prisoner ward, I felt the penetrating gazes through the large iron grills that ran vertically along a vast section of the wall. I occasionally heard random, generally inaudible comments. Thereafter, there was laughing. On some days, when there were fewer convicts or if they had not spotted me approaching, I was able to sneak a peep into the male ward—an inaccessible area. In most instances, traversing the length of the wall with the iron grills was a humiliating experience that I eventually learned to overcome. My best tactic was to continue conversing with the female guard who accompanied me. This allowed me to ignore the glances. I ignored the remarks, jeers, and laughter. In recounting their first arrival into the female ward and their future journeys to the main office, a number of female convicts remarked about navigating this vast male convict ward. When a female prisoner went by this ward, the jeers, catcalls, remarks, and looks were unchecked. Many did what I did—paid no heed. Others said that they became accustomed to this attention over time. A female prisoner informed me, "We also converse with them, respond, and flirt a bit. It is harmless."

I narrated my exchange with Renu didi to one of my closest friends in the female ward, and she told me I should stay away from Renu didi as she had heard that some prisoners have seen her allowing male prisoners to grope her, touch her breasts in return for money, or anything else they may have. As this was within the realm of gossip, I had no way of verifying it. In earlier readings, analysis, and presentation of my fieldnotes and the analysis, I had excluded such instances, with typical methodological concerns of veracity. These encounters and prisoners' narrations hinge exclusively on the "body" of the prisoner. How is this body to be maintained and presented? What kinds of impressions must the body give off? What relationships are established and communicated between the body and personal belongings and between the bodies of prisoners? Seeking answers to these questions point to the imbricated relationship between emotion, body, and the prison experience. The corporeal body, the body in the way it marks out a specific private space, and its presentation in a larger public space—this is the material world that the prisoner accesses the most and with relative ease. Through the body, the prisoner and the warder convey acquiescence to structures of, and people in, authority. They also express disdain for prison rules and quiet derision for those with power.

The use of the prisoner's body and bodily waste as a weapon of last resort is well documented in Erving Goffman's (1961) work on life in the asylum. When prisoners are stripped of their belongings, they are inclined to utilize their bodies to resist and express themselves. I discovered numerous cases of this—male convicts refusing to shave or bathe upon entering prison and voicing their refusal as a means of opposing the prescribed daily routine of prison life. Such refusals were also a rejection of their pre-prison lifestyles marked by similar cleanliness and hygiene efforts. This was amplified in jail when warders and other convicts frequently stressed prisoners' need to maintain clean bodies. Any opposition to this would be construed as a challenge to the jail authorities and hence as acts of indiscipline to be punished. A female prisoner also similarly used bodily fluids when she was being forcibly held after she had attempted to escape during a hospital visit. When she was brought back into the female ward, she was flailing her arms and trying to fight off the warders holding her down and taking her to her cell for solitary confinement. She spat at the warders as a way of fending them off. Other women prisoners who saw this narrated it with a sense of appreciation, as though this woman prisoner had succeeded momentarily in demeaning the warders.

The granting of sexual favors to warders and other prisoners was considered a common strategy to gain privileges. While there was plenty of talk around this matter of sexual favors, most of it revolved around people talking about others rather than themselves—ethnographic content in the realm of rumor and gossip. I draw on two ethnographic instances that demonstrate the use of the prisoners' bodies for the sexual pleasuring of those in positions of power in return for items of need. The first instance concerns the sexual harassment of two young women prisoners by a male warder. The male warder supervising the cleaning of an unused ward by two young women prisoners promised them "Christmas cake" if they would lift their skirts and show him. The two young women complied but were later beaten up by other women prisoners for committing an act that gave the entire female ward a bad name (Bandyopadhyay, 2010). The other ethnographic evidence came from a young male prisoner who was apprehensive about speaking with me, the researcher, fearing that I was a journalist. He shared that in the initial days of incarceration, he was asked to be a partner of one of the senior and influential male prisoners in return for protection, food, a better place to sleep in, and other benefits that a new prisoner could not otherwise have. He refused and had narrated this to a visiting journalist. The young man's harassment only increased after this. His fear of speaking with an outsider was palpable.

One of my informants, an ex-political prisoner, spoke about life in prison in the seventies when the jail was filled with political prisoners. He said that this practice of getting protection and other privileges in return for sexual favors was known as *chokrabaazi*. The use of the body for sexual favors and in chokrabaazi was exploitative and violent, reinforcing the violence of everyday prison life. Prisoners could feel violated in specific contexts, in being asked to use their bodies for sexual favors, for instance, or they may choose to use their bodies and their substances to assert agency, express disrespect to authority, and acquire items of need. Tracing the connections between material objects, the body, and the abstract notions of identity and agency enables different explanations for corporeality in institutions of confinement. While corporeality is targeted as a medium of punishment, it is also used creatively by individuals to create everyday practices, defy order, and defile normative conceptions of body and its use. Conveying this domain of corporeality, both punishment and its navigation, is fundamental to the craft of ethnography in prison. These instances demonstrate that communicating embodiment of the researcher is critical for understanding the use of the body to generate systemic chaos, subversions, and the renewal of everyday prison life.

Order, Prison Sociality, and Crafting

In the preceding section, I argued that destabilizing bodily experiences enfold incoherence and chaos and shape the character of prison sociality. Ethnography in prison necessitates paying close attention to the embodiment of incarceration for both inmates and fieldworkers, albeit in circumscribed ways. Though vastly different, the embodied experiences of incarceration for the prisoner and fieldwork for the prison ethnographer share common ground in terms of limiting solidarities, exposing the "body" to scrutiny and surveillance, and placing an immense responsibility on defending the body from harm. A focus on these destabilizing experiences also reveals aspects of chaos in everyday prison life. In this part of the chapter, I explore how prison sociality may be theorized through the lens of order and chaos. Using social science studies on sociality, I demonstrate how criticisms of function and order and an emphasis on the material aspects of the social permit alternative conceptions of sociality. This conversation provides hints as to how prison ethnography and an emphasis on disorganization have the ability to express various meanings of the social, as opposed to presuming an obvious set of networks and relationships.

Sociality is usually understood as connections between people (Long & Moore, 2012). In social interactions, things aren't privileged (Leach, 1961; cf. Strathern in Ingold, 1996, 2005). Ethnographic accounts show how material items can frame organizational routines and convey organizational hierarchies. They can also be used to defy both. An overarching critique of sociality is the dependence on the functionalist argument as an explanans, which uses the biological analogy to claim that systems and organizations serve certain functions. Emile Durkheim, Bronislaw Malinowski, and Edward Radcliffe-Brown considered these structures as contributing to solidarity, coherence, and stability. Talcott Parsons (1951) theorized the social universe as four sorts of action systems: culture, society, personality, and organismic or behavioral, with associated functional demands of delay, integration, goal accomplishment, and adaptability. Robert Merton (1948, 1968) noted the problematic presupposition of social harmony when examining the persistence of societies. He responded with "dysfunction" and its significance for social order. However, the image of society as a system with diverse elements, each with a particular role, remained imprisoned within the larger concept of these parts contributing to systemic stability. This was the substance of functionalism and what social science was trying to unravel, portray, and theorize at the time.

Despite the waning influence of the functionalist perspective in understanding society, the force and hegemonic manifestation of the interest in order, its perpetuation, maintenance, and theoretical explanation, implied that the making of the "social" came to be seen mainly as a process of creating meaning and order. The act of creating was attributed to humans, as they could make meaning, understand the implications, and then represent and communicate this meaning. This process of sense-making is also crucial to another theoretical strand, symbolic interactionism (Blumer, 1969). This strand is complex in its layered understanding of how social order is made, focusing on language, communication, and symbols through which we learn to engage in our worlds and construct our realities. As a perspective, symbolic interactionism values the multiple identities and roles of the actors, their definitions of situations, and their cognitive processes. The shared nature of values and understanding of roles, the universality of reflexivity, and the processual yet cementing nature of these constructed realities are central aspects of symbolic interactionism. It also attempts to destabilize some of the certainties of the functionalist model of social order and persistence of societies. Critiques of the hegemonic notions of sociality and a focus on exclusions, thus, reveal alternate ways of conceptualizing the social. What follows is not an exhaustive documentation of these alternate conceptions of the social; rather a sampling of ideas of what it means to problematize human agency and order in discussions of sociality and attribute significance to the world of objects and its interface with human actors.

Ethnography is replete with instances of acknowledging the "thing" and the creation of value through circulation. Gifts, totems, and sacred groves play an important role in interpersonal relationships (Mauss, 1966; Strathern, 1988). Marcel Mauss'

(1966) work on the morality of the gift economy affirms the value of the item or object that makes relationships reciprocal and ensures long-term commitments between people and collectivities. Mauss mentioned three elements of the gift in Polynesian society: tonga, oloa, and hau. Things that are fixed in place are referred to as tonga. Tonga therefore represents inherited items that should be returned. The oloa are moving commodities, and hau is the spiritual power that all things have. As the object transfers from one individual/collectivity to another, the spiritual force moves with it. The object must return to its original owner because of its spiritual strength, and it is this spiritual power that keeps the thing in a continual motion cycle. The item's spiritual power fills the receiver's life with each motion, even as the receivers leave their mark on the thing. Accepting anything from someone entails accepting a fragment of his spiritual nature, which must be repaid at some point. As a result, objects have a magical and spiritual effect on the receiver. Without things, values, commitments, and lasting relationships would be incomplete. For the purposes of confinement and the establishment of regular routines in prison, objects and the organization of physical spaces are critical. Locks, keys, and bolts, the "lathi" (a stick carried by warders and used arbitrarily to chastise prisoners who break the rules), and big registers in which all information is recorded, are all important in keeping discipline and managing convicts. Inmates also utilize the objects to break laws, earn modest privileges, and reimagine their daily lives in jail. So, a new prisoner may sell the soap she receives from the administration to a warder in exchange for some advantages inside the jail, or a prisoner may give away a sari she received from her house to a warder in exchange for certain benefits within the prison. Relationships in prison revolve around things, and therefore, things and the material realm are significant in structuring everyday prison life. In terms of methodology, it's critical to recognize the importance of tangible items and the power with which they facilitate connections within jail. Hearing the voices of the marginalized is complemented by cultivating a meticulous sensitivity to the significance of material things and how they are utilized by various individuals within the jail to shape their everyday lives.

Whether the resistance to conventional notions of sociality lies in discovering the connections between multiple sites (Marcus, 1995), or in articulating the significance of things that contribute to enduring human relationships, or in destabilizing the apparent ways in which the collective is presented as a coherent whole—these are all significant questions of empirical research and theorizing in social research. Recent debates on the question of the Anthropocene have invigorated these concerns with the non-human environment, bringing them to the forefront of our academic exercises. Latour has been critical of the presumptive nature of "social" in the social sciences. One of the central ways of articulating what the social means rather than presuming an obvious set of networks and relationships is to focus anew on sociology of associations without privileging human actors. What are the ties that bind humans and non-humans within a particular setting? The location to observe and follow these connections lies in the hitherto unobserved. Events, cases, or situations that are destabilizing, incongruent, and contribute a sense of incoherence, rather than coherence, are rife with possibilities of discovering meaning, understanding, and grounded concepts. Such incoherent aspects are often omitted in the analysis of the social, or included as outliers, within a more general, encompassing analysis. In Latour's words,

> Every account . . . also consists of a decision about what the social should be . . . Rare are the group formations today that are not equipped and instrumented by economists, geographers, anthropologists, historians, and sociologists, who are hoping to learn how the groups are made, what are their boundaries and functions, and how best to maintain them.
>
> *(Latour, 2007, p. 258)*

Charles Perrow's (1984) attempt to decode the play of human and non-human agency is significant because he relies not on ordered situations but on rigid and risky ones to articulate the intricacies of the connections between human and non-human actors. In using high-risk technologies, such as in nuclear power plants, which are tightly coupled systems, accidents are normal, not in terms of the frequency with which they occur, but because of the inherent property of the system to experience such a breakdown. The accident would not typically fall under the rubric of the "everyday." But in this conception of normal accidents, they come to be seen not as extraordinary events but as part of everyday life. Tightly coupled systems are set up to experience catastrophic cascading effects, and accidents result from multiple failures. Perrow (1984) recognizes the non-human elements in making an accident. When an accident occurs, there is a tendency to find a human operator to blame, even though accidents are never really the sole responsibility of operators. Perrow's idea of the normalcy of accidents enables us to rethink sociality. It reminds us that in modern tightly coupled systems, understanding sociality requires us to consider the materials, substances, and organization of physical spaces and human bodies. Further, the accident, the disruption is not necessarily an extraordinary event in such systems; instead, disruptions are a part of the "normal" and the "everyday." In prison, escapes attempted escapes and other minor infractions and subversion of prison rules are normal accidents. The structuring of everyday life is oriented toward preventing these normal accidents, but they are constitutive of everyday prison life. Violent arguments often erupt during the distribution of food on certain days. Younger and less privileged prisoners are punished for the infractions of rules. One instance of this was the beating of two young women prisoners when they dared break a moral code in engaging with a visiting male warder. If contraband articles are discovered with prisoners, it disturbs the equilibrium between warders and prisoners, and a conflict ensues between them. Such moments of conflict and disruption hold clues to understanding prison sociality and order and its tenuous nature. Escape attempts and successful escapes have a spectral presence in everyday prison life. They enable a rethinking of the social in prison as being shaped by the ever-present possibility of the normal accident (Martin & Chantraine, 2018; Bandyopadhyay,

2018). For such rethinking to be enabled, the ethnographer must train one's eyes and ears to seek out elements of disruption and chaos in a seemingly ordered, and tightly structured everyday routine.

These ideas animate the discussion on prison sociality and the question of crafting ethnographic fieldwork in prison. How is prison fieldwork to be done? What does it mean to craft fieldwork? Is this crafting different in prison from other sites, such as an urban neighborhood? I probe these ideas further in the context of prison sociality. Simple, taken-for-granted understanding of sociality tends to privilege the agency of human actors and signify certain definable aspects of human relationships, such as interpretation of meanings and intersubjectivity, the network of relations, the dynamic flow of relationships of power, and ultimately the multiple ways in which people connect. The focus on people's connections with each other presumes linkages between order and sociality. Yet sociality is also about disorder and chaos. The braiding of order and chaos, normality and the abnormal, ordinary, and extraordinary aspects of everyday life play a role in making a distinctive sociality. Prison life symbolizes the extraordinary, as it contains a population whose performance in everyday lives was either deviant or at least suspected to be so. The prison also stands for an extreme form of social organization, where everyday life is performed in batches, uniformity of routine is maintained at all costs, discipline and the system of strict, dehumanizing punishment that enforces discipline is paramount. At the same time, prison life is chaotic, never stable, and rife with unpredictability and the transience of relationships. Due to this paradoxical nature of the social, the prison provides a unique location for understanding sociality.

Here, regular social interactions are impossible and personal identities are jeopardized by the institutional design. This provides fertile ground to reassess the model of human beings on which sociologists and social anthropologists frequently rely implicitly and uncritically. I have argued that the prison's uniqueness as a location for social interaction is contingent upon the researcher's ability to uncover prisoners' interaction with the prison's material reality. It is analytically significant to re-examine the materiality of prison experience through things such as locks and bolts embedded within prison walls, the high and imposing iron grill gates, the restricted personal items, the posters on the walls, the graffiti, the ropes, handcuffs, sticks, guns, sandbags, and uniforms.

The forms of prison sociality depend on how these elements emerge through the interconnected ties between individuals and various groups of participants within the jail. What might the ethnographic accounts earlier teach us about observing and recording daily life in prison? The craft of ethnographic fieldwork involves close observation, not unlike the kind that has been extolled since Malinowski's evocation of the imponderabilia of daily life. However, what is different is the experience of repression, subjugation, and surveillance in doing prison fieldwork. Recording this sensory experience of repression and surveillance and its impact on prisoners' sense of self is what most prisoners attempted to communicate in their conversations and interviews. The messy domain of intimacies linked to the physical closeness of bodies, the needs of bodies for warmth, love, and affection, what bodily expressions suggest—these aspects complicate and even compromise notions of prison discipline and ordered institutional space. The interactional space of the prison appears fraught with these struggles with the body, with hopes of liberation and freedom, or at least the hope of experiencing uplifting moments of freedom embedded in the experience of captivity.

This everyday sensory world is what ethnography can access, with the ethnographer as mediator. Making full use of oneself would then mean immersing oneself in the sensory experience of surveillance, repression, and control. Several directives of how I should do prison fieldwork influenced me and left their mark on my physical body. These included the anxieties I felt as a fieldworker, the hidden, ineffable dangers of being questioned by a male prisoner or warder, the catcalls and comments I overheard as I crossed the male wards, the restrictions on how my body was to be presented while in prison, and the distance that I was required to maintain from all prisoners. These directives were expressed in the way I dressed (wearing muted colors, conservatively dressed, always covering the front part of my body with a large scarf), my demeanor and my openness to always being questioned and ordered to do or not do something. I was quick and eager to please—a complete transformation of some aspects of my personality. This sensory experience of the fieldworker held clues to the experience of subjugation and the ensuing negotiations with this experience. Three aspects are crucial in terms of crafting ethnographic fieldwork in prison. It involves documenting the sensory experience of surveillance, repression, and denial. Observing and describing the modalities of the exercise of power by human actors are important. Being attentive to the use of the body and the material world in the display and experience of this power is a critical tool for the prison ethnographer.

Notes

1 Convict warders are convicted, and long-term prisoners tasked with various daily, routine responsibilities of management of prisoners and administration of prisons, in order to keep the convict prisoners gainfully employed and to help prison warders.
   This practice of employing prisoners to perform duties comparable to those of the warders resulted in the fusion of functions and consequent entanglements of power and privilege.
2 All names have been anonymized to protect the research participants' identities.
3 Didi means elder sister. Most prisoners addressed me as "didi." It was a way of marking familiarity and closeness as well as respect.

References

Abu-Lughod, L. (1996). Writing against culture. In R. G. Fox (Ed.), *Recapturing anthropology: Working in the present* (pp. 137–162). School of American Research.

Bandyopadhyay, M. (2010). *Everyday life in prison: Confinement, surveillance, resistance*. Orient Blackswan.

Bandyopadhyay, M. (2015). Deviation and limitations of (prison) ethnography: Postscript to fieldwork in an Indian prison. In D. Drake, E. Rod, & J. Sloan (Eds.), *The Palgrave handbook of prison ethnography* (pp. 442–462). Palgrave Macmillan.

Bandyopadhyay, M. (2018). Prison escapes, everyday life and the state. In T. Martin & G. Chantraine (Eds.), *Prison breaks: Toward a sociology of escape*. Palgrave Macmillan.
Blumer, H. (1969). *Symbolic interactionism; Perspective and method*. Prentice-Hall.
Clifford, J., & George, E. M. (1986). *Writing culture: The poetics and politics of ethnography*. University of California Press.
Drake, D., Earle, R., & Sloan, J. (Eds.). (2015). Palgrave studies in prisons and penology. In *The Palgrave handbook of prison ethnography*. Palgrave Macmillan.
Fairbrother, P. (1977). Book review: Experience and trust in sociological work. *Sociology*, *11*(2), 359–368. https://doi.org/10.1177/003803857701100207
Geertz, C. (1973). *The interpretation of cultures: Selected essays*. New York: Basic Books.
Goffman, E. (1961). *Asylums: Essays on the social situation of mental and other inmates*. Garden Books.
Gupta, A., & Ferguson, J. (1997). *Anthropological locations: Boundaries and grounds of a field science*. University of California Press.
Ingold, T. (1996, 2005). *Key debates in anthropology*. Routledge.
Latour, B. (2007). *Reassembling the social—an introduction to actor-network-theory*. Oxford University Press.
Leach, E. R. (1961). *Rethinking anthropology*. Athlone Press.
Long, N. J., & Moore, H. L. (2012). Sociality revisited: Setting a new agenda. *The Cambridge Journal of Anthropology*, *30*(1), 40–47. www.jstor.org/stable/43610888
Marcus, G. E. (1995). Ethnography in/of the world system: The emergence of multi-sited ethnography. *Annual Review of Anthropology*, *24*, 95–117. www.jstor.org/stable/2155931
Martin, T., & Chantraine, G. (Eds.). (2018). *Prison breaks: Toward a sociology of escape*. Palgrave Macmillan.
Mauss, M. (1966). *The gift: Forms and functions of exchange in archaic societies*. Cohen & West.
Merton, R. K. (1948, 1968). *Social theory and social structure*. The Free Press.
Moczydlowski, P. (1992). *The hidden life of polish prisons* (Bloomington: Indiana University Press).
Moran, D. (2013). Between outside and inside? Prison visiting rooms as liminal carceral spaces. *GeoJournal*, *78*(2), 339–351. www.jstor.org/stable/42006323
Parsons, T. (1951). *The social system*. Free Press.
Perrow, C. (1984). *Normal accidents: Living with high-risk technologies*. Basic Books.
Strathern, M. (1988). *The gender of the gift: Problems with women and problems with society in Melanesia*. University of California Press.
Strathern, M. (1996, 2005). The concept of society is theoretically obsolete. In T. Ingold (Ed.), *Key debates in anthropology*. Routledge.
Whyte, W. (1955). *Street corner society: The social structure of an Italian slum* (2nd ed.). University of Chicago Press.

4

SITE JUXTAPOSITION AND CONSTITUTIVE COMPARISON IN PROVISIONAL ENCAMPMENTS

Andrew M. Jefferson[1]

Crafting Comparative Relational Ethnographies

Over the last couple of decades or so, social scientists have sought to breathe new life into comparison as a legitimate tool of social inquiry and analysis (e.g., Abramson & Gong, 2020; Bowen & Peterson, 1999; Gingrich & Fox, 2002; Herzfeld, 2001). In the introduction to *Thick Comparison: Reviving the Ethnographic Aspiration*, Niewöhner and Sheffer (2010) argue that this is a much-needed antidote to the threat posed to qualitative social inquiry by the self-doubt induced by "reflexive debates" in anthropology in the 1980s and the more recent seductive rise to prominence of big data-oriented reductive models of analysis. Their call is for "thick comparison," a means through which to ethnographically generate and juxtapose objects of comparison in the interests of greater analytical precision. Comparability—that is the opportunity to compare—is not, for them, a predetermined feature of a research field but is produced "*through* the research process" (ibid.: 3, my emphasis). In the same vein, this chapter explores the utilization of comparison and the way comparable objects of inquiry are produced by the ethnographer. This is an extension of earlier work "putting comparisons to work" where I advocated for an orientation to comparison which includes processes and relations as key dimensions, perhaps anticipating some of the more recent scholarships on the generative potential of comparison (Jefferson, 2011). In this work, I leaned mostly on anthropologists to argue for the importance of "theorizing contexts," a practice that Gingrich and Fox (2002, p. 21) characterize as "indispensable for any explicit comparison."

A more reflexive approach to the relations between different kinds of comparison in specific projects is overdue. In their helpful overview of types of interpretive comparison, Tavoy and Timmermans (2020) describe the shadow comparison that takes place when researchers situate their work in the light of

DOI: 10.4324/9781003275121-6

existing literature. I stretch this notion of shadow comparison to other kinds of relations including those between ethnographer and informant and ethnographer and field to look more closely at the different plays of light and their effects, and to advocate for increased recognition of the *constitutive* role comparison plays in ethnography and in people's lives.

A key task of the ethnographer is to search for the question that the material gathered provides answers to (Tavoy & Timmermans, 2020, p. 200). My material is about forms of life and entangled encounters[2] and thus takes the form of relational ethnography bearing a resemblance to the work of Veena Das and others on forms of life interlaced with social suffering, violence, and deprivation (Das, 1998, 2007; Segal, 2016; Singh, 2015). But it also provides answers to questions about the craft of comparison during and after fieldwork, that is, to comparison as a field-driven analytic craft.

"Comparison" state Niewöhner and Sheffer (2010, p. 5) "is omnipresent in everyday social practices . . . There is no single occupational activity that is not in some sense using comparison in order to forge relations and produce order and meaning." Every relation or encounter features comparison, either up front or in the shadows whether in the form of positioning, sizing each other up, projecting, or in other ways formulating answers to the unspoken questions posed by the presence of the other.

In this chapter, I make a case that juxtaposition and mutual illumination are legitimate and necessary forms of analytic comparison. I see juxtaposition, with its allusion to the bringing together of objects/phenomena/sets of relations and the resultant "contrasting effects"[3] as imbued with comparative force. Mutual illumination alludes to the way discrete (though analytically adjacent) sites can be made to cast light on one another. To first identify meaningfully juxtaposable relations and then bring them together to display contrasting effect(s) is a core element of the analytic ethnographic craft. Like the meanings of social life, "(T)he meanings of ethnography emerge through difference and reference" (Tavoy & Timmermans, 2020, p. 185). Comparison is the mechanism through which difference is registered, recognized, and acted upon.

In what follows I present and discuss constitutive comparison as a phenomenon and an analytic strategy, as something that people do when narrating their lives, and as an indispensable tool of the ethnographer. Comparison is not a method or a technique; comparison is a verb. It will become clear as I describe various ethnographic encounters that my orientation is not toward comparison as a kind of neutral, procedural, programmable, and controllable endeavor but to comparison as contingent, processual, and intuitive. Comparison constitutes the social lives that people live and the social field that the ethnographer delineates.

This chapter unfolds as follows: I begin by explaining the chapter's genesis before moving on to introduce the two "camps" that form the chapter's empirical platform. Subsequently, in a section called fieldcraft, I illustrate how comparison plays out as an expression of difference between ethnographer and research participants during fieldwork before moving to illustrate how comparison can creatively be put to work. A section on analytic craft identifies the precarity of shelter; hyperbolic victimhood versus everyday suffering; and the significance of temporalities and stubborn hope as important and generative comparative dimensions.

Into the Field

In response to the editors' call to be reflexive and autobiographical about encounters in the field, this chapter is based on a revisiting of material gathered a decade and a half ago in 2006–2007 during fieldwork in Sierra Leone. My ostensible topic was imprisonment during and after the civil war (which spanned 1990–2001) but true to form the open-ended ethnographic endeavor led me in directions I had not foreseen.

Ethnography is contingent on presence and participation (be this proximal or from a distance)[4] but presence is mediated, and participation is circumscribed by people and forces largely beyond the ethnographer's control. Research fields are often circumstantial; they emerge as we occupy specific places and engage with particular people. The starkest example in relation to the subjects of this chapter is the way I discovered the Liberians while I was in the prison or, more accurately how they discovered me. We make our own luck—the sites and people, and thereby the relations, that find us do so when we are predisposed to discover them through presence in other sites. While I am sympathetic to Tavoy and Timmermans' (2020) abductive, sequential approach that involves the deliberate identification of new field sites (not for the sake of volume alone but only when essential), my sequencing was not deliberate but contingent on the research process itself and my sequences—if it is right to call them that—were overlapping.

My two primary field sites were the central prison in the capital Freetown and a poor urban neighborhood that I initially hung out in because I presumed I might find some former prisoners there. But fieldwork was not limited to these sites. I traveled across the country visiting other prisons; I "patrolled" the streets of Freetown with people I met in the poor neighborhood; I traced the paths of former fighters to their jungle camp; I visited the border areas between Sierra Leone, Liberia, and Guinea across which refugees had fled in multiple directions at different times in the 1990s. Further, I accompanied notorious former soldiers and politicians, as well as senior prison officers and community leaders, to rural villages and I often hung out at the law courts, following cases, talking with people who had a stake in them and observing the arrival, departure, and treatment of detainees.

In drafting this chapter, I have reread fieldnotes, re-listened to recorded interviews, and revisited a book chapter and two journal articles, the contents of which both overlap and serve as a springboard for further reflection. I draw most explicitly on my experiences "getting to know"[5] two groups of people, namely, the occupants of one small area of the poor urban neighborhood (that they referred to as "Camp Diva") and a group comprising 43 Liberian refugees whom I met in prison and whose court case I subsequently followed. This led me from the prison to the offices of the United Nations High Commissioner for Refugees (UNHCR), and to their homes in the city and in what was once a designated refugee camp some distance away.

In recent years, encampment studies have expanded—in tandem with and cross-fertilized by confinement studies (Turner & Jensen, 2019; Weegels et al., 2020)—to cover sites that are not camps in an orthodox sense.[6] I examine forms of life in two such "camps" echoing Simon Turner (2015) in drawing attention to sociality, temporality, and contestation. Following Mathew Desmond, I turn aside from sites (the camp) and groups (refugees, or marginalized urban dwellers) as such and embrace and explore instead the "configurations of connections, transactions, and unfolding relations" (Desmond, 2014, p. 574) that constitute the forms of life in which subjectivities are imagined.

Introducing Camp Diva and Its Residents

The urban "camp" consisted of around 40 single-story rooms made of bamboo poles and zinc sheets often lined with newspaper, and two *baffas* (open-sided shelters) where (mostly) youths congregated, socialized, smoked *djamba* (cannabis), and passed the time. The land on which these rooms were situated was reclaimed from the sea, a process that involved the dumping of garbage and then "banking" with sand and mud. The inner *baffa* looked onto an open space used as a football pitch, the outer *baffa* onto the sea. The *baffas* were linked by two narrow alleyways from which people's rooms could be accessed. There was no sanitation or running water and no cable-led electricity. Occasionally, the chugging sound of a generator could be heard powering light and perhaps a sound system for a party. The tide-swept garbage-constituted land between outer *baffa* and sea functioned as a natural sewage system. One of the residents wrote for me an "official history" claiming with it that he was the camp's "first resident." It is a single-page handwritten sheet that describes the establishment of the camp, its destruction, and re-establishment at the current location as well as fires, floods, routine conflicts with the police, and fights between residents. The text reveals how the youths who built the camp felt misrepresented by the wider society ("they say we are street boys, but most of us have basic education"). At the same time, it describes them as being like "wild animals" with a propensity to "fight each other any time."

There were around 76 adult residents with an average age of 25 (range 18–60) and around 14 children with an average age of 6 (range 1–14). Most residents were born within just a few kilometers of the camp. As I hung out in the outer *baffa* gazing at the ocean, or at the inner *baffa* watching basic necessities being bought and sold, sometimes chatting, often just listening and observing, struggle and conflict were plain to see. Livelihoods were sustained through irregular casual labor, hustling, pig-rearing, and fishing as well as extra-legal activities including drugs, the handling of stolen goods, and rumor has it, weapons. Corporeal discipline and networks of patronage created some sense of order and security. My conversations with residents, and a modest room-to-room survey, evidenced fragmented histories of loss, displacement, and war-related violence revealing a highly disparate group who either fought with, were abducted by, or otherwise suffered at the hands of various factions during the civil war.

Introducing the Liberians

I did not initially meet the 43 Liberians at their homes but during a routine visit to the Central Prison in Freetown. They were charged with violence and damaging property at the local UNHCR office. It was around 18 months later that I visited the neighborhood where most had stayed when they first arrived in Sierra Leone up to 18 years before, following hazardous journeys from war-torn Liberia. At that time, it was an UNHCR-run refugee camp located on a disused airfield built by the British adjacent to the main road linking the Freetown peninsula with the hinterland.

At the time I went there, UNHCR was no longer servicing the camp and the court case which dragged on for a year had been dismissed. Throughout that year the 43 had been obliged to attend court—a 2-hour ride away on public transport sometimes weekly, with the threat of imprisonment hanging over the whole group should one member fail to attend. The backstory to the court case seen from the Liberians' point of view was their continued neglect by the UNHCR and allegations of corruption within the local office that involved the literal selling of their stories of hardship and suffering to Sierra Leoneans who were subsequently resettled in third countries. I carried messages between prison and court and helped draft press releases and advocated on their behalf with the UNHCR, all to no avail. They had become persons no longer "of concern." Their status as refugees was denied and instead, they were labeled former rebels and troublemakers.[7]

In the stories recounted to me and a researcher colleague (Maya Mynster Christensen) during a series of interviews what was emphasized was their sense of abandonment; they regularly faced mockery, discrimination, and threats of violence. To avoid violence some of them chose to stay silent in public places for fear of having their accents recognized. Their livelihoods were sustained by irregular labor—laundry, selling soap or other goods for others, making clay pots, collecting or chopping wood, and sex work, and for some through marriage to better socially situated Sierra Leoneans. Occupying the position of most victimized was important to their sense of who they were and what they hoped to become. A sense of victimization dominated their narratives and served as an organizing principle of their struggle for recognition and resettlement. Like, but not identical to, the residents of Camp Diva, their stories also featured severe loss and displacement. To my consternation despite the court case, despite the misery, despite their disavowal by the UNHCR (or perhaps because of all three factors), the discourse of the 43 was infused by an insistent hope that they would one day be resettled. This hope was also projected onto me. Despite my protestations of powerlessness and insistence that my presence was research-related, there was a very strong expectation that I might be the solution to their problem. When in interviews we asked about futures, our own role in ensuring those futures was blatantly displayed:

> (Our) future lies with God. And with you, Andrew! We wanted you to come and see. There's a difference between hearing and seeing. And now you have seen for yourself. We pray for prosperity and to get out of here.
>
> *(Interview, December, 2007)*

In both sites, my presence served as a foil or a screen upon which the Liberians especially, but Diva residents also, could project themselves and perform their identities sometimes almost in caricatured—hyperbolic—fashion. This left me puzzled, implicated, and occasionally moved to action as I consider further later.

Fieldcraft

Within some strands of research, the presence of the researcher is seen as necessary but problematic; in the kind of comparative relational ethnography I practice, the researcher is indispensably disruptive.[8] This is part of the process of generating comparability and identifying the object of study that Desmond has argued strongly is something ethnographers often neglect (2014, p. 549). In this section, I look at the play of disruptive difference between my research participants and myself with a focus on performances of positionality and relative privilege and the way these were enacted.

The relationships I developed were within fluid "communities of practice" (Lave & Wenger, 1991). My knowledge is provisional, partial, and pixelated, for which I make no apology. My "infiltration" of the field was enabled by strategies of cajolement, accompaniment, and gatecrashing (Jefferson, 2015): Sometimes I had to almost beg for an audience, other times I was invited to join in, and still other times I simply showed up. When the opportunity arose, I gave consistent accounts of who I was and what I was doing but I did not have a standard introductory script. Initially, I invited myself to Diva with the help of at least two gatekeepers[9] where I slowly "imposed" myself; the Liberians, on the other hand, invited me (insistently) to engage, first by delivering a note to relatives at the court about their delayed arrival from the prison, then by helping draft a press release documenting their complaints, and later even trying to get a handful of them released from police custody.

My presence among both groups was reflexive, doubt-filled, and hesitant. As I engaged, I was particularly conscious of the demands put on me and I worried about whether I was being told the truth. The Liberians demanded I help deliver justice and resettlement and make their allegations and their plight visible. Diva residents demanded tarpaulin and cement and sometimes money—for medicine, to allay hunger, or for parties. This often left me conflicted. I was an ignorant and reluctant patron, unaware of the extent to which the obligations of patrons to clients lubricate social relations in Sierra Leone. I overlooked the contrast between my position and status as a white, foreign, mobile, professional researcher and their position and status as black, autochthonous, relatively impoverished, marginalized people living a hand-to-mouth existence. I failed to acknowledge the significance of this difference and while its symptoms—especially in the form of my discomfort at requests for assistance—haunt my notes, I still did not grasp how the difference situated me as first and foremost a patron in their eyes and themselves as potential (natural and legitimate) "clients." I was aware of my privilege, but I wanted to bracket it off, to come to them as innocuous, implying a strange vision of disembodied neutrality and innocence.

My presence represented the embodiment of difference or distinction. This distinction was actively appropriated and sometimes co-opted by both communities. They were putting comparison to work. Rather than naively and inadvertently adopting the role of "white savior"—I definitely did not feel I was there to rescue anybody—I found it projected onto me. The expectations were disconcerting, and I found myself identifying with a character in a novel by acclaimed Canadian author Robertson Davies whose "chief difficulty was that he did not, himself, place much value on comfort . . . Because he mistrusted comfort, he could only recommend endurance" (1988, p. 970). I found myself discomfited by the call for comfort if that is what it was, in the sense that the hopes often expressed in both communities resembled false hope. My recommendation to the Liberians to endure (rather than maintain their hope of reparation and resettlement) was rejected by their chairman in no uncertain terms. For them, recommending the suspension of hope was unequivocally unpalatable.

I now see that I was inserting myself into a field where my position was (partially) predetermined and decidedly not neutral or innocuous. In the end, I muddled through, sometimes helping, sometimes refusing, sometimes triggering or exacerbating jealousies and rivalries in the process. But slowly I suspended the need to check veracity and came to accept the performativity of narratives and the negotiations around position as meaning carrying. I came to see social interactions as performances that were as much directed at the wider audience as at me. Slowly it dawned on me that I was not the center of attention, even as I was foregrounded and exposed.

DeGloma understands autobiography "as an articulation of one's relational standpoint in a contentious field" (DeGloma & Papadantonakis, 2020, p. 97). This is the story my fieldnotes tell about me. But it is also the story told by the Liberians. They firmly situate themselves in a very concrete instantiation of a contentious field that they have lived in for almost two decades. It is also the story of the dwellers in the urban camp, though their accounts of contention are less focused on a single actor. Also noteworthy is the fact that neither Diva dwellers nor the 43 Liberians presented me with ahistorical accounts, or simple "cross sections" of their lives. Rather, they performed their "intimate identities" (Holland & Lave, 2001) through our mutual encounters, as situated, embodied subjects embedded in history, engaged in contested social practices, and constituted by acts of comparison, including, as we shall consider further later, comparison of their place in time.

In this section, I have shown how comparison (as an expression of difference) haunts fieldcraft. I turn now to consider more explicitly the work of comparison in analysis and I do so by juxtaposing the two camps across a range of emergent dimensions.

Analytic Craft: Identifying and Exploring Comparative Dimensions

Tavoy and Timmermans (2020) characterize the work of Niewöhner and Scheffer and colleagues (2010) as an examination of "how and when layers of comparison shift, overlap and respond" and where "the theoretical construct forms the *comparative hinge* that connects multiple sites" (ibid.: 204) (my emphasis). A collateral effect of writing this chapter has been the development of some theoretical constructs for the purpose of comparative analysis. The issues I choose to dwell on pertain to shelter, articulations of suffering (expressed as hyperbolic victimhood and everyday struggle), and the confines of time (expressed as lives on hold *contra* stolen lives). But I begin this section with some examples of the way members of both communities constituted themselves through comparison with others, near and far. I have already considered how my presence created one encounter through which identities could be displayed. A further illustration of how this played out via comparison involves the single night I spent in the camp. When I passed through the front of the camp the following morning the Chairman proudly announced, "here is Andrew the first white man to sleep in Camp Diva." In my notes written later the same day, I observe that my overnight stay was "clearly as significant for them as it is for me." Color or race was a highly significant parameter for the Chairman who regularly displayed an internalization of racial and societal exclusionary stereotypes, once telling me how he regretted being born black invoking a sense of shame and self-stigma. On another occasion, he offered a poignant—for me—commentary on my presence in the camp: "Do you know why we like you here in the camp?" he asked me rhetorically, "It's because you come and join us, treat us like brothers, *not like others* who think we live in the dirt who would prefer to avoid us, you come and are with us, you join in our burials" (Fieldnote, July 3, 2006). I had indeed joined in their burials, joined in their daily life, suspended judgment as best I could, and perhaps even treated them like brothers (and sisters). Here, my apparent significance is achieved via comparison with those who think they live in the dirt and avoid them as a result. I was with them while others were against them.

The Liberians shared this conception that others were against them, while I was with them, the latter impression produced perhaps by a combination of their desperate hope to escape and a belief that I might help. My persistent though sporadic curiosity about their situation implied I cared, though from my point of view that care was more *about* them than *for* them. Yet, while others (most pointedly the UNHCR) clearly did not care it seemed as though I did. Through such a comparative lens, I appeared to them in a very particular light that no number of declarations to the contrary could extinguish. That is, to adopt the language of this book, I was rendered an "imagined subject" by the participants in the research.

Both communities were partially constituted through their relations with the authorities including the police and the judicial system. Camp Diva featured more regular skirmishes with the law and the police than the Liberian's camp (despite the ironic fact that I met them in prison). Diva was so unruly it had its own rules, codes, and system of discipline and punishment, and the police were a regular presence there, either as their place of residence, their regular hangout, or the place they occasionally raided and trashed. In contrast, the Liberian's camp had a police post adjacent to it, though it offered scant protection. Aside from the court case and the riot, arrest, torture, and detention that preceded it, the Liberians' most significant external authority was the UNHCR, the agency that had once protected, sheltered, and provided for them but had ultimately let them down. Let me turn now to the theme of shelter.

Comparing the Precarity of Accommodation

Encampment presupposes some form of shelter, however temporary. Ideas related to shelter, sanctuary, and having a home have deep existential resonance; having or not having a place to call home relates in a quite fundamental way to a sense of how welcome or unwelcome one feels in the world. A notion of accommodation, in the sense of being accepted or belonging, was significant for both populations and affected their relations. For example, the conflicts around which social life was constituted in Diva often related to accommodation. One instance involved an altercation resulting from one of the four "landlords" promising a room to three different sets of new tenants and presumably extracting a deposit from each of them (he needed the money to fund an abortion for his wife, I learned later). One of the prospective tenants showed up as darkness fell, angry and frustrated, to find the room already occupied. Earlier I had noticed the couple who had just moved in playing Ludo on a board decorated with Nigerian soccer players, a scene I characterized in my notes as "an image of tranquility and contentment." This was now shattered by the young man's protestations, though in the end he was calmed and the situation did not escalate. Salim, who accompanied me, was bored by the drama implying this was nothing out of the ordinary for him.

Another family moved within the camp, shifting from one corridor, which they said was noisy and full of arguments, to what they hoped would be the quieter side. The precarity of accommodation was also illustrated by the situation of a somber young man, I interviewed, who faced eviction, unable to pay the rent due after 2 years of rent-free living. His work preparing *djamba* for sale was unlikely to help him earn enough to avoid having his belongings and himself turfed out of the single room he occupied.

On another occasion, I witnessed the aggressive posturing of two young men who were in conflict with a woman about who had begun "banking"[10] the exposed garbage first. Clutching a jar of palm wine in his hand one of them cursed the woman, ranting about her being a witch. Later, the other told me to bring my camera the following day so I could watch someone die: "I have my cutlass, I will bring my cutlass, someone will be killed tomorrow, someone will die tomorrow," he declared referencing the woman who was contesting his claim to the land. Remember too, the precarious nature of the land itself, built on a foundation of refuse, reclaimed from the sea and leased from the council under a tenuous arrangement that offered no long-term certainty or security.

The Liberians' accommodation issues are on a different scale. They were made homeless by war in their home country; and later displaced from the refugee camp by Sierra Leone's civil war, warned by UN officials that they should flee if war came but could return without losing entitlements when conditions allowed it. Some who did flee were housed temporarily in another camp at Jui before later returning to discover their plots at the airfield site had been occupied in the meantime by Sierra Leoneans. It is also noteworthy that while the Diva residents had reclaimed their land, the Liberians' camp occupied a former airstrip, another example of repurposing. Both camps were created ex nihilo—out of nothing—the airfield turned into a refugee camp, the ocean rebutted, and the land occupied at Diva. In time, both camps expanded and transformed in different ways, Diva continuously reaching further into the sea, the refugee camp becoming something more like a suburb of the nearby town, a "village" encroached upon by non-refugees, no longer a safe space of protection for persons of concern to a UN agency.

Juxtaposing these relations to the land reminds us of the tenuous forms that "shelter" can take and how for people living under compromised circumstances,[11] it cannot be taken for granted; such forms of encampment have an interminably provisional form, as alluded to in the title of this chapter. But we are also reminded that even under compromised circumstances, people's relations to land and issues of shelter are not identical.

Hyperbolic Victimhood and Everyday Struggles

The people whom I got to know in the two camps suffered, there is no question about that. It was common to hear Camp Diva residents refer to themselves as sufferers, but I did not witness or experience the same degree of victimhood displayed there as I did among the Liberians. There was need and desperation, but it was rarely if ever overstated, not even when directed toward me.[12] My experience among the Liberians was rather different and at first highly puzzling. I came to characterize their displays of suffering as "hyperbolic victimhood." By this term, I did and do not mean to dilute or deny their suffering but rather to highlight the work their displays of victimhood did in constituting their identity as a collective and as individuals. The tropes used were powerful: it is better to be a slave than a Liberian refugee, said the Chairman during a speech at a meeting arranged on my behalf in the camp; the women of the camp were raped or had to work as sex workers, he declared purposefully. The ignominy and stigma they faced as discarded (former) refugees cut off from work (and marriage)[13] opportunities left them exposed, abandoned, and abject.

Anthropologist Mats Utas (2005) has turned critical attention to the inevitability of being given embellished or under-stated stories (scripted or formulaic versions of social life) when occupying particular social or organizational positions in situations of extreme poverty or post-war desperation. A young person approaching a program for the demobilization and reintegration of child soldiers is likely to play up the parts of their story that will enable them to receive help; a woman ex-combatant associated with the rebels is likely to play down her combat experience (her agency) if that leaves her a better chance of getting help to build a different life. This is not mendacious but reflects varying degrees of "revelation and concealment" (Jefferson & Schmidt, 2019) that are a common feature of any discursive, interactional practice. Researchers diving in too quickly risk overlooking this, especially if utilizing reductively styled surveys unaccompanied by any form of field presence or when over-emphasizing veracity at the expense of meaning.

My interpretation of the "scripts" directed at me was aided by my increasing levels of embeddedness and participation. Over time (18 months) I was not only subject to scripts addressed to me but also witnessed scripts that were self and other directed. Recall that I met the Liberians in dire need in prison; I witnessed firsthand the delays to their court case and the disavowal and stigmatization of them by the UNHCR. I was also obliged to help a woman who had been gang-raped receive medical attention. But the important point here is not about truth-seeking or triangulation but to note that scripts themselves are both performative and revelatory. The displays of hyperbolic victimhood I witnessed were expressions of who the Liberians had become. I drew on anthropologist Veena Das and philosopher Stanley Cavell for help in making sense of this:

> I do not believe the claims are only discursive strategies. It is not just rhetoric. Or even if it is rhetoric, it is rhetoric with significance beyond their engagement with me and my research assistant. Cavell links the idea of having a voice with having a political existence (1995, p. 161). It is, as if, drawing on Das (1998, pp. 185, 191) and Cavell, that language is a "bodying forth." The words, expressions, and performances of victimhood are almost "wrenched out" of the Liberians. They are perhaps controlled by the words they speak to a greater extent than they control the words. They cannot help themselves.
>
> *(Jefferson, 2014, p. 232)*

There is ambiguity in the phrase "they cannot help themselves'" as I used it here. In context, it was about how words were issued forth (involuntarily) but it also indexes their perceptions of their situation of isolation and abandonment—they could not help themselves but were dependent on others for help.

I have dwelt mostly on the more puzzling display of suffering of the Liberians, but juxtaposing their hyperbolic victimhood with the forms of victimhood in Camp Diva enables me to think anew about the experience of Camp Diva residents, another example of putting comparison to work. If the dominant trope of the Liberians was hyperbolic victimhood, then that of Camp Diva residents was "everyday struggle." Everyday struggle captures the mundane realities of making a living, dealing with conflicts, and simply surviving that characterize the lives of the "sufferers." These two parameters or concepts emerge as dimensions of comparability that have been generated via specific encounters and particular histories; they may serve as pertinent concepts in other compromised settings.

Comparing Temporalities

One of my academic preoccupations has been with conceptualizing confinement, also beyond the walls of prisons. It was engagements with the residents of Camp Diva—as well as readings of other scholars' work—that drew me toward notions of stuckness and relative immobility and the significance of temporality. I began thinking about how lives lived under the compromising circumstances of poverty and everyday struggle can be conceived of as stuck in time (as well as place) and about the "confines of time" itself (Jefferson & Segal, 2019). For the purposes of this chapter, I choose to draw a distinction—a comparison—between "lives on hold" and "stolen lives."

The idea of stolen lives emerged from the Liberians' allegations of how their life histories (via their UNHCR files) had literally been sold to others who had been repatriated in their stead. I characterized the result of this like this:

> The refugees seem only knowable to themselves through the attributed category of refugee and hoped for resettlement. Robbed of the attribution, they are robbed of a self.
>
> *(Jefferson, 2014, pp. 229–230)*

Diva residents' lives were not stolen from them literally or metaphorically; they may however be thought of as "pending" or "on hold," "on standby." Some of them are in the process of "claiming" their lives, establishing themselves independently, distinct from their families whom they have either lost or fled from. There was a general sense from interactions and interviews with residents, that something better might be just around the corner though mostly out of reach and the waiting was a rather tiresome and tiring form of treading water. I described this as follows:

> Listening to their talk of the long-hoped for windfall which would mean they could pursue their dream of escape it was hard not to hear a sense that

> they really felt destined never to move beyond the actual. There were no realistic horizons of possibility.
>
> *(Jefferson, 2013, p. 57)*

If Liberian narratives were of loss, injustice, and calls for reparation, those of Diva residents were of basic survival and struggle. Another way of comparing the two forms of life is in terms of "economies of abandonment" (Povinelli, 2011) and "economies of getting by/making do." The Liberians defined themselves in terms of what they had had taken from them; Diva residents struggled the best they could with the cards they had been dealt. Where the Liberians might be characterized as predominantly living in the light of the past, Diva residents were living in the light of the present and an unpredictable unknown future. Where the Liberians were sustained by the obsession with resettlement, Diva residents dreamed (literally) about everyday violence. In my fieldnotes, I recorded a conversation where I was asked by a young woman whether I had dreamed. I replied that I had not, but another young woman interjected sharing she had dreamed she was being beaten by a man. "Your own man," joked the first woman. This was laughingly denied but a subtext of gendered violence was clear.

Of course, the distinction between backward-looking, fixated Liberians, and forward-looking/caught in the moment Diva dwellers does not fully hold. The Liberians were certainly in thrall to their status as neglected, abandoned refugees and a sense of what they had lost, but this was always directed toward the expectation of a resolved court case and a resettled future. They too were hopeful, perhaps in some ways more hopeful, more expectant, more oriented to a change of circumstances than Diva dwellers whose lives I portray as "on hold." In fact, the hope of the Liberians is another puzzle I still grapple with. It has drawn me to think about the obstinacy of hope, a kind of hope which withstands reality testing, a hope that is maintained even as circumstances seem hopeless, an impossible hope forging an "imagined subjectivity" (Gubrium, this volume), a hope arising out of what singer/songwriter/musician/performer Nick Cave (2021) characterizes as "known suffering . . . (as a) defiant and dissenting spark that refuses to be extinguished . . . (as) wised-up and disobedient." I was confusing the Liberians' hope with optimism which Cave in turn characterizes as featuring a denial of suffering, "a fear of facing the darkness, a lack of awareness, a kind of blindness to the actual," as something "fearful and false." In fact, the obstinacy of their hope was not optimism but faith.

Conclusion

I began in search of questions that my field experience and "accumulated observations" (Tavoy & Timmermans, 2020, p. 200) might answer. Italian philosopher Giorgio Agamben (1998) asked "what is a camp . . . that such events could happen there?" Some answers to that question have been implied earlier, but the material I have selected also answers questions about what is ethnography, given the particular ways it is called forth by the specific fields in which the ethnographer is engaged, and what is comparison given the way it is conducted and simultaneously rendered possible through the ethnographic enterprise.

With this chapter, I have made a case for a more explicit comparative ethnography. I have drawn attention to the ways in which both ethnographies and the social worlds of research participants (and ethnographers) are constituted through comparison. This has not been about delineating procedures or outlining criteria for comparison in a formalistic, mechanistic, recipe-like fashion. Rather, on the contrary, this has been about reflexively sensing the ways in which comparison is endemic to the production of social worlds, to the "discursive contours of subjectivity" (Gubrium & Holstein, 2000, p. 95), and to ethnographic relations.

I am advocating for a version of comparison that is not necessarily by design or according to a strict set of methodological protocols but is the deliberate product of the "emergent and fluid process of ethnographic practice itself" (Marvasti: Pers Comm).[14] I did not set out to compare two camps but my discovery of them, my getting to know their occupants and their ways of engaging with me and accounting for their lives, and my subsequent analysis of their circumstances has enabled me to juxtapose them so that respective forms of life may mutually illuminate each other, and thereby our understandings of lives lived under compromised circumstances.

Ethnography, in its classic sense of exploring taken-for-granted social worlds, is dependent on difference. Comparison is integral to the ethnographic endeavor though not always acknowledged as such or utilized to its full capacity. Deconstructing the taken-for-granted and eschewing explanation in favor of illumination is imperative for an interpretive, fieldwork-based form of social inquiry, despite the objections of realist scholars (cf. Abramson & Gong, 2020, pp. 13–17). Procedural and mechanistic modes of comparison that end up reducing differences to sameness in pursuit of causal pathways and generalizable explanations fail to capture the complexities of social life. Ethnographic comparison, as outlined in this chapter, is a viable and generative craft that is in keeping with the emergent and fluid nature of fieldwork.

Notes

1 I am deeply grateful to Jaber F. Gubrium and Amir B. Marvasti for their perceptive comments on earlier drafts of this chapter and for this opportunity to look back and think through encounters that have formed me—professionally and personally—in ways that remain imponderable. Thanks also to Maya Mynster Christensen for being an inspirational co-researcher during parts of the study and to the residents of the two camps I discuss in this chapter and particularly Salim Johnson whose presence granted me both access and security. All errors of interpretation are, of course, my own.

2 This was a term I first began to use in connection with a study comparing the *relations between* human rights NGOs and prison systems in three different countries, my first deliberate foray into the comparison of relations (Jefferson & Gaborit, 2015).

3 Juxtaposition definition—Google Search.

4 See Schatz (2009); and Gaborit (2019) on the merits of nurturing an "ethnographic sensibility" toward sites in which one cannot participate or observe in the orthodox sense.

5 For an elaboration of "doing trust" and "getting to know" see Jefferson (2015).

6 Kublitz (2015), for example, follows her interlocuters in identifying Danish urban housing projects occupied predominantly by migrant families as camps.
7 See Jefferson (2014) for a longer analysis of the relationship between the 43 and the UNHCR characterized as oppositional performances of allegation and disavowal.
8 See Abramson and Gong (2020, p. 18).
9 Baaz and Utas (2019) call importantly for gatekeepers to be given greater prominence in ethnographic accounts. Without the backing of Mats Utas and his networks in Sierra Leone, the research on which this chapter is based would have come to nothing.
10 Banking is the emic term used for extending the shoreline out into the sea through combinations of garbage, sand, and mud.
11 For further elaboration on "compromised circumstances" as a concept see Jefferson (2022).
12 One exception to this was when the Chairman tried to ease the pressure of expectation that lay on his shoulders deflecting the demands of his "dependents" onto me with the help of exaggerated rhetoric.
13 See Coulter et al. (2008, p. 35).
14 I am grateful to Amir B. Marvasti for the latter formulation.

References

Agamben, G. (1998). *Homo Sacer: Sovereign power and bare life* (Daniel Heller-Roazen, Trans.). Stanford University Press.

Abramson, C., & Gong, N. (2020). *Beyond the case: The logics and practices of comparative ethnography*. Oxford University Press.

Baaz, M. E., & Utas, M. (2019). Exploring the backstage: Methodological and ethical issues surrounding the role of research brokers in insecure zones. *Civil Wars*, *21*(2), 157–178. doi:10.1080/13698249.2019.1656357

Bowen, J., & Peterson, R. (1999). *Critical comparisons in politics and culture*. Cambridge University Press.

Cave, N. (2021). *Nick cave—the red hand files—issue #178 — Do you have hope?* The Red Hand Files.

Cavell, S. (1995). *Philosophical passages: Wittgenstein, Emerson, Austin, Derrida*. Blackwell.

Coulter, C., Persson, M., & Utas, M. (2008). *Young female fighters in African wars. Conflict and its consequences*. Nordiska Afrika Institutet, UPPSALA.

Das, V. (1998). Wittgenstein and anthropology. *Annual Review of Anthropology*, *27*, 171–195.

Das, V. (2007). *Life and words: Violence and the descent into the ordinary*. University of California Press.

Davies, R. (1988). *The Cornish trilogy part 3: The lyre of Orpheus*. Rosetta Books.

DeGloma, T., & Papadantonakis, M. (2020). The thematic lens. A formal and cultural framework for comparative ethnographic analysis. In C. Abramson & N. Gong (Eds.), *Beyond the case: The logics and practices of comparative ethnography*. University Press.

Desmond, M. (2014). Relational ethnography. *Theory and Society*, *43*, 547–579.

Gaborit, L. S. (2019). Looking through the prison gate: Access in the field of ethnography. *Cadernos Pagu*, *55*, 1–25.

Gingrich, R. G., & Fox, A. (2002). *Anthropology, by comparison*. Routledge.

Gubrium, J. F., & Holstein, J. A. (2000). The self in a world of going concerns. *Symbolic Interaction*, *23*(2), 95–115.

Herzfeld, M. (2001). Performing comparisons: Ethnography, globetrotting, and the spaces of social knowledge. *Journal of Anthropological Research*, *57*(3), 259–276.

Holland, D., & Lave, J. (2001). *History in person: Enduring struggles, contentious practice, intimate identities*. SAR Press.

Jefferson, A. M. (2011). Comparisons at work: Exporting 'exceptional' norms. In T. Ugelvik & J. Dullum (Eds.), *Penal exceptionalism? Nordic prison policy and practice*. Routledge.

Jefferson, A. M. (2013). Conceptualizing confinement: Prisons and poverty in Sierra Leone. *Criminology and Criminal Justice*, *14*(1), 44–60.

Jefferson, A. M. (2014). Performances of victimhood, allegation and disavowal in Sierra Leone. In *Histories of victimhood, the ethnography of political violence* (pp. 218–238). University of Pennsylvania Press.

Jefferson, A. M. (2015). Performing ethnography: Infiltrating prison spaces. In D. H. Drake, R. Earle, & J. Sloan (Eds.), *Palgrave handbook of prison ethnography*. Palgrave Macmillan.

Jefferson, A. M. (2022). Prison reform and torture prevention under "compromised circumstances". *Criminology and Criminal Justice*. Online First 1–17. https://doi.org/10.1177/17488958221105.

Jefferson, A. M., & Gaborit, L. S. (2015). *Human rights in prisons: Comparing institutional encounters in Kosovo, Sierra Leone and the Philippines*. Palgrave Macmillan.

Jefferson, A. M., & Schmidt, B. S. (2019). Concealment and revelation as bureaucratic and ethnographic practice: Lessons from Tunisian prisons. *Critique of Anthropology*, *39*(2), 155–171.

Jefferson, A. M., & Segal, L. B. (2019). The confines of time: On the ebbing away of futures in Sierra Leone and Palestine. *Ethnos*, *84*(1), 96–112.

Kublitz, A. (2015). The ongoing catastrophe: Erosion of life in the Danish camps. *Journal of Refugee Studies*, *29*(2), 229–249.

Lave, J., & Wenger, E. (1991). *Situated learning. Legitimate peripheral participation*. Cambridge University Press.

Niewöhner, J., & Sheffer, C. (2010). *Thick comparison: Reviving the ethnographic aspiration*. Brill.

Povinelli, E. A. (2011). *Economies of abandonment: Social belonging and endurance in late liberalism*. Duke University Press.

Schatz, E. (Ed.). (2009). *Political ethnography: What immersion contributes to the study of power* (1st ed.). University of Chicago Press.

Segal, L. B. (2016). *No place for grief—Martyrs, Prisoners, and mourning in contemporary Palestine*. University of Pennsylvania Press.

Singh, B. (2015). *Poverty and the quest for life. Spiritual and material striving in rural India*. University of Chicago Press.

Tavoy, I., &Timmermans, S. (2020). Sequential comparisons and the comparative imagination. In C. Abramson & N. Gong (Eds.), *Beyond the case: The logics and practices of comparative ethnography*. Oxford University Press.

Turner, S. (2015). What is a refugee camp? Explorations of the limits and effects of the camp. *Journal of Refugee Studies*, *29*(2).

Turner, S., & Jensen, S. (2019). *Reflections on life in ghettos, camps and prisons: Stuckness and confinement*. Routledge.

Utas, M. (2005). Victimcy, girlfriending, soldiering: Tactic agency in a young woman's social navigation of the Liberian war zone. *Anthropological Quarterly*, *78*(2), 403–430.

Weegels, J., Jefferson, A. M., & Martin, T. (Eds.). (2020, Spring). Confinement beyond site: Connecting urban and prison ethnographies. Special Issue *Cambridge Journal of Anthropology*, *38*(1), 1–14.

PART II

Selves

5

IS ETHNOGRAPHY ONLY FOR EARLY CAREER RESEARCHERS?

Tarja Pösö

Introduction

A common characteristic of ethnographic research is that it is often conducted by early career researchers or PhD candidates. More established or senior researchers tend to move on to supervise younger people's fieldwork or switch to entirely different research approaches. There must be a variety of reasons for this, one of them being that ethnographic fieldwork is embodied work: the older you get, the more tiresome you might feel it is to negotiate social contacts to get to the "field," take notes, be constantly observant, and give up your personal routines in order to become included in the groups and communities you study. It might also feel strange to practice the mindset of "anthropological strangeness" if you, as a more mature researcher have already some experience and knowledge of the topics you study.

While there might be many reasons why ethnography is well suited to young researchers, I focus in this chapter on the age of the researcher and ponder how it shapes the mundane doing of ethnographic fieldwork. Rather than viewing age as an individualized asset of the researcher, I am more interested in looking at age in a methodologically tuned way and how the age of the researcher intersects with field relations and, at the end of the day, the understanding of the topic under study. My particular focus is on "old" age as it is more uncommon in ethnography than "young(ish) age" and thereby encourages a reflection on age-related matters. This chapter also explores the temporal nature of ethnography in a wider sense. Time and temporal dimensions are always embedded in ethnography (as they are in all aspects of social life), yet the overwhelming frame is to emphasize "the ethnographic present" which often suppresses time (McLeod & Thomson, 2009; Atkinson, 2017). The "present" is regulated by a variety of academic traditions, methodological fashions, research ethics standards, and other similar issues of academia which the researcher of whatever age has to take a stand on and

DOI: 10.4324/9781003275121-8

incorporate into research. Moreover, the ethnographic present is not free from temporal layers and their continuities and discontinuities which may shape fieldwork in a variety of ways of which the researcher may be more or less aware. Some external factors shaping fieldwork become visible for reflection when revisiting the same site (e.g., Boelen, 1992; Burawoy, 2003).

This chapter explores the age of the researcher through a research design of revisits. Between the revisits to the site, the conditions and customs for doing research change and so does the researcher. This happened in my research as I revisited my field sites, which in my case were reform schools for troublesome young people 10 years after my first study. In the first study, I was a PhD student of the age of a "big sister" in relation to the young residents; in the later study, this then changed to a position of an associate professor and the age of a "mother" to the young people. More than only reflecting past ethnographic work, I will be shifting between the lived and imagined fieldwork of the same research site as I play with the idea of doing it once more: as a person soon to retire. What would it be like to do an ethnography of the same reform schools for young people now? What would it be like to stay in the institutions for several months and talk with young people and staff in the ethnographer role as a retiring professor of social work? What impact would that have on ethnographic relations and understanding?

The Context: Institutions for Troublesome Young People

Human service institutions are typically differentiated by age—kindergartens versus adult education, care homes for the elderly, and adult versus youth prisons, among others. What tends to typify ethnographers in this regard, regardless of the field, is adulthood. As adults, ethnographers often observe other adults in different settings. On some occasions, if care homes are studied, for example, adults may be defined as being "the elderly" but otherwise adulthood is shadowed by the other identities attached to the people in the field (e.g., inmates, patients, or care workers). When children are studied in kindergarten, school, or other similar contexts, adulthood is not shared but it is still taken for granted as a feature of the ethnographer: ethnographers are adults unless child or youth-led research designs are implemented (e.g., Delgado, 2006). According to Allison James (2011), as the researcher is not a child, there always exists a power differential between the child and the adult researcher, and this dilemma is handled in a variety of ways in research which aims to "understand" children; however, in the end, the inevitable differences between children and other ethnographic selves have to be accepted (James, 2011).

This is evident in the human service organizations presented in this chapter. They are Finnish residential child welfare institutions in which children and young people under the age of 18 are placed on the grounds laid out by the Child Welfare Act. The placement is made for the welfare and protection of the child. Nevertheless, it makes sense to translate the name of the institutions into English as "reform schools" as they are not ordinary child welfare institutions. During their long history, going back to the end of the nineteenth century, they have had a special standing among the variety of child welfare institutions as ones for "high-risk" troublesome—asocial—young people who need special measures of education, upbringing, and care (Bardy et al., 2001; Pekkarinen, 2017). Over time, they have established an image as last resort institutions; on the other hand, they have in recent years claimed to be institutions with special expertise in "high risk young people" (Pekkarinen, 2017). They are the only child welfare institutions governed by the state as other institutions are governed by municipalities or are outsourced by them to private care providers. Unlike other child welfare institutions, there is also specific legislation defining their role. There are currently five state-run reform schools, with approximately 150 children residing in them and 130 members of staff working with them. In 2022, the website providing information about the reform schools presents them under the headings "Reform schools—on a path towards positive growth" and "All children and young people have the right to education, treatment and care," described in more detail as follows:

> The care, education and teaching provided at reform schools form a rehabilitative whole that emphasises factors protecting growth and mental health. The experiences young people and their families get of fairness and being heard are an important part of a successful care process in a reform school. As a premise, young people are strongly and equally included in the planning concerning their own lives. To safeguard the age-appropriate development of young people, reform schools employ specialists in care, education and teaching. The work carried out with families aims at helping the young people build workable relationships with their loved ones, and makes the placement a shared process that the whole family is involved in.
>
> *(Valtion koulukodit, 2022)*

Any study of reform schools is in one way or another informed by the long history and competing treatment philosophies about how best to work with troublesome young people. The description of the reform schools is rich in the vocabulary of rehabilitation, care, participation, mental health, and family relations which reflects their present emphasis on treatment. Interestingly, the wording avoids "high-risk youth" terminology such as petty crimes and drug abuse which previously characterized the public presentation of the institutions. At the beginning of the 1970s, for example, the reform schools were targeted by the radical criticism of the time as they, as "total institutions," were seen as acting against the rights and liberty of residents, in similar fashion to the mental health hospitals and prisons of that time. Later, the testimonies of ex-residents have highlighted their experiences of tough discipline and even abuse (Hytönen et al., 2016). On the other hand, their treatment philosophies also record an interest in art-based and empowering therapies for young residents (Känkänen, 2013). What has remained unchanged is that the residents are children—or young people as they will be called in the chapter—up to 18 years of age.

Revisiting and Imagining Reform Schools

In methodological terms, revisiting can imply two different types of research: follow-up studies or the archiving and reanalysis of existing studies or data (McLeod & Thomson, 2009). Follow-up "revisiting" studies, as one type of longitudinal qualitative studies, include those

> where the original researcher reviews a previously completed study through a different temporal and conceptual lens, or extends the original study with another way of research, or subsequently returns to a research site or follow up participants.
>
> *(McLeod & Thomson, 2009, p. 122)*

Revisiting follow-up studies may provide insight into social processes at different points in time and capture the crisscrossing of the past, present, and future (McLeod & Thomson, 2009, p. 138). The different time periods provide the revisiting researcher an opportunity to compare them and analyze change. Changes do not, however, belong only to the past. McLeod and Thomson (2009) propose two temporal strategies for qualitative research on change: memory and imagination. Memory is about the past; imagination is about the future. For someone interested in ethnographic fieldwork and the impact of the ethnographer's age on it, they provide a unique platform: the memorized fieldwork is about the younger "me" and the imagined future fieldwork is about the older "me." Revisiting sites provides material for memories about what it was like to "be there"; imagination provides material for thinking about what it could be like to "be there."

Both memory and imagination can be contested because of their subjectivity. Nevertheless, I will build the following sections on them in order to reflect upon the age of the ethnographer and its impact on field relations on the one hand, and the temporal contexts of ethnography on the other hand. I will look at three issues, all stereotypical for any ethnographic report, that being, roughly speaking, entering the field, the embodied fieldwork, and relations in the field. The focus on those typical themes is an acknowledgment of the essence of ethnography as a method: one has to be "there" and "being there" requires access, observations, and taking notes among other similar tasks. In their revised textbook, Hammersley and Atkinson (2019, p. xii) state that while introducing "new approaches and innovations" to ethnography, the differences between past and current principles and practices are often exaggerated. Whatever new approaches to ethnography are introduced, one still has to be "there" to problematize everyday life at the chosen site. This continues to be a constant methodological challenge for ethnographic handicraft (e.g., Jacobsson & Gubrium, 2021), also evident in revisiting and imagining ethnographic work.

In what follows, memory is used for remembering what, for example, the relations in the field were like during my visits to the reform schools and imagination is used to draft an agenda for a return to the reform schools in the near future. In order to support my memory of the revisiting fieldwork periods, I have reread the reports written about those periods. Both reports (Pösö, 1993, 2004) include long chapters about fieldwork, following the idea that the reader of the reports really needs to know about the doings in the field in order to evaluate the quality of the research data and interpretations of it. I have also reread other texts that I wrote at the time. The texts are re-interpreted for this chapter as at the time of the first study in particular I did not think much of my age and its impact on the ethnographic relations although I was deeply aware of my different ways of being in the field during the two research periods. All memories are not, however, written as notes; instead, some memories "emerge" and become a part of the study when memorizing the past and present (Plummer, 2019)—I take some freedom to include them as well. When imagining the future fieldwork, I use my best knowledge of the present state of the reform schools, research ethics, and governance and troubled childhood as well as child welfare practices and play with the thought of what it would be like to enter the institutions as an ethnographer. It is a sort of "time travel" or just a reminder of the humanistic nature of ethnographic research in which there is not only the past and present but also the future (McLeod & Thomson, 2009).

Meeting Points: Researcher Biography and the Reform Schools

Between periods of my first and second episodes of fieldwork in the reform schools at the turn of the 1980–1990s and in the early twenty-first century, the number of reform schools in Finland had declined from ten to six, and the number of residents had declined accordingly, not to mention changes in treatment rationales and professional ethos. One of the schools of my first study did not exist anymore, demonstrating that even the institutions with a long history are not fixed or unchangeable as noted also by a revisit of child welfare institutions in England (Berridge & Brodie, 1998). That first study was my PhD study, published in 1993 (Pösö, 1993), focusing on the social constructs of "deviance" of the young people placed in three reform schools. The second study was 10 years later in two of the reform schools involved in the first study, now looking at the lived experiences of the young residents (Pösö, 2004), with a separate interest in their understanding of violence (Honkatukia et al., 2003, 2006). Both times I stayed in the institutions for several months and took part in the daily activities of the institutions in a variety of ways, carried out interviews, some recorded, some not, read documents, and asked young people to take photographs, that is to say, whatever there was to do when you study 24/7 out-of-home care ethnographically. I returned to the institutions later to do some focus group interviews with young people about restrictive practices as well as for some occasional visits for other purposes. This later study was not ethnographic and is not therefore given much attention here.

When revisiting the reform schools for my second study, I realized that my age had become an issue. First, it was an issue for other people, including research colleagues and child welfare practitioners as they commented on my study expressing doubts about whether I could understand the teenagers' language and their ways of being as I was so "old" (as if age was the only uniting or separating factor in our encounters). When doing my first ethnography, I did not think much of my age. Other people did not remark on it either, as assumably a PhD student in her late twenties was not very different from other students doing research in the reform schools or similar contexts. An associate professor in her late thirties, involved in educating future professionals for social work, is different in many ways. The remarks about being "old" included concerns of social distance and barriers of communication and understanding. More experience could of course also give more assets for communication skills and flexibility to move around the ethnographic site but the comments excluded those aspects. Although I do not agree with the binary views that age as such is either a resource or an obstacle to fieldwork, I fully agree that age-related matters have their impact on fieldwork but in more mixed ways as they are intertwined in the very ways of being in relations, listening, asking questions, hearing, and making sense of it all.

The complexity of age-related matters became evident in the first hours of my first visit to the second study. I returned to the reform school where I had spent many months in the first study and was picked up by a familiar staff member in a minibus from the railway station. This institution was—as they all were and still are—located far away from urban centers and public transport. The journeys between the station and the institution, sometimes together with young residents returning from their visits to home, were always important opportunities to catch upon news during both studies. This time the driver of the minibus remembered me and I remembered her. Together we discussed the years between the past period shared and the present. I was told that the young people ending up in the reform schools were in much more difficult conditions "now" than they were earlier. She told, for example, about young people who entered the reform schools without any reading skills, which, in the Finnish society of that time, was a very unusual indicator of being lost in the education system. The stories of the present residential life were emotionally rich, loaded with sadness about the fates of young residents. She told about her own children, born after our previous encounters, and contrasted them with the young residents, again with sadness about the differences in care and love they experienced. We also shared some experiences of the impact of having children of one's own on the ways how one meets children in care; this was a new topic for both of us as 10 years earlier neither of us had children of our own. The portrait painted to me was full of concerns and worries about the deterioration of the lives of young people ending up in reform schools and the services provided to support them, making a clear distinction between the past and present.

This portrait became intensified during the periods of stay in the institution. There were also other staff members whom I remembered well and who remembered me and the discussions circulated around the same topics of things being more difficult than 10 years previously. The very fact that I had been there before made these accounts possible; they also shaped my understanding of the present at that time. The talks with young people did not change that portrait of sadness and concerns as I will describe later. The portrait was only intensified by the fact that the young residents were just some years older than my own children, yet they had gone through so much, and the child welfare system, the topic of my teaching and other university activities as an associate professor in social work, had failed them in so many ways. As an ethnographer, I had changed as I knew more about research in general but also in relation to the young residents as a private person from the age of a "big sister" to "a mother" and in relation to the institution from a student to an expert. In consequence, what I "saw" was very different in these two studies 10 years apart. Playing with my idea to return there still once is an issue to consider, personally, academically, and morally. What would be certain, however, is that the position of a retiring professor of social work, at the age of a grandmother to the young residents, would leave its mark again on doing ethnographic work.

My age—or myself—is not, obviously, the key issue here but rather the relations it enables; it is more or less directly an intertwined and influencing factor in the "interpersonal field" (term: Coffey, 1999). It is also a factor that one cannot do much about as age acquires its meaning in social interaction; nevertheless, ethnographic data cannot exist without it. Age in a general sense is also an institutional topic which is problematized in current guidelines of academia when setting the platform for studying children. This will be demonstrated in the next section before going into more detail with regard to relational dynamics of ethnographic fieldwork.

Regulated Field Relations and Risk Awareness About Adult Researchers

In contrast with the previous fieldwork periods, being an adult studying children and young people is nowadays tightly regulated by the current research ethics codes as are the very relations and practices in research encounters. Previously, a variety of formal and informal permits were required but they did not specify the adult–child relations as a topic for negotiations or scrutiny as they do now. My own research started by contacting the reform school leaders in the late 1980s to discuss the opportunity to do an ethnography there. They all welcomed me and especially the idea that it would not be a short visit. I have recorded notes saying that their view was that a long-lasting ethnography would give a fairer analysis of the complexities of the institutions. There was one condition: I should not participate in any situations against the wishes of the young people. I visited all reform schools and decided to include three of them in my study. As gender-related constructions of troublesome behavior were the focus of my research at the time, I chose two single-sex institutions and one that was mixed. The Ministry of Social Affairs and Health granted me permission to do my study. I shared information about my study in the institutions by attending classrooms to meet all the young people residing in those institutions at that moment as well as staff meetings, handing out short leaflets, and spending time in the residential common rooms to introduce myself. As I also wanted to study the case files of young people, I was given a key to the office where the files were kept and spent several evenings there coding information. When it was time to talk with someone or attend a treatment session, I always asked whether it was alright for me to join; if it was, I stayed. I think I had a "business card" of some kind to give to the parents who shared the guest rooms with me for overnight stays to show who I was. We did not exchange any signed contracts about talking together.

It was equally easy to obtain access to the reform schools 10 years later: I contacted the head of the reform school that still existed and was immediately welcomed. I chose the other institution to represent some of the new features of the reform schools at that time: the chosen institution included some family-run units in addition to the reform school wards. The permission granted by the reform school leaders gave me formal access, and other types of access were negotiated in a similar way to earlier. Permissions to interview or to attend meetings, for example, were then negotiated on a case-by-case basis, and the negotiations varied during the fieldwork periods, suggesting a situational and relational approach to research ethics (Alderson & Morrow, 2011).

The entry and access to studying reform schools would be very different now as research in general and research with children in particular are more regulated (e.g., Alderson & Morrow, 2011). If I started a new study now, the review of an ethics committee would be needed first and after that, the permission to do the study would be granted by the National Institute of Health and Social Affairs. According to their current instructions, they would need the application plus 13 compulsory appendices. These requests for material follow not only common research ethics as well as data integrity and security guidelines (as for all studies at the moment) but also norms for people working with children. I should include a certificate of my criminal record (or the lack thereof) to show that I am not a risk to young people. I should also provide consent forms for young people to sign to prove that they participate voluntarily in the study, drafts of the interview schemes as well as details of data security and data management to show how I would store and work with the data. I should also contact the parents of those children who are under the age of 15 and have their permissions and consent forms signed to complement those signed by the young people and staff members. I might also have to contact the children's child welfare agencies that placed them as well to ask for further permission to speak with the children. It is likely that I would not have any easy access to read the case files—other permissions would be needed and specific data security, highly priced, would be required.

In the current frame of regulations, as a researcher and an adult entering the institution, I pose a possible risk to children against which they should be protected and the gate-keeping bodies need to minimize the risk I might pose. As I have previous experience with ethics regulation based on minimal bureaucracy and on trust and situated negotiations, I imagine that I could be a very hesitant ethnographer as I would enter the field with a multitude of forms and formalities in my mind, and with a mindset which categorizes people and situations into those where "permission to study" has been granted and formalized and those that are beyond my rights as a researcher. Hammersley and Atkinson (2019, p. 44) use the term "rude surprises" to describe unwelcome episodes involved in entering the field; for my imagined study, indeed, the new formalized practices and regulations are "a rude surprise" even before entering the field. Furthermore, if proposing a revisiting study to reform schools, the very idea of ethnography would also need to be considered in relation to the adult–child relationships in theoretical and methodological terms. There is a growing body of literature highlighting the ways in which adult researchers objectify children and how the design of an adult as the researcher and a child as the one researched may reflect symbolic violence and that these issues should be of particular concern for research in child welfare (Kiili et al., 2021). Adult-led research as such could thus be seen as being a risk or academically problematic, suggesting that in order to obtain academic approval for my imagined study, there would be a need to solidly argue for the way of being an adult researcher and the relevance of knowledge emerging from these relations, or, alternatively, to introduce a design of a non-adult ethnography.

The requirements for proof of non-risks and the arguments for adult-led research would, however, be a task for any *adult* researcher, not only for an older one. For older researchers, the current (risk) awareness of child–adult relations in research and the emphasis on children's rights to produce knowledge on their own mean that they need to problematize the traditions and customs of doing research learnt and established earlier in their careers. My notes and (nostalgic?) memories about trust and negotiations in research relations, for example, may exclude the age-related power imbalance there must have been but which, at that time, were seen as any relations between the (adult) researcher and the (adult) researched. The younger researchers may have internalized the rights of children as knowledge producers as part of their (academic) life course and have positioned themselves in the studies with/about/by children (Lundy & McEvoy, 2011; Thomas, 2021). This is related to academic generations and how they learn to think of their roles as researchers. However, regardless of the age of the researcher, age is indeed more than the individual asset of the (adult) ethnographer as it currently defines the formal preconditions of the design for ethnography in a human service organization for children, that is, the relations in the site and the very right to be there.

The Mundane (Embodied) Doing of Fieldwork

While writing about the embodiment of ethnographic fieldwork in her textbook about the ethnographic self, Amanda Coffey (1999) writes about the presence of the body in fieldwork relations and its textual representations, and highlights issues varying from the sex of the ethnographer to his/her appearance. However, the age of the ethnographer or age-related issues of embodied fieldwork seem to be a topic that has been given relatively little attention in that book or elsewhere. Assumingly, the adult body of the ethnographer as the standard body is taken for granted, and other elements of the body are seen as being more methodologically influential and interesting.

The few self-reports that explore the impact of the aged body on fieldwork highlight the methodological interrelations between the age of the body and the field relations. This is evident, for example, in the reflections of a late middle-aged researcher studying ethnographically the military service of young men in Finland ethnographically (Hoikkala et al., 2009). He, along with two younger colleagues, took part in military training activities, including long marches and camping in the woods in the middle of the Finnish winter. He writes about the age difference and how his body stood out as an exception among those more than 30 years younger than himself, even more so during physically tough exercises. When reading the report, it is obvious that the age—and in this case, the aging—of the body indeed shapes field relations and it becomes intertwined with his role as a man among other men, and consequently, the interpretations of the field. Age and its impact on his body is indeed the topic which the researcher elaborates in detail, possibly even more than other individual traits, in relation to his understanding of military service and its approach to health education.

Studying reform schools is different from studying military service or any such sites in which the body of the researcher is at risk and therefore likely to be reflected on. Nevertheless, regardless of the site, ethnography is embodied work and so is reform school ethnography. Its embodied nature is also temporally structured—as any social practice is (Moran, 2015; Atkinson, 2017). Residential life is 24/7—it is very much a temporally intense social practice (Moran, 2015)—and nighttime has a special status in the daily running of residential care: the beginning and end of nighttime are regulated (young people needed to go to their rooms and wake up at certain times), nighttime regulations differ according to the days of the week (weekends had looser regulations) and time of year (school terms were more strictly regulated than holiday seasons), and there are (or there used to be) special members of staff doing night shifts, among many other factors. It is a very private period of residential life as everyone is in their own rooms, surrounded by quietness and darkness. It is also a sensitive period of loneliness, longing, fears, and nightmares. For an ethnographer of residential care, it is a period not to be missed. As a young researcher during my first study, not feeling sleepy in the middle of the night, I managed to talk with the people on night shift and sense the atmosphere of the nighttime wards. Later, during my second study, I did not even try to visit the units during nighttime as the physical space had been changed to be very private: the units were small and some of them were located in the family homes of the staff. How could I enter those private spaces during the night? I did attend some early morning activities in the wards when everyone was getting ready to have breakfast and go to school but missed night hours. If I ever visit the institutions again, I would struggle—due to my age and its impact on me—to stay awake to do those ethnographic night shifts. This would introduce some weakness to the data as I would miss the chance, for example, to see how much of nighttime security has been replaced by technical monitoring, a topic that was discussed during my previous field period as a future alternative. Technical monitoring is often remarked upon by young people who have exited these institutions in recent years; ethnography on a reform school would be quite thin if it lacked firsthand observations of technical monitoring in nighttime action, especially without seeing how technical monitoring is linked with the institutional aim of providing a platform for "positive growth."

Staying awake at the night is one tiny and mundane example of embodied fieldwork. The literature is rife with much more exciting examples of embodied fieldwork and risks related to violence, harassment, or accidents which (young adult) researchers encounter in their work. Staying awake is, however, a reminder that ethnographic fieldwork depends on the body in a variety of ways. The recent interest in walking methods (e.g., O'Neill & Roberts, 2020) builds on the idea of body competencies of the ethnographer as one who can "walk" and "move." There are many issues related to the competencies of the body that have been taken for granted, some of which are not age-related at all, although they enable on the one hand, and limit or exclude, on the other hand, opportunities to be in field relations. However, doing ethnographic fieldwork is not only "about being" in one's body "there" but also about thinking about what one sees and remembering it, or, as Coffey (1999, p. 27) puts it, it is "about experiencing and remembering, ordering and giving frameworks to our memories." Taking notes, intermediating, and ordering experiences and remembering have changed over the years with the emergence of new equipment and ways of thinking of note-taking (Hammersley & Atkinson, 2019, pp. 152–153). Hardly anyone writes notes with a pen on endless notepads as I did during my first study and even the progress I experienced in my second study of having a personal laptop to record notes might not be so cherished nowadays; instead, many researchers may just audio or video record their observations and even ask the ones researched to do that themselves in less researcher-led designs. Taking notes is about capturing and re-representing the ethnographic site for later use, which can be done systematically or non-systematically, and consequently, ethnographic memory is not only supported by note-taking but also shaped by it. Notes can be destroyed by accident or by institutional regulations regarding the norms of data storage or other reasons (as my notes of the first and second periods had to be destroyed), whereas the human memory of the ethnographer functions differently: it cannot be destroyed by external commands, and neither can one control what is forgotten and what (and how) is remembered. For revisiting ethnographic sites, remembering, forgetting, and the archives of notes of different kinds are essential resources. The temporal layers of memories and forgotten people, buildings, and episodes of interactions are, however, not fixed but dynamic objects for re-interpretations (e.g., Misztal, 2003). The more years you have and the more visits to the site you have done, the more opportunities for forgetting and re-interpreting you have.

Generational and Professional Relations

When entering the reform schools for the second time, 10 years after the first ethnographic period, I was reminded that I might not understand the "youth culture" of that time due to the age difference between the young residents and myself. For me, the age difference was an issue, among other issues, to negotiate during the fieldwork—the very reason for doing ethnography was to learn to know what "youth culture" was when focusing on young people's views and experiences of reform school life. Obviously, there was a need for translations of different kinds, one of them being the translation between generations (but I also struggled to understand that the pictures of flowers drawn on young people's notebooks resembled cannabis leaves and thus had more meanings than just being "pretty drawings"). That is why I provided cameras to the young people to take pictures of what was important in reform school life. The pictures were to be shared with me and explained in words. When it was time to discuss the pictures, many of which were of the young people themselves, or of other young people and some details of the reform school buildings (e.g., windows, fridges), I noted one overall message: loneliness. The pictures showing young people having fun in the classrooms or in the living units were not merely about being in peer relations but about being outside those relations, which is about being lonely. This clash between the words and the pictures is a challenge for any researcher (Pink, 2001); I followed the interpretation of loneliness as it emerged in many episodes during my stays there: the young people spoke about it—in length or in passing—when I met them in the interview sessions; peer relations were described as conditional, and parents were spoken about in very limited words. The staff told that it was very rare for young people to have visits from their family members, and the previously important family-centered working methods had lost their meaning due to the lack of contact with families. I did not meet many parents during the fieldwork periods, which was in stark contrast to the evenings spent with visiting parents in the guest rooms 10 years earlier when parents visited their children frequently. The interpretation of loneliness was indeed tested and further elaborated in many field episodes and many encounters and became of the key findings of the study. I imagine that I would equally need translations for many words and signs used by young people if I ever start a new ethnographic period. However, I would not see the reason for the need for a variety of translations as only my "old age" or generational differences; instead, the very nature of ethnography requires the ethnographer to learn how the social world is accomplished in his/her particular site and to be alert about the emerging interpretations and constantly test and elaborate them. In fact, "old age" could give the privilege to ask silly questions as generational differences are so obvious in relation with teenagers.

In fact, my professional mindset as a social work professor troubles me more than my age and age-related issues if I ever start the third period in the reform schools. When doing my second period, I, as a mid-career social work university teacher, felt ashamed of not having understood the transformation of the welfare services and the ways in which some young people had been excluded from the services during their childhood troubles. There were, as mentioned before, young people who had not learnt to read properly as they had been running away from their school for so many years—truly an anomaly in the Finnish education system—suggesting that there were children who had dropped out of many ordinary childhood environments as was later documented in research highlighting childhoods during the years of economic recession in Finland. I should have known about those changes as a university teacher, but my research activities had focused on other issues. Therefore, the stories I heard in the reform schools surprised me and troubled me professionally. During the first period, 10 years earlier, I was free from such professional self-criticism as I was just a PhD student interested in (gendered) social problem constructions. These positions must have been reflected in the fieldwork and in my relations with the residential actors. During the first period, I observed staff (how they acted and contributed to the problem constructions), but during the second period, I needed them to explain to me what had happened during the 10 years. My professional self-criticism was strengthened by the new strong role of psychiatric discourse evident in some parts of practice. When reading the case files of the young people, the overarching frame for approaching the young people's needs for residential care was worded with psychological and psychiatric terminology in clear contrast to the frame of norm-breaking behavior 10 years earlier. For making sense of the residential life of that time, it was quite a mixture of competing frames: my self-criticism about not knowing the recent changes in society, the institutional frame of disorders to position young people and their needs in the reform schools, and the frame of loneliness, emerging in many parts of the fieldwork.

Ten years earlier, as a junior researcher, I "saw" more rebellion and protest against social norms, and, consequently, young people as protestors and ones to rebel (and staff as those trying to cope with the protests). It was supported by my theoretical background—the social constructionist reading of "deviance" and social problems—and I did not much doubt my interpretations. To support my interpretations, I collected a solid data set, stayed for several months in the institutions, analyzed my data systematically, and reported in detail how I came to my conclusions; in other words, followed all the steps which at the time were required for a valid qualitative analysis, supported by the variety of textbooks on ethnography of that time. There is no way to know now how much my age and short experience of child welfare and research influenced my interpretations. I only know that it would be different if I ever start a new project. I find it difficult to imagine what "a path towards positive growth," the present frame worded on the website, would look like in the everyday practice of reform schools. What I know is that if I ever enter the reform schools again, I would be more aware than before that it is the *present* frame, taking place in a certain temporal and social context instead of being "the" frame for reform schools. This would certainly be reflected in the relations with staff and young people alike: there would be even more questions asked. If I anticipate the answers, I would be inclined to assume that staff and young people would take some time and effort to explain this "new" paradigm to someone who is an "old academic", ignorant and distant from the current way of doing residential care. As a retiring academic, at the margins of the field of child welfare policy, I would not pose any threat as an expert to the staff. For young people, my grandmother age would most likely emphasize my interest as an ethnographer to listen to their accounts of residential life without any hurry and judgment.

The researcher being treated as ignorant is not necessarily a bad thing for ethnographic data as it helps to make contextual practices "known". The essence of contextual practices and their meaning-making is demonstrated by a recent study looking at adult–child touch in residential settings (Warwick, 2022). The study argues that adult–child touch should not be isolated from the relations in residential settings as touching as a bodily contact acquires its meanings in those relations in that particular residential context. This is to say that the appropriateness or inappropriateness of touching, for example, is far from binary in nature in the residential context and the task of an ethnographer would be to capture the spectrum and variability of those meanings. It is the task of the ethnographer not to know the meanings before the fieldwork but to learn to know them as being constituted (e.g., Buckholdt & Gubrium, 1979; Bengtsson, 2012). To do that, generational or age-related sameness could be equally problematic or beneficial as generational and age differences. It is, after all, the relations which constitute most of the data in residential settings, and there is no fixed way of what they would or should be like.

Concluding Remarks

Although this chapter was initiated by my memories of revisiting residential care as an ethnographer and my interest in doing it once more, the intention has not been to provide an autoethnographical account. "My old age" is not really "me" but it is one of the many ethnographical assets which crafts ethnographic fieldwork. It might not be one of the most essential assets, but it is an inevitable feature of any ethnographer and any field site and more so in age-divided human service organizations. I have demonstrated earlier some issues related to age and generations which might not be so evident (for young researchers). I have also concluded that "my old age" would not be any better or worse than "my young age" (or vice versa) as all ethnographic fieldwork is shaped by relations in the field and the ethnographer in any case influences those relations and the emerging data. That is why I do not necessarily agree with the proposals that children and young people should be only studied by other children and young people for the sake of democracy of knowledge production. Whether young or old, the ethnographic data is situated, relational and contextual.

While being situated and contextual, also temporally, ethnographic follow-up studies could indeed be helpful in challenging the "ethnographic present" and its temporal limitations. I have demonstrated how "rebellion", "loneliness", or "paths towards positive growth" are time-related frames for ethnographic understanding of residential life. Despite being time-related, there is also continuity: year after year, fieldwork period after fieldwork period, the institutions provide a place of residence for young people who are seen to be in need of care out of their homes and they employ staff to work with these young people as they have done for the last 140 years or so. If one agrees that the task to understand the continuities and discontinuities of residential life is a task for ethnographers and not only for historians, it provides a sound methodological challenge for those both younger and older among us. Ethnographic research is not at its strongest when exploring the social and political factors shaping the different rationales and frames for residential care, but it is at its strongest when highlighting how they are accomplished in practice in their specific temporal contexts.

References

Alderson, P., & Morrow, V. (2011). *The ethics of research with children and young people: A practical handbook*. Sage.

Atkinson, P. (2017). *Thinking ethnographically*. Sage Research Methods. Retrieved January 6, 2022, from https://dx.doi.org/10.4135/9781473982741

Bardy, M., Salmi, M., & Heino, T. (2001). *Mikä lapsiamme uhkaa? [What threatens our children?]*. Stakes.

Bengtsson, T. (2012). *Youth behind bars: An ethnographic study of youth confinement in secure care institutions in Denmark*. Københavns Universitetet.

Berridge, D., & Brodie, I. (1998). *Children's homes revisited*. Jessica Kingsley.

Boelen, M. (1992). Street corner society: Cornerville revisited. *Journal of Contemporary Ethnography*, *21*(1), 11–51.

Buckholdt, D., & Gubrium, J. (1979). *Caretakers. Treating emotionally disturbed children*. Sage.

Burawoy, M. (2003). Revisits: An outline of a theory of reflexive ethnography. *American Sociological Review*, *68*(5), 645–679.

Coffey, A. (1999). *The ethnographic self. Fieldwork and the representation of identity*. Sage.

Delgado, M. (2006). *Designs and methods for youth-led research*. Sage. https://dx.doi.org/10.4135/9781412983884

Hammersley, M., & Atkinson, P. (2019). *Ethnography: Principles in practice* (4th ed.). Routledge.

Hoikkala, T., Salasuo, M., & Ojajärvi, A. (2009). *Tunnetut sotilaat [The known soldiers]*. Nuorisotutkimusverkosto.

Honkatukia, P., Nyqvist, L., & Pösö, T. (2003). Sensitive issues in vulnerable conditions—studying violence in youth residential care. *Young*, *11*(4), 323–339.

Honkatukia, P., Nyqvist, L., & Pösö, T. (2006). Violence from within the reform schools. *Youth Violence and Juvenile Justice*, *4*(4), 328–344.

Hytönen, K., Malinen, A., Salenius, P., Haikari, J., Markkola, P., Kuronen, M., & Koivisto, J. (2016). *Lastensuojelun sijaishuollon epäkohdat ja lasten kaltoinkohtelu 1937–1983 [The failures and abuse of children in substitute care 1937–1983]'*. Reports 22. Sosiaali- ja terveysministeriö.

Jacobsson, K., & Gubrium, J. (Eds.). (2021). *Doing human service ethnography*. Policy Press.

James, A. (2011). Ethnography in the study of children and childhood. In P. Atkinson, A. Coffey, S. Delamont, J. Lofland, & L. Lofland (Eds.), *Handbook of ethnography* (pp. 246–257). Sage Publications. Retrieved January 10, 2022, from https://dx.doi.org/10.4135/9781848608337

Känkänen, P. (2013). *Taidelähtöiset menetelmät lastensuojelussa—kohti tilaa ja kokemuksia [Art-based methods in child welfare—towards space and experience].* Terveyden ja hyvinvoinnin laitos.

Kiili, J., Moilanen, J., & Larkins, C. (2021). Child-research relationships in child protection research. An integrative review. *European Journal of Social Work.* https://doi.org/10.1080/13691457.2021.2016648

Lundy, L., & McEvoy, L. (2011). Children's rights and research processes: Assisting children to (in)formed views. *Childhood, 19*(1), 129–144.

McLeod, J., & Thomson, R. (2009). *Researching social change: Qualitative approaches.* Sage.

Misztal, B. (2003). *Theories of social remembering.* Open University Press.

Moran, C. (2015). Time as a social practice. *Time & Society, 24*(3), 283–303.

O'Neill, M., & Roberts, B. (Eds.). (2020). *Walking methods. Research on the move.* Routledge.

Pekkarinen, E. (2017). *Koulukoti murroksessa [Reform school in change].* Nuorisotutkimusverkosto.

Pink, S. (2001). *Doing visual ethnography.* Sage.

Plummer, K. (2019). *Narrative power.* Polity.

Pösö, T. (1993). *Kolme koulukotia. Tutkimus tyttöjen ja poikien poikkeavuuden määrittelykäytännöistä koulukotihoidossa. (Three reformatory schools. A study on the practices of defining girls' and boys' troublemaking in the context of Finnish residential child welfare).* Acta Universitatis Tamperensis. Ser A Vol. 388. University of Tampere.

Pösö, T. (2004). *Vakavat silmät ja muita kokemuksia koulukodista [Serious eyes and other experiences of reform schools].* Report 133. Stakes.

Thomas, N. (2021). Child-led research, children's rights and childhood studies: A defence. *Childhood, 28*(2), 186–199.

Valtion koulukodit [The state reform schools]. Retrieved January 10, 2022, from https://valtionkoulukodit.fi/en/

Warwick, L. (2022). "Depends who it is": Towards a relational understanding of the use of adult-child touch in residential child care. *Qualitative Social Work, 21*(1), 18–36.

6

SENIOR ACTIVISTS AND AGE AFFILIATIONS IN ETHNOGRAPHIC PEERING

Gary Alan Fine

In what ways does an ethnographer's demographic and cultural similarities to informants matter? Does access result from resemblance? Is rapport inevitably dependent on the match between researcher and researched? Can we only learn that which we have already experienced? These challenging questions have intrigued and bedeviled fieldworkers for generations, but they have become ever more salient in an age in which identity politics has become a source of concern, conflict, and anxiety. While this challenge may be stated too strongly, relationships within a field setting are crucial to what we know and what we report. What is learned in the field shapes what is transmitted on the page.

Debates on the importance of the researcher's identity have focused most frequently on the role of race and gender in qualitative research. Much has been shared on the challenges that female ethnographers have faced in interacting with male informants. Male ethnographers may, in turn, not be sufficiently trusted by female informants and their groups to produce candid and textured data. Race, too, has a central issue but has played out differently as typically it was the more structurally powerful White ethnographers, embedded in elite universities, that examined communities of color. Ethnographers must confront the dynamics both of less powerful scholars studying "up" and more powerful scholars studying "down." We recognize all too painfully that how these issues are framed—up and down, more and less established—reflect a society in which bias, oppression, and privilege are commonplace.

Still, a broader issue emerges, and it is one that I discuss in this essay: Must one be a member of a chosen category in order to establish productive rapport and to establish trust? How much does demography matter? Does one need to be a potential member of the group to be a full-fledged ethnographer? What are the benefits and the costs of similarity with one's colleagues/informants/subjects?

DOI: 10.4324/9781003275121-9

This issue applies to many social categories: not just race and gender, but ethnicity, class, sexuality, education, politics, even region, and, in my case, age. The linkage of researcher and informant matters in several ways. I point to three components that either benefit or limit the ethnographic enterprise: Access, Rapport, and Insight.

Access. How one's presence can be negotiated has proven a thorny topic for researchers who desire to gain entry to a group that controls its borders, either through formal approval or by common consent. On what basis will a community permit an outsider to observe its inner workings? As Everett Hughes (1971) pointed out, all occupations and organizations have an underside, and it is often necessary to keep these practices shaded from those who have not been initiated. The researcher, with large ears and thorny eyes, can expose the group to public opprobrium. Entry demands trust, a collective sense that the observer will take care to tidy up any dusty or disreputable corners of the interaction order. On what basis can ethnographic trust be established to allow entry, particularly prior to the researcher being tested? A crucial allowance occurs if the researcher is seen as one of "us," or at least as a person who, by virtue of experience, is seen as someone who is likely to be sympathetic by having experienced some of the same affronts that members of the group have experienced (Goffman, 1989). This is particularly evident when the group has been the target of some measure of discrimination or oppression.

Rapport. Having achieved entry into the desired social world, the ethnographer is soon put to the test. How should this person be treated? Can the "dirty little secrets" of group life be shared? This edges into the domain of rapport. Will the emotional connection prove to be a productive one? One can be permitted to enter into a group space, but what is shared may be a misleading picture of what group members believe and how the group truly operates. Sexual talk or offensive jokes are rarely shared at first, as I learned in my examination of Little League baseball teams (Fine, 1987). This represents the ethnographic equivalent of a "Potemkin village." The community seems to obey desirable norms, however, without the establishment of rapport much has been missed. Facing this dilemma, one searches for a "key informant": someone who can unlock the unstated rules that the core members understand. The problem of rapport constitutes a commitment to likeability. However, the concern is something other than a personality trait or a form of pleasing interaction. Rapport often develops from being able to refer to shared experiences that are part of a shared habitus or background culture.

Insight. Some 50 years ago, Fred Davis (1973) wrote of a fundamental division in ethnographic research: the divide between the Martian and the Convert. By these memorable concepts, Davis addressed whether the researcher wished to become as full a member of the group as possible (the convert) or whether being an outsider provided insight that insiders would inevitably lack because it challenged their taken-for-granted reality (the Martian). Ethnographers disagree as to which is preferable, a debate that is evident in science studies as to whether one needs transactional knowledge (Collins & Evans, 2017) or whether, given the impossibility of gaining full experience, transactional ignorance can be a blessing to keep the focus on sociological knowledge (Atkinson & Morriss, 2017). The truth is that there are advantages to both strategies; each provides a distinctive orientation toward the development of theory: from the inside out and from the outside in. The choice is between a phenomenological, reflexive understanding—in the extreme a form of going native—and an external behavioral and cultural explanation of action. This divide, of course, is not identical to the issue of whether it is necessary to be a part of the same demographic category, but demographic overlaps certainly make becoming a convert easier and more difficult to be a Martian. While there are cross-cutting categories (being African American, a woman, a professor, LGBTQ, a cancer survivor, a Catholic, or a Democratic Socialist), the basis of the theory of intersectionality, the more overlap, the fewer Martians in our midst. The smaller the overlap, the less can researchers rely on their own reflexive phenomenology.

Ethnography and Age

To explore the way in which access, rapport, and insight shape the relations between the fieldworker and informants, I focus on the importance of age in ethnography, describing one of my recent ethnographic projects (Fine, 2023). What are the benefits and the drawbacks of examining an organization in which members are age peers, while the organizational staff are not? I describe my immersion in an organization of senior citizen progressive activists, a group that I observed and participated in during my late sixties, a time that I was a generational peer, but whose organizers were younger women (and one younger man).

Age is a salient issue in political organizing, as it is in ethnography. Most ethnography has been conducted by younger scholars. Ethnography is not capital intensive, but, when done properly, is labor intensive. One must constantly be "in the field." This provides a benefit to those who are at the outset of the careers and explains why so much iconic ethnography is conducted by young scholars. This is true of studies of senior citizens (Hochschild, 1973; Gubrium, 1975; Abramson, 2015). For these researchers, the elderly were treated as akin to a somewhat distant tribe, known of but not a part of one's experience. The question emerges as to whether this distance is a desirable stance for understanding or whether it constitutes a block on experiencing the world in a way that one's informants do.

When analyzing senior worlds, this often creates the ethnographic role as akin to a child or grandchild, rather than a peer: a chronological outsider. In this research, conducted with a progressive political group that I label Chicago Seniors Together, I was able to embrace that my age was similar to that of members, while I differed from the younger staff. Although my relationship with the members was as an equal, gaining easy camaraderie, the staff, as I discuss, were more skeptical of my role as my age did not overwhelm the reality that I was an outsider to the movement.

I have advanced the methodological justification for ethnographers taking on the stranger role, a perspective that I still embrace. However, being a stranger to a group may take several forms. The virtues of age peering were balanced in my attempt to understand the activities and the culture of these seniors from a skeptical perspective by the reality that I conducted this research without having previously been a member of the organization or a political activist myself. As a result, my age provided me with rapport, while my distance in terms of the substance of the activity allowed me to have the ethnographic distance that allowed for what I have termed a skeptical ethnography (Fine, 2019).

Observing Seniors

For decades I had been teaching students about social movements and have instructed graduate students in the rigors of conductive ethnography. However, aside from brief ethnographic forays into the world of political party activists (Fine, 2012, pp. 14–15, 141) and observations of a group that supported families accused of child abuse (Fine, 1995, pp. 138–142), I had not conducted a fully focused ethnography on a social movement group. As I became a senior citizen, I felt that it was time to bring the two interests together. But which group should I study? Ethnography necessarily involves a search for the proper site for discovery. In this, it is inevitably both a personal and a practical endeavor. As a result, one's personal equation is often crucial for one's ability to see. Further, one's public identity to define is crucial for one's future friends to be willing to be observed and to share.

As I neared age 65, soon to receive my Medicare card, although not ready to retire, I determined to observe a group of senior citizen political activists. How would people, much like me, but more committed to the rigors of challenging inequity, push for social and political change? Not all of my research has been with age peers as I have studied Little League baseball players and high school debaters, even though I have typically studied across in terms of social class, rather than up or down.

Having decided to theorize the political commitments of vulnerable seniors who act to promote change within the public sphere, I faced the question of where to find these activists, engaged seniors, men and women who were my age peers. The search for the right site proved more challenging than I had anticipated. The activist organizational field has few movement groups that specifically recruit the elderly, although many social movements happily accept seniors as participants, even if they do not adjust the culture to address their vulnerabilities. Seniors have long been involved in fights for social justice or, from another perspective, in attempts to prod the state to be a conservative bulwark for morality. However, organizations that explicitly recruit seniors and that are designed to mobilize them are rare.

After searching, I found a suitable organization, and I reached out to the executive director, a woman in her late fifties. Her not (yet) being a senior proved to be a source of joking in the organization. (She retired as executive director before she reached age 65.) We met in a local coffee shop, where I explained that I wished to understand how seniors, given their age-related vulnerabilities, operated as political actors. I felt that the meeting went well, and I was surprised when approval was not immediately granted. I was asked to go through a set of evaluations, meeting with both the board of the organization, a group of seniors, and attending a staff meeting, with the group's community organizers who were younger women in their twenties and thirties, committed to direct action and progressive activist engagement. After these meetings, I was quickly welcomed by the seniors who were delighted that someone wished to participate in their world, but the responses of the staff were notably cooler, even if never hostile. After reaching out to one of the organization's co-chairs, a retired professor at a local community college, I was allowed to attend meetings, but the staff meetings were not immediately open as there was concern about what I might uncover. I was seen as an ally of the seniors—being one of them—but, as I learned later, the staff meetings often involved critical comments on how to deal with some of the more "troublesome" seniors as well as criticism by one staff member of another. It was only at the end of the research that I was allowed to attend four consecutive staff meetings, and this occurred only after I had befriended the newly hired staff. This experience revealed that age shapes access and rapport, and serves as a marker for allegiance.

The project involved ethnographic research during a 30-month observation of the group that I name Chicago Seniors Together,[1] conducted from fall 2015 until spring 2018. This group proved to be a particularly appropriate site to examine how narrative, history, and shared experience are resources for collective action. Because the larger project addresses well-publicized issues and events that are easily traceable, I specify that the organization is based in Chicago. However, minor details and names have been altered to respect the anonymity of informants, especially those who engaged in unlawful civil disobedience.

My research is based on extensive ethnographic field observations, supplemented with document analysis and with in-depth interviews. I approached the project using the grounded theory methodology that involves looking for comparative cases and writing interpretive memos, building on extensive fieldnotes (Glaser & Strauss, 1967). My focus shifted at various points during the 30 months as different issues rose to prominence as reflected in the organizational agenda.

During this extended ethnography, I observed numerous committees and public meetings and participated in some demonstrations, marches, and other protests. Since I had not previously been involved with the organization, I began as an outsider; however, in the course of the research I engaged in actions and activities with fellow seniors, although, like most members, I chose not to engage in civil disobedience. I attended board meetings, staff meetings, finance committee meetings, and issue-oriented committees. On each occasion, I took fieldnotes, focusing on those interactions that developed the group culture, transcribing stories, anecdotes, and other narratives. I explained to participants that my presence was for research purposes. As noted, I had the advantage of dealing with the activist members in that I was a chronological peer. We had experienced the same range of historical events, even if my position as a professor of sociology provided a different perspective. However, as any good ethnographer, I attempted to gain their trust so that they would share their stories, share their concerns, and share their world. Social seduction is necessary for gaining trust and data. I hope that I returned that trust with respect.

During the research, I developed friendships with senior leaders and staff. After a few months, members and the seniors who were organizational leaders treated me as a full participant, although, as I describe, it took longer for the staff to accept my presence without suspicion. In the last months of the project, I conducted 35 interviews: 10 with staff and 25 with members. Interviews lasted from 1 to 3 hours and were tape-recorded and transcribed. Having spent years with the group, I was able to ask questions about the events in which they and I had participated, building on the rapport that we shared, my local knowledge, and, perhaps, a decreased need to present socially desirable responses to someone who had shared their world. Throughout the research, I wrote memos that contrasted their explanations and my observations with those from previous research projects and tested my ideas and their claims against data that seemed to contradict them.

I joined the organization, paid dues, participated in phone banks, and contributed to fundraising, but I was never a leader of the organization. I listened but did not direct. My role in meetings varied. In meetings of the board, the finance committee, the leadership committee, and staff meetings, I remained quiet. There were two exceptions: at the start of the meeting in which the leader asked those present to introduce themselves (I announced my role as professor and researcher) and presented a relational question or posed a relational exercise. In these responses, I attempted to be both honest and supportive of the group beliefs. Often at the end of the meeting a feeling word was requested to evaluate the meeting (my word was never negative). I rarely spoke in larger committee meetings, but in smaller meetings planning actions, I participated more directly and also participated when we were divided into small discussion groups. As an ethnographer, I made an effort—one I judge to be largely successful—to befriend members who were part of my generation (or the one earlier) and with the staff, younger but with several trained in the social sciences or in social work.

As I describe subsequently, in the 30 months, a few moments of tension emerged, particularly in light of my level of involvement. Many seniors urged me to participate more actively, valuing my insights as an insightful peer. In contrast, others, particularly a few staff members, felt that I should remain a silent observer and rarely an active participant. I had to negotiate this balance. I admit to being broadly sympathetic to the values of Chicago Seniors Together, although not on every issue or with every tactic.

Peer and Peerless

For this chapter, I focus on the relations that developed in the course of my research, both relationships with my age peers in the organization and relations with the younger staff members. In this, I draw from my extensive fieldnotes to explore the dynamics of access and rapport. I then address how what I learned—my insight—resulted from these sets of relations.

Being With Seniors. It should be noted that while similarity of identity made life easier, my age was rarely addressed directly. No one said, "You are a senior too." Rather it was a sense that I belonged, and that being there was of unquestioned value. This allegiance occurred from the first board meeting that I attended, in contrast to the first staff meeting. Perhaps being a sociology professor with the politics that the position implied helped me to gain access to the staff, but the trust was immediate.

At that first board of directors meeting, I was introduced by the organization's co-chair, Jerry, a retired humanities professor at a local community college. After this meeting, my incorporation into the life of the organization was swift. I explained to the board (comprised of the senior citizen leaders of the group) that I was a faculty member at Northwestern University, who was interested in how seniors participated in political life and how we as seniors attempted to change the world. This project was greeted with warm enthusiasm. Like so many groups, these seniors felt unrecognized and underappreciated, even by their ostensible, though younger, allies. After the meeting, having been asked questions about the ways that I would participate and about confidentiality, several members told me that they were glad that I was present and that I would be sharing their experiences in my research findings. Many wanted to know if I would be writing a book that they could purchase and share with family. Several asked if I was retired or planning to be so. This same welcome was evident at the first "action" that I attended, a demonstration at the Chicago Board of Trade. The organization had arranged buses from senior housing projects and I arranged to travel on one, where I met some dozen other members of the group, several of whom became friends throughout the research. Our cultures, experiences, and memories were sufficiently similar that we could (and did) talk about events from the 1960s without having to explain what we meant. In these early activities, I gained both formal and interpersonal access to senior members as someone whose perspective might be valuable, or at least interesting.

One senior leader made this explicit in our interview, claiming (to my pleasure),

> I was glad someone was that interested in what the group was doing. . . . So to have an individual similar to you in a position at least outside and looking at us who could give us suggestions about how to do things better and that is very, very useful. So I was glad to see you every day because you were going to analyze things. . . . So to have inspiration from someone, I like that. To have inspiration from someone like you.

In his view, I already had a place that justified my presence. Others spoke similarly. Jerry joked at one meeting that in order to portray them in a balanced way, "He leaves his bias at the door." Because of my similar background, I could translate their activity both to the group itself and to those who stood outside.

In time, this open access developed into rapport. I was frequently asked to help with various projects, such as making posters for demonstrations (an activity that reminded me of preparing for a Junior Prom), handing out signs, and taking photos (many of these seniors did not snap "Selfies," but asked others to do the job). I would do those favors that I could. Similar to my early research on Little League baseball (Fine, 1987), I offered to drive my new friends home or to appointments when my schedule allowed. I also routinely brought in food on those occasions on which there were pre-meeting pot-luck gatherings. Those informal discussions in my car or sitting around tables eating our shared contributions both provided insight and built friendships. On one occasion I was asked to take notes for an organizational meeting, although my formal acceptance by the Executive Director was based on the fact that I would observe and not take on the roles of members who were being trained (sometimes without their explicit awareness) to be activists.

As the months went on, I made friends, developed key informants, and was invited to lunches and coffees on several occasions or to sit at their table during organizational parties. While I reached out to all members and became friends with many, I recognize that these close relationships developed more rapidly with White members and male activists, although my close connections were not limited to members of these groups. My Jewish ethnicity (and urban cultural style) helped as well, as many activists had a Jewish background and some wished me Shana Tovah (Happy New Year) on Rosh Hashanah. On one occasion, traveling with two other senior members, one of them described us three as "troublemakers together." All of the seniors that I asked to interview readily agreed. (Most staff agreed to interviews, but not all.) I knew that I was accepted when, after attending the bimonthly board meetings, I was described as being an "honorary member" of the board, reminding me of the time 40 years previously when I was studying Little League baseball teams that one player called me an "honorary kid." Indeed, of all my research projects, the study of senior activists was most similar to my study of preadolescents.

The connections began early in the research as I made a point of attending as many meetings as possible, and in arriving early and staying late. Ethnographers realize that the penumbrae immediately prior to and immediately after formal gatherings are often the most insight-rich moments. But the best indicator of belonging occurred when I missed meetings. When I returned after travel, senior members would inquire where I had been and even shared that they noticed my absence. I was not an occasional presence, but an integral part of group life. Given organizational turnover after 30 months, I had become a regular.

Perhaps the most dramatic instance of my acceptance by the seniors occurred when the organization had planned to make an endorsement in the election for governor. Luisa, the staff member in charge of the endorsement committee, wanted the decision to be made in a closed committee meeting (i.e., without my presence). As Luisa, the staff member responsible for the committee, explained, "I would prefer if it were just the endorsement committee. It might be a difficult conversation." Luisa wanted to insure that she could direct that they did not make an endorsement as she believed that none of the candidates showed the organization sufficient respect. After the decision had been made, which, as Luisa wished, was to withhold any endorsement, one of the key members of the committee, Richie, approached me, and whispered in my ear, "We're not supposed to mention this, but I will anyhow. We decided not to endorse anyone." When I determined in winter 2018 that I needed to end my research (although I subsequently showed up for a few events), I was hugged, told that I was always welcome and needed, and asked about the plans for publishing my research.

This access and subsequent friendship provided the material through which I could understand the passions, the frustrations, and the vulnerabilities of these senior activists in light of my similar generational experiences. In a previously published paper (Fine, 2020), I argued that it is important to understand social movements in light of the memories, experiences, and shared histories of the participants. However, in making this case, I did not address how my shared experiences helped me to understand the group dynamics. But the process is not that of an outsider looking in—no matter the shared background of that outsider—it is also dependent on the fact that I could fluidly participate in the interaction order of the members. Even if I had not previously committed myself to the Saul Alinsky-inspired activism that the organization believed in and even if I had not engaged in provocative civil disobedience, I shared enough in common that I could understand how their experiences during the Civil Rights movement and the Anti-War movement of the 1960s shaped their perspective. This bolstered the arguments that I wished to make about how history inserts itself into morality and activity. Further, I was not looking at any age group, but rather an age (my age) in which health and bodily concerns come to matter, often in consequential and crucial ways. Each participant had their own health concerns, some more insistent than others, but the idea of bodily decline and physical incapacity affects all seniors to a greater or lesser extent. An ethnographer from a different generation would not appreciate the same worries in a similar fashion, no matter how empathetic they might be. For these younger researchers, the seniors were always, in some important sense, others: a tribe whose membership was not fully open. In a study that emphasized how histories and vulnerabilities affect one's civic participation, the ability—indeed, the necessity—of sharing these concerns enriched the analysis. So, being a peer of these seniors was instrumental in the analysis that I was able to conduct (Fine, 2023). But, as I now describe, "hanging with seniors" was not all that this research involved. I now turn to negotiations with the staff, sympathetic members of a younger cohort.

Engaging With Staff Across a Suspicious Divide. As noted, Chicago Seniors Together as a relatively stable and fairly adequately funded social movement (with an annual budget of approximately $500,000) had a staff of five-to-seven, plus an office manager. My engagement with the younger staff was not always as smooth or readily accepted as with the seniors. I had to attend a staff meeting at first where I was questioned about my politics and what I would do for the organization.

I was aided by a brief article in the Northwestern University alumni magazine that touched on my research with Chicago Seniors Together during the research. Although I was somewhat anxious about how the project might be reported, the staffer who had seen the article was pleased and shared it with others, leading to support for my presence.

While access was granted, rapport had to be delicately negotiated with the staff as a group and with each staffer as an individual. The turnover among staff further complicated this effort as only two staffers—one being the Executive Director—remained throughout the 30-month research project. Further, as staff members had the responsibility to direct the various "action" committees, notably the Housing Committee and the Health Care and Economic Justice Committee, I had to gain the approval of the lead staff member in each case, even though there was no concern by the members. Eventually, I gained access to each of these committees, as I had hoped, although the staffer brought the approval to permit my attendance to the members of the committee.

I lacked the same depth and richness of relationship with these committed organizers from a younger generation. The new staff had to determine what they could properly share with me. When I wished to interview an intern with whom I had friendly relations, she was willing but explained that she needed to talk with senior staff as to what topics about which she should refrain from sharing. This difference was magnified as all but one staffer was female. Unlike the seniors, who never raised the issue, the staff was concerned that my male (and White, class, and professorial) privilege might bias the story that I would tell. One staffer was quite direct in our discussions. She asked, "What is your perspective as a White Jewish male senior." These were the categories that mattered to her. Of course, she was not wrong in asking the question, even if the answer was rather blurry. Were those the categories on which my insight would depend? In part, no doubt. As they were outsiders to my world, could I appreciate theirs? For these activists my biography—my habitus—was at issue.

Further, even though I was explicitly an observer, they worried that, given my identity, I might attempt to shape the activities of Chicago Seniors Together in ways that they found undesirable. At various points, Jane Tate, the Executive Director, emphasized, especially to the staff, that "Gary is just here to observe," preventing me from answering the opening relational question at one of the staff meetings. Prior to a committee meeting of the Racial Justice Leadership Team, a group that addressed racial bias within the organization, in which the group was facing defections, a sense that they were not contributing sufficiently to the organizational goals, and had to decide whether to continue, Jane took me aside and reminded me that I was there only to observe. I could watch, but I was not to speak. On several occasions, Jane chided me for making comments in meetings with seniors that she felt directed their attention. Perhaps the greatest strain resulted from a committee meeting where, after no one was willing to create a future agenda, I volunteered. Jane was disturbed by this, saying that I should not have become involved as this was an opportunity to train a member of the committee to gain the skills allowing them to become leaders. Despite the fact that I was a senior and that I was a dues-paying member, I was not to think of myself as a full member of the organization. For the staff, I did not truly belong. The absence of impact was the basis on which the staff permitted me to have access to committee meetings and engage in political actions, both those that they directly controlled and those that were ostensibly run by seniors. Because the staff perceived (correctly, in some measure) that I was an outsider and not one of "them," not someone who was committed to community organizing, they were (reasonably) suspicious of my intentions. For my part, I had to learn what it meant to be an organizer, particularly one who was organizing people who were distinct from themselves. Significantly, later in my research, one of the newer staffers commented that she wished that I had spoken more in committees because she found my perspective to be particularly valuable. This was a balance that I had to negotiate as being a senior, an outsider, and a scholar of social movements.

It was clear that in the course of the research that one of the staffers, Luisa, had more trouble with my presence than others. She was described to me as someone who had "issues with boundaries." While we developed a cordial relationship, there were places where she felt that I did not belong and comments that I should not be asked to make. When she left the organization, my relations with the staff improved. However, the issue of whether I could attend staff meetings proved problematic. In the middle of the research, I was allowed to attend a staff meeting, a time at which staffers could discuss the challenges of dealing with senior members and with their own and others' frustration. I had assumed that these meetings would be open to me, but it turned out that I was only permitted to attend one meeting because this was a private space. I was not (yet) to be trusted. A year later my relations with the staff had developed to the point that I was permitted to attend a month of staff meetings, despite my perceived alliance with senior members, and I did discover that the staff meeting was a time and place in which venting and the sharing of anxiety were legitimate. It was not that I was too old, as such, to be in these spaces, but rather that my affiliations did not allow for comfort by the staff. At one point, I was told that my presence dissipated the "creative tension" of the meetings. Participants felt that they had to be "on their best behavior" for fear of what I might learn, and, perhaps, because the interaction style of a senior, such as myself, might differ in noticeable ways from those who were younger. My age—and the relations that developed as a result—constituted my organizational identity, which both opened doors and closed them. Admission to the staff meetings was the primary issue of access with regard to staff, but rapport proved an issue at times.

With some 15 staffers working during the course of my several years at Chicago Seniors Together, I developed a range of relations. Some of them became quite supportive, particularly those who had graduate degrees or were particularly interested in the social sciences. Others were careful and cordial, but distant. Further, for the new staffers I was a figure who was already present, someone that they couldn't invite in, but someone who they must deal with: a senior, but one with access to publication outlets who might possibly shine a negative light on the organization.

Beyond the issues of access and rapport, I had to determine what was possible to learn. How could I gain insight into the lifeworlds and the commitments of these younger, female activists in a way that contributed to sociological knowledge? Of course, some of these come naturally, however adequate it might be. Ethnographers routinely assume that they can figure out the perspectives of those others who differ from themselves. This is the basis of anthropological fieldwork and, to be candid, how sociologists are able to engage with gangs and with other groups that are distant from their home spaces. We typically do this well enough that we persuade other sociologists, whether or not we can persuade those in the community that we examine.

To examine community organizers from the standpoint of an academic sociologist is, after all, not so much of a leap. Age is not the only basis for peering and Othering. While I never developed the rapport that I developed with my senior friends, I do believe that I understood the anxieties and strains that these young organizers felt as they were unable—again and again—to change the world. Like so many of us, they dealt with failures, strategies that just did not work or at least could not be demonstrated to be effective. This anxiety is shared by academics and is a basis of a commonality of insight. Further, the challenge of working with seniors—those of a different generation—in which one was supposed both to lead and to follow was a topic that I was able to appreciate. Chicago Seniors Together was an organization that claimed that it was run by seniors and for seniors, but this could only happen if organizers provided the direction. This concern with competing authorities is something that appeared in several of my research projects. My insight, while imperfect, was no less imperfect than when I observed Little League baseball players or high school debaters.

The Challenges of Peering

The problem of overlap between researcher and researched would not have the implications that it has if ethnographers, in their private selves, thought or felt like the rest of the population. However, we recognize that this is not true. Despite some measure of diversity in the backgrounds of academics and in their current commitments, researchers do not share the moral code, political perspectives, or experiential stances of the wider public. In some regards, this is not surprising. Using our current political imagery, there are red jobs and blue jobs, red towns and blue towns, and red degrees and blue degrees. The challenge comes when one group claims to have the expertise to explain the perspectives of another. Thus, when conservatives speak of liberals as "socialists" or "Marxists," this does not reflect how these targets see the world. The critique of White scholars attempting to understand Black communities or male scholars attempting to understand female communities reflects this difficulty as well. In ivied academic quarters, the challenge is for those on the left to understand those on the right. It is a test that is often failed, even despite sincere attempts (Hochschild, 2016). Perhaps there is no way around this, but it is a dilemma to be recognized.

While these demographic barriers are important, we must also recognize the diversity within groups. The world is intensely intersectional. Few groups have members that fall into a single category. The group that I examined, Chicago Seniors Together, was composed of men, women, gays, lesbians, straights, Blacks, Whites, professionals, homeless people, young old, old old, long-time activists, and newly minted protesters. It was not only that the group had to fit these individuals together to be cohesive and coherent but, as the researcher, I had the same challenge as my own experience did not connect to many of these intersecting categories. Inevitably, no matter how close we might wish to be to embrace various sub-categories, we have not had the experience of all. As a result, making a sharp distinction between known experience and unknown, if imagined, worlds will be fundamentally misleading, even if we recognize that some of these categories will be more phenomenologically salient than others. And, as ethnographers, we must be accepted within the group, embraced by the members, and then understand what might be seen as a buzzing confusion.

Ultimately, there is no single or simple answer to the question of whether prior affiliation is essential. As ethnographers say so frequently in reference to their methods, there is no one right way. Ethnography—and our understanding of the world—is bettered when we as a community approach our topics of study in multiple ways with respect and with an open mind, willing to be surprised, comforted, and dismayed. What I describe as "peering" is but one way, but even when we imagine that we are peers, there is no perfect concord. This is particularly true with the recognition of a segmented and relational social world (Desmond, 2014). Still, the recognition of a zone of shared knowledge and common allegiance, as well as shadows creating a penumbra, allows the ethnographer to avoid being either a convert or a Martian, but a sympathetic outsider for whom both distance and closeness are the basis of insight.

Note

1 An earlier article (Fine, 2020) labeled the group the Alinsky Senior Coalition, because of their reliance on the strategies of Chicago activist Saul Alinsky, but the Executive Director, after reading another manuscript and believing that the group did not fully rely on Alinsky's tactics, preferred the name Chicago Seniors Together as the pseudonym for the group that she directed.

References

Abramson, C. (2015). *The end game: How inequality shapes our final years*. Harvard University Press.

Atkinson, P., & Morriss, L. (2017). On ethnographic knowledge. *Qualitative Inquiry*, *23*(5), 323–331.

Collins, H., & Evans, R. (2017). The bearing of studies of expertise and experience on ethnography. *Qualitative Inquiry*, *23*(6), 445–451.

Davis, F. (1973). The Martian and the convert: Ontological polarities in social research. *Urban Life and Culture*, *2*(3), 333–343.

Desmond, M. (2014). Relational ethnography. *Theory and Society*, *43*, 547–579.

Fine, G. A. (1987). *With the boys: Little league baseball and preadolescent culture*. University of Chicago Press.

Fine, G. A. (1995). Public narration and group culture: Discerning discourse in social movements. In H. Johnston & B. Klandermans (Eds.), *Social movements and culture* (pp. 127–143). University of Minnesota Press.

Fine, G. A. (2012). *Tiny publics: A theory of group action and culture*. Russell Sage Foundation.

Fine, G. A. (2019). Relational distance and epistemic generosity: The power of detachment in skeptical ethnography. *Sociological Methods and Research*, *48*, 828–849.

Fine, G. A. (2020). Now and again: Eventful experience in senior activism. *Social Movement Studies*, *19*, 576–591.

Fine, G. A. (2023). *Fair share: Senior activism, tiny publics and the culture of resistance*. University of Chicago Press.

Glaser, B., & Strauss, A. (1967). *The discovery of grounded theory: Strategies for qualitative research*. Aldine de Gruyter.

Goffman, E. (1989). On fieldwork. *Journal of Contemporary Ethnography*, *18*(2), 123–132.

Gubrium, J. (1975). *Living and dying at Murray Manor*. St. Martin's Press.

Hochschild, A. (1973). *The unexpected community: Community portrait of an old-age subculture*. University of California Press.

Hochschild, A. (2016). *Strangers in their own land: Anger and mourning on the American right*. New Press.

Hughes, E. (1971). *The sociological eye*. Aldine.

7

SHIFTING CODES, CONTINUAL VETTING, AND RECURRENT RAPPORT-BUILDING IN ETHNOGRAPHIC FIELDWORK

Brittany Presson

Introduction

> I walk down the sunlit hallway toward the conference room with my senses on high alert. I pass by two mothers sitting in blue armchairs. One is crying while sharing what sounds like the story of her son. "And that's when I knew . . ." The other mother lifts up a tissue. A few steps away is a small group of mothers laughing in front of a convention banner. They ask me if I will take their photo. "Of course." My previously somber face lights up with a smile to match the mood. The mothers grin and bend their knees. In other circumstances, their uniform stance and all white clothing could be mistaken for a sorority reunion picture. The camera click, click, clicks. The smiles relax. "I took a few. Hopefully one works." They gather around the camera remarking on their looks depicted back from the digital screen. "Thank you" one replies. I am dismissed. I continue my path down the hall, listening to the voices around me. "Is it time to go in?" "I saved you a seat." "Have you seen Kay this morning?" From the side, I notice a shorter older woman with curly white hair that seemingly defied gravity. "Can you help me with the coffee?" she asked the person next to her. Together, grief, joy, and the mundane coexist in the hallway, steps away from one another. In a few moments, they all enter the conference room, converging the three together during the pomp and circumstance of the opening welcome.

I knew when choosing to study gold star mothers—those whose sons and daughters died while serving in active-duty military or as a result of their service—that emotional moments would occur. I expected to hear tragic stories and to witness a few tears. In choosing the convention as a field site, I knew those emotions would be somewhat limited by the constant transitions of events, ceremonies, and business. It was this juxtaposition of the emotional, familial, and organizational that sparked my sociological curiosity in the first place. Anticipating emotional

DOI: 10.4324/9781003275121-10

displays from others is different than navigating the rapidly changing emotionally expressive sites I would come to know. In the notes earlier, I was performing what I considered to be researcher appropriateness. I matched the mood of each scene, stayed aware of the constant flow of data around me, interacted and participated when I could, and jotted down memory joggers, quotes, and reflections whenever possible. I focused on the external rather than my own internal and I assumed that if I centered the participants as I should, that I would be protected from genuinely feeling the emotional atmosphere. It was not that I was afraid of emotion. Rather, I interpreted my position as being distant from it, not wanting to cloud my scientific observation with sadness, anger, or joy. I challenge this notion later in this chapter, demonstrating how this perspective was a little misguided.

This chapter details the challenges of researching social worlds that are saturated by heavy and shifting emotional expression. Emotional performances reinforce the organizational identity. The national board relies on emotional order and use devices such as music, volume, seating, dress, rituals, and coordination of the events to evoke, suppress, and manage emotion for the group and individuals. In this sense, the conventions serve as emotionally expressive sites—that is sites where emotional expressions and performances are brought to the forefront and actively cultivated.

The fieldwork discussed centers on the Gold Star Mothers Organization, namely its annual convention as a social world. This world is constructed during convention, chapter and national events, and through its journal and social media platforms. It is both formal in terms of bylaws and congressional approval, and interactional in its "sisterhood" as many participants described it. I focus, here, on the national convention, drawing from four conventions across 6 years. I handed out badges, picked mothers up from the airport, attended tours, participated in various events and ceremonies, shared meals with gold star mothers, and interviewed in hotel lobbies and hallways. Still a graduate student at the time, I followed what I took to be the traditional route for entering ethnography. What I came to find was a constant vetting process by members long after I had organizational board access and a complicated emotional landscape that necessitated an acute attention to emotional management and performativity on an organizational and individual level. This chapter covers some of the challenges and experience of navigating emotionally expressive social worlds, learning the emotion codes, and negotiating emotional performances in times of conflicting codes and order. I fold in some of the skills that worked for me, namely emotional adaptability, approachability, how I learned to feel more in the field.

Entering Into Ethnographic Research—Entry, Trust, and Rapport

We read many ethnographies during my graduate school years. I loved the way they read as novels, gaining a sense of who their participants were as people. To me, ethnography was an edgework methodological process, designed for and by risk takers. Edgework refers to voluntary risk-taking and managing expertise (Lyng, 1990). For an edgeworker, control, knowledge, and ability were key to success. In ethnography, there is risk within the field, risk of losing oneself to the field, and risk of public perception once published. I imagined ethnographers with leather jackets, shiny shoes, and that air of coolness about them that others just couldn't touch.

I began reading ethnographies of more mundane everyday life. These still had their risks, but they altered the way I viewed ethnography. It transitioned from something completely inaccessible to something still daunting yet entirely achievable. Ethnography is often placed on this pedestal, needing to be as captivating as a novel, accessible across audiences, and scientifically rigorous. In between page-turning scenes, one has to balance theoretical and conceptual conversations that feed the scientific audience while not alienating other readers. This piece, in line with the overall book, focuses on the challenges of ethnography that are not typically covered in a methodological- or ethnographic-specific textbook.

I found my opening into ethnography by accident. Still captivated by the excitement of edgework ethnographies, I considered a research project that would have placed me in a hang-gliding commune in Florida. While thinking about research, life occurred. I married. We went on our honeymoon camping across the United States and were asked on our return to accompany my mother-in-law to a convention she was a part of for Gold Star Mothers. While there, I participated in events, talked to members, and toured a few places. It wasn't until some months later after the Khan family spoke on the Democratic National Convention stage (Bruton, 2016) that I realized that more research and knowledge was needed about gold star families.

Everyone seemed to be talking about gold star families except the gold star mothers I had become acquainted with. Most of those espousing their stances and values on the topic were unfamiliar with the lived experiences of gold star families or the intricacies of both individual gold stars and the organizational units. They didn't realize that gold star mothers have an important and complicated role in US History connecting back to the suffragette movement (Budreau, 2021), or that the creation of the gold star was designed to reconstruct the narratives of the public surrounding war and national morale (Budreau, 2010; Fenelon, 2010; Wilson et al., 1966). They did not know that gold star mothers played an instrumental role in the creation of the Vietnam Veterans War Memorial also known as "The Wall" (VVMF, 2019, 2021), or that there are positions specifically for gold star mothers in the Pentagon, various State and National legislatures, and on the board for the national Veterans Affairs, effecting veteran and service member care across the country. Commenters were also uneducated on the degree that gold star mothers at an organizational level aim to perpetuate patriotic narratives, construct motherhood within the organization, model military family bereavement practices, and have contested formal conversations of what types of death should "count" for membership—designating a social hierarchy of valor. If the commentators had understood these things, and more, they would have realized that the structure of gold star mothers in relation to national and political strategies is far more complicated than the narratives at the time acknowledged.

Encouraged by my advisor and my family, I followed the textbook steps of IRB, organizational permission, trust, and rapport and was confident in my ability to gather data. Once "in" I realized I underestimated the amount I would be vetted by individual members. I received numerous inquiries through face to face, over the phone, and via emails from gold star mothers. They asked me to clarify my goal and intent. They were skeptical that I was another news interviewer or columnist who might misrepresent their stories or besmirch their name. I quickly became smoother at conveying my connection and intent.

Having married into a gold star family seemed to help significantly as I was seen as someone who, while not a gold star mother, recognized the reality and significance of the weight of that symbolic gold star. Because I was not a sibling, I was able to ask questions as an inquisitive novice without the expectation of sharing a related loss experience or without them feeling as if they have to also comfort me for a loss or grief. Once I became a mother myself, they used phrases like "oh well you know" in reference to motherly love, parent–child bonds, and those little memories. That latter note also meant their experiences of grief connected on a deeper emotional level, striking at my deepest fear.

My cultural capital of being raised in a southern evangelical setting also helped. The convention is one that relies heavily on Christian narratives and themes. To many, their duty is similar to that of Mary, whose son sacrificed his life for the common good. Events reinforce this through reading scriptures, prayer, and hymns, organized by the Chaplain. My particular identity and experience provided me with a foreknowledge of many of the cultural norms, religious language, and even expectations on dress.

Going Concerns, Emotionally Expressive Sites, and Adaptability

The organization's national conventions and events serve as a social world where members organize their interpretations, meanings, perceptions, and purposes. Social worlds give context to how a person or group of people make sense of their experiences which speak representationally toward their own realities (Gubrium, 1975). Individual members may experience some aspects of the social world differently than others. The emotions are felt in different ways and are expressed in a variety of ways, with members both constructing emotional order and responding to those codes.

Expanding beyond individual stories, the convention itself, is an emotionally expressive site, relying on emotional codes, and multiple forms of emotion work for all involved. Organizational meetings require complicated, rapidly shifting, and intense emotion work. These are emotionally discursive and expressive environments where discourse is drawn on and expressions are evoked, suppressed, and managed. As the events shift, so do the codes. Unspoken emotional codes or expectations transition rapidly. Members require emotional stamina and resilience to volley between the emotional codes within various events. They go from moments of laughter, camaraderie, curiosity, and business to public reminders of their gold star status via memorials, photographic attributes, and names.

Staging, props, and organizational scripts code the order. Emotion codes are codes or rules that order when, how, where, and what emotions are appropriate, to whom they should be directed, and for how long these should be outwardly expressed (Loseke, 2017). These may be conveyed to others in an attempt at evoking the desired emotion from them. Participants adhere to these codes often through emotion work including changing one's thoughts, bodily postures, and facial expressions (Hochschilds, 1979).

Studies on political communication find audiences respond more positively when they feel emotionally connected to the message (Grader, 2005; Loseke, 2017; Roser & Thompson, 1995). The politics of the organization are similar. They rely on emotions as a form of membership bonding also referred to as the "common bond," emphasizing their shared experiences of grief, the convention orders events in terms of themes and emotions, mixing in the joyous occasions with the mundane, bureaucratic, and grief. Doing so exemplifies a going concern. A going concern is a pattern of interaction that orders discursive environments—places of interaction with particular interpretive perspectives—and influences one's self and identity (Gubrium & Holstein, 2000). People make sense of their worlds in part based on their interactions with institutions and their relationships within them. These social institutions influence social construction and reconstruction between those simultaneously experiencing and effecting the reality (Holstein & Gubrium, 2000; Wästerfors, 2011).

The gold star organization and convention itself serves as a space for going concerns (Hughes, 1984), that of shared grief, motherhood, and service. The emotional codes communicated and devices used indicate the active construction of events, atmosphere, and definition—that is how they honor, remember, grieve, and serve. The members, adherence to the codes, decorum, and schedules, demonstrate their commitments, investment, and active participation in meeting those values. Heavily influenced by the organization, members have a choice whether and to what degree to participate. This is also evident in the organization's constructions of what it means to be a mother and what constitutes valor. They construct the meaning, and it remains so long as members continue to agree to it. Those who reject it may leave the organization, stay, and push against it by expanding definitions for their chapters, or by attempting to pass amendments to change this. The membership itself plays an active role in the organization's construction.

Emotion codes, emotional order, feeling rules, and framing are crucial to the maintenance of the convention and the organization itself. Shifting events, rules, frames, and codes requires awareness and resilience. As I describe later, there are even moments where some members outright reject the structure of the event by breaking emotional codes. Adaptability is necessary for both researchers and members between these shifts and when an emotion code is breached. In the scenes later, I demonstrate different convention events with separate and sometimes converging emotional codes.

An Occasion for Joy

> We arrive late to the smaller hotel banquet room. There are looming palm trees made of fruit. Shoulder to shoulder, we are crammed together in this space with mothers trying to find a place to sit and be heard. Some mothers have pregamed with alcoholic beverages, taking advantage of the vacation aspect of the convention. We squeeze our way through the crowd to sit with other gold star mothers and fathers. The president projects over the loudness of the crowd and introduces the entertainment. It is a Polynesian dance school. Music and drums blare over invisible speakers. The crowd cheers as children line through the tables, shaking their skirts and moving their arms expertly in traditional dance. The teacher explains the meanings to some of the dances. The crowd shifts and stretches their necks to witness this show. "Look at them go!," "I'm getting tired just watching them.", "She looks like my granddaughter."

The large palm tree inspired decorations of fruit, the colorful crepe paper ribbons, and the loud music cue those entering that this is a fun environment. The lack of space and volume in the room prevents any meaningful conversation, and outbursts would likely go unnoticed or be brushed off as a result of the available alcoholic beverages. The dress of participants is even casual, with some wearing what are commonly known as "Hawaiian shirts." At a later convention, this event exchanges the Polynesian dance for an Elvis impersonator. Participants wear red, white, and blue clothing, styled as if attending a Fourth of July barbeque or an outdoor classic rock concert. The impersonator engages with the crowd and a group of women begin dancing at the cash bar. There are smiles and an expectation of entertainment and fun. Similar techniques are used during the Polynesian event. Alcohol is available. Dress is casual. Music is loud, blocking out any potential for swapping sorrowful and/or meaningful stories. Seating is pushed together, crowding attendees.

These events serve a few functions:

1. It sets the tone and breaks some ice. Going in, moms may wear their grief close to their hearts, literally and figuratively. At this event, the accosted senses force one to be in the moment.
2. It shares some of the local cultures and attempts to entice spectators out of the hotel to explore the local area.
3. It provides a [hopefully] positive shared experience and talking point beyond their shared loss or group political endeavors. Even if it is mildly negative, such as complaints over lack of food or space, the group still has that knowledge and experience to converse over.

The emotional management techniques used signal that this is not a place for sharing sad stories, having deep conversation, or strategizing politically. It is instead a place for fun, expressions of joy, and closeness.

An Occasion for Remembrance

> The wind sifts through the trees, gently blowing the leaves. I hear the water falling from the bubbling memorial fountain nearby. Large banners of fallen service members wave from towering light poles. Attendees are gathering in this luscious, green courtyard toward the makeshift stage. Surrounding us are the brightly painted apartments of elderly gold star parents. I take my seat at the rear and notice the mingling of people. In front of me, two mothers browse through the program. Another edges down a row of metal folding chairs to sit next to her friend. Behind me is a bucket of roses and a growing line of mothers. These mothers are serving as representatives for the deceased. Each grabs a pre-determined amount of roses, some white for gold star mothers who passed away the previous year, and the yellow for the gold star fathers who passed. Light music begins to play as the crowd hushes and the line at the back forms. I glance back one more time. I watch as a mother who was previously joking with a friend bows her head in silence until the smile fades. Her head remains down a few more seconds as her overall composure changes. She lifts her head, face now solemn. Others are solemn too.
>
> The chaplain, standing at the front says a prayer before calling the names of the recently departed gold star mothers and known gold star fathers. Organized by state chapter, the representative mother walks in slow procession down the aisle to the table. She pauses. A white rose is placed for each mother she is standing in for. A yellow rose is placed for the father. The representative mother then gives pause and takes a step back after placing her last rose. The chaplain and mother then meet eyes and signify acknowledgement, either by a head nod, a whispered "thank you," or a hand over the heart. Tears may well up for the mothers who were especially close to the representative or chaplain. The representative mother walks to the side and the next mother is called to begin her slow procession. This continues until the last name is called.
>
> A folded American flag is brought out and unfolded. Gold star dads step up to unfold, "in recognition of a grateful nation," meant to honor the mother's sacrifice of their child. The chaplain steps aside as the Americanism Chair presides. She explains each fold of the flag as the dads carefully work. A prayer is said for the families of the now departed gold star mothers and fathers represented on this day. A reverend is called up and he reads from the book of Isaiah and speaks about pain, loss, and remembrance.

The tone here is somber. The setting is calm, peaceful. We are surrounded by reminders of loss and grief. The dress is formal. The hymnal music is soft and low. The seating focuses one's attention on the memorial display, a black sash draped, a candle lit, and a bible open. The words spoken are reverent and denote a degree of sacrality. Here, one is expected to reflect, to experience a slight level of grief, and to perform solemnity. Quiet tears are common. Emotional order is maintained.

An Occasion for Business

> The morning sun filters through the hotel hallway as people step into the large conference room. The mothers are dressed in their more formal whites. Those who wear open-toed shoes, shorts, or capri pants that are too short may be asked to leave. Until the aughts, those who wore pants would have been out of dress code as well. Gold, red, and purple gleam from the pins on their stark white blouses. Purple is for those whose children were killed in action. Gold is for those whose children died by other means. Shiny gold is for the national and past national board badges. Dog tags and pins with their children's faces are also common. Two women serve as pages, wearing white hats, white gloves, and ushering people in. The banner guard and flag guard move their flags and signal where the board will line up. Other mothers mingle and find their seats, organized by their state chapters. Dads, guests, and other non-mother attendees are asked to stand at the back. They are contrasted in dress, with the unofficial "dad" uniform being short-sleeve shirts and khaki shorts or jeans. Ball caps are also common. The dress codes do not apply to nonmembers as they are already going to be escorted out.
>
> A designated mother stands at the front to signify the start of the ceremony. The crowd turns to face the back as the banner guard and flag guard step in and walk down the aisle, one going left, the other right, to place the flags. The current national board follows and sits at a table on a platform at the front of the room, facing the crowd. Their titled name plates are staged in front of them. The organizational president gives a speech. In some years, a guest may be invited to speak or give a presentation. Then, the president announces that it is time for the dads and guests to leave on their tour. Only the mothers are allowed to stay for the business meeting. The rest of us are shipped away by bus or car to tour another facility, eat, and stay occupied until the evening.

One year, I managed to gain permission from the organizational president to sit in on the business meeting. "Yes, but you have to be very quiet and not make a sound." She told me over dinner the night before. I sat in the back, quiet, with only my notebook. I made it all of 20 seconds in before I was approached by a page. I quietly explained that I had permission to be there. She said she would be right back, checked outside, and then returned to tell me, "No, you have to leave." Not wanting to cause a scene, lose credibility, or access to the rest of the convention, I stood up politely and allowed her to escort me out just as the members were standing and beginning a pledge to the organization.

When it comes to ethnography, access does not always mean complete access. In the four conventions I attended, I was never able to penetrate the elusive business meeting. I did hear from mothers after the fact about topics they found noteworthy, including a heated debate on who should count as a member of the organization and a recounting of a physical altercation between a member and the President. Prison ethnographer, Andrew M. Jefferson (2015; see also Jefferson's chapter in the current volume) described the fear of losing access to the field while in the field. In one section, he described an encounter with inmates outside the director's office. While he was given permission to speak some with the inmates, he worried that the position was too blatant and that it might jeopardize his standing in the field. Similarly, the feeling of "getting in trouble" or overstepping bounds in the field can result in one taking extra caution later. For me, that meant fighting my avoidant nature later in the convention and not allowing myself to hide from interactions, including with the page. Helmes-Hayes (2010) argues that the act of research itself is a going concern and one must be willing to adapt to the institutional and contextual environment that they choose to study.

The ceremony leading up to the business meeting sets the tone. The clothing and jewelry communicate not only positions and titles but also hierarchy. Within the organization is a social hierarchy based on constructions of valor, socially marked by type of death of loved one (killed in action, friendly fire, accidental, cancer from service related toxins, and the most contested—suicide), type of mother (biological, adoptive, step, foster), and era of death (Korea, Vietnam, Desert Storm, Pre-9/11, Post-9/11 conflict, and in-between eras). The formality of the entrance might mirror that of the memorial, except there is no serene music being played. The design is that of business, voting, and exclusion. The strict dress code signals a demand for decorum. Here is not the place for partying, crying, and meandering. Here is a place of business.

Learning Emotional Codes and Codes Allowing Myself to Feel

The preceding sections describe the ways in which emotionally expressive events at the convention are managed and the evocative devices used to help encourage the desired emotional expression and maintain emotional order. Language, tone, music, setting, dress, and even the layout of the event itself double as devices that evoke particular emotive themes, such as joy, unity, grief, and business. Even within those emotion codes, the degree to which one might feel this grief is limited. If one were to say fall out into the aisle sobbing during the memorial service, that would break the emotional code even though it is in line with the grief being evoked. Hochschild (1979) argued that one of our societal feeling rules involves degree of emotions. In this case, the intense order of the organizational event, the perfectly positioned chairs, and the muted sadness performed by those in the spotlight signal the degree of acceptable emotional performance. Degree of emotion is one of the feeling rules that the organization relies on to maintain that emotional order of each event.

When and how does one learn these emotional codes? This is something that is tricky on a researcher level as well as on the attendee level. Some of the mothers I spoke with joined the organization through stumbling upon the convention. For them, it was something they heard about advertised in the media leading up to a convention happening in or near their hometowns. "And I said, that sounds like me! I'm a gold star mother. Though, I had never heard of that phrase." At least two of these mothers then checked out the convention, wandering in almost lost. By the time we spoke, they had been attending regularly for over a decade. For them, learning the symbolic and emotional codes occurred through a deep immersive experience. However, for most of the mothers, there was some foreknowledge given before attending their convention.

Typically, the convention occurs later in a gold star mother's story with the organization. Instead, most become aware of the organization soon after the loss of their son or daughter. Gold star mothers have been known to attend funeral viewings with pamphlets, write letters to newly minted gold star parents, call, email, or reach out later on down the road. At least one mother recounted gold star mothers attending the burial service. In a lot of cases, individuals sought out community and gold star mothers themselves. One mom in particular was googling the national organization within days of her son's passing.

The standard process for mothers interested in joining the organization is to:

1. Connect with local members.
2. Attend a chapter meeting or event.
3. Apply for national membership.
4. Receive the national newsletter.
5. Attend a convention if able.

Mothers who follow this more standard approach come to know the expectations well before attending the event. Some of them will have interacted with mothers who have attended conventions for decades. The following account will elucidate this a little more.

We are at a French restaurant, and I am sharing the family-style meal with three mothers, referred to here as M, S, and T. Of the stories told during this meal, one in particular stands out in terms of socialization. M tells me that before the trio's first convention, some years prior, she counseled S and T on how to wear their whites, the members' signature color. "We knew we had to wear whites, right?" But I knew, and I said, "you can't wear white under white. It will show. You have to wear beige." Discussing undergarments may seem trivial at first, but it indicated something that I would pick up on later, that being the socialization process. Other moms told of hearing stories about the convention before attending themselves. Many roomed and traveled with former attendees. Through these stories, they learned what occasions to anticipate and gained insight into the varied emotional expectations.

> I see a mother crying in the hotel hallway. She is alone and I heard she is new here. A couple of mothers approach her. One puts an arm around her. They, "take her under their wing." Her socialization process continues.

As an outsider, I was at a little disadvantage in terms of expectations. Like the two mothers who stumbled into the convention, I learned by immersion. In a way, I was also taken under some mothers' wings. In my first attendance, I expected the convention to be a grief fest. I quickly adjusted my assumptions. Upon arrival, we were immediately greeted with laughter and large smiles. Inflatable palm trees and décor lightened the "hospitality" room. I also found that the lighter events made the more somber ones feel even more stark. I was told they had to have fun sometimes. They invited me to eat, to sit with them, and even explained some of the upcoming events. Even still, at my first convention I committed a faux pas by not standing during the Armed Forces Medley, that garnered glares and head turns. Later years, I watched as other guests were gossiped about or re-guided based on their attire, attitude, interactions, or attempts at leaving or evading some events. While learning these codes, I also served as an unofficial photographer, validator of looks, and a person they could chat, gossip, complain, or share their stories to. I was their listener.

During that first year, I found myself, a non-smoker, spending a significant amount of in-between time at the smoker's tables. There, I learned about the political underbelly of the organization and picked up on tensions and hierarchies within the group. One evening, a mother asked if I would stay with her a little longer. We sat at the outdoor table as the moon rose and those in the pool began to exit. She told me her story and about her son. She also shared how those who have never experienced that grief tend to react. How they seem afraid of feeling any emotion or a need to apologize if they do. As a result, the conversations surrounding her son are typically avoided by others, dismissed, or discouraged. It struck me how one's instinct to protect their emotions or the emotions of others can be as detrimental in conversation as a listener becoming overcome with emotion. Cerwonka and Malkki (2008), drawing on insight from Passaro (1997) and Gadamer (1999) interpret this as a juxtaposition of objectivity versus subjectivity and a desire for scientific integrity.

Over time, I adjusted what I previously thought of as researcher appropriateness from calculated surface acting to some genuine feeling. This furthered in later years, after hearing more stories, and becoming a mother myself. The weight and significance became heavier and I understood not only the mechanics of the arranged emotional order but also some of the latent significance of it, that is sharing a grief, forcing attention shifts to something more joyous, and mothers being seen more as whole people, who can play and cry, who have ambition, and who may get angry. At the convention, no conversation was out of bounds, only the timing of which conversations could be had was regulated. In a way, my feeling was also a way of connecting and giving back. It aided in my approachability. This does not mean that I fully gave way to emotionality. There was and is still a sense of researcher responsibility toward objectivity and the emphasis on centering participants. Instead, my realization mirrored one similar to Cerwonka and Malkki (2008) in that embracing some emotionality provided more insight into the work and allowed me to connect as a human. Recognizing my subjectivity requires me to consider on a deeper level how my positionality plays into my interactions and interpretations (Bettie, 2003).

Rapidly Shifting Codes

The scenes described until this point have demonstrated some emotional management and performativity of the organization and the individuals within it. They have depicted scenes where emotional codes last throughout the entire event. However, for a significant portion of the convention, emotional codes are less static. A tour with the fathers has them lackadaisically walking through a museum one moment, only to turn the corner and see a funeral video and caisson horse the next. Followed shortly afterward by a bus ride to a gym and then lunch, perhaps with beer, shifting from tourist mode to grief, reverence, and then back to tourism. Installation services of new officers shift from business, sentimentality, and sometimes grief with the giving of a dedicated honor and remember flag, back to business. This shifting of emotional codes can also be seen in the single event that is the final banquet, where the expectations shift in stark ways.

> Attendees arrive in the grand ballroom ballgowns and tails and ranging down to "Sunday best" or a casual polo shirt and jeans. There is an intended air of elegance to the atmosphere, including the fine china and the multi-course meal. Depending on the year, one may need to find a place card with their name on it for arranged seating. Once seated, you make conversation over dinner rolls and sweet tea. The conversations may cover things one has seen, speakers one enjoyed, to stories of loss, and back up again to food, or entertainment. One does not appear to stay in the grief too long in this setting.
>
> The entertainment begins during the entre, loud enough to block out meaningful conversation. At some point, there is a pause and the explanation of the "missing man table" (The National League of POW/MIA, 2017) occurs, sobering the crowd as they are called to recognize the reason they are there and the loved ones no longer in attendance. The entertainment then starts back up, shifting one back to the regality of the environment, and evoking more of the lighter emotions. Sometimes the outgoing and new Presidents may make some speech, shifting tones again. In the most recent convention, a slide show was played with the pictures of the deceased children of attendees.
>
> The sentimental country music accompanies the slow transitioning PowerPoint. It is quiet. One can hear if a glass is set down two tables away. Each picture displays and the mother may react. Some will stand while their son or daughter is on display. Many have tears in their eyes. I watch a mother's hand raise to her chest. Another mother lets out one audible sob. Another mother stands and salutes her son's picture. One mother walks away, whispering, "It is just too sad", to me as she leaves. We have quickly shifted to a thick layer of grief displayed. The music, pictures, and attention evoking this heavy emotional expression.

> Soon after the slide show has ended, the board members and planning committee members are thanked for their assistance. We shift out of the grief momentarily and finish the last bit of desert and coffee. From the speakers, we hear the beginning of Lee Greenwood's "God Bless the USA", beginning the now traditional final salute of the convention. This ritualistic moment is important to the organization as what I describe happening next solidifies the organization's authenticity as a space that honors and remembers the fallen, cares about the mothers left behind, and maintains patriotic beliefs. Everybody stands. Usually, one mother will call out and direct everyone to hold hands. Most are already walking forming the large structure that will fill nearly the entire room. "Don't leave" one mother calls to a guest. The expectation here is participation and the significance is heavy as this ritual is meant to evoke a sense of unity, collective effervescence, and to honor their losses.
>
> Hands clasped even during a pandemic. Arms thrust upwards during the lyrics, regarding standing up. The hands lower and raise throughout the song until the finale when the arms stay raised. Several mothers sing the words. Some angle their heads upwards, eyes closed, as if attempting to speak directly to the heavens. Tears are not uncommon. The atmospheric emotion is tangible. The tone is one of utmost respect, honor, and unity. This is the last official moment of the entire convention and the point that attendees will walk away from. This connection, patriotism, and emboldening is designed as a convention take away. To a newcomer or outsider, this ritual can evoke some stereotypical cult associations. The music ends, heads lower, hand clasps break, and the circle separates. The tone rapidly shifts again. There's laughter, exchanging of contact information, happy hugs, and farewells. Some take this time to go over the last-minute departure plan for the next day.

Ending on this note allows attendees to leave on an emotional high just having participated in a bonding ritual. This last event validates their parenting work in honoring their children, it folds into their legacy work that their child is one that should be honored in this collective and physical way, and it deepens the significance and emotional connection of patriotic discourses. The performance itself is instrumental in the authenticity of the organization, and its adherence signals a group membership. While great lengths are taken to manage these emotions, such efforts are not guaranteed to be effective in every case. The next section demonstrates when these codes are broken or when the performance falls.

Emotional Chaos—Be a Helper

Moments of emotional chaos do occur. In some cases, they are moments when there are less clear restrictions on the degree of emotions expected. One example of this was during a visit to a memorial park. After being fed a barbecue-style dinner, participants were asked to walk around the park's loop 2.2 times in honor of the estimated 22 veterans who die by suicide each day. The walk itself was varied in emotion with mothers chatting, smiling, and kneeling for pictures, while others teared up and posed stoically behind signs with their children's names. Every other sign set up by the organization issued some value statement—"valor," "honor," and "sacrifice." Once finished, the participants were led down a short path through a memorial site before reaching the stage and seating area. The memorial spot and this transition from one event to the next provided a space for some unchecked expressions of grief.

> Mothers rushed around one another frantically, trying to find their children's names. Some mothers sobbed, others asked for help, one read some of the names aloud. A mother reached out and grabbed my elbow, asking me to help her find her son's name. In the distance, I hear a mother cry that her son's name isn't there. Only those killed in action are engraved on these black stone pillars. As the crowd thinned, one mother was left sitting, silently staring at the names in front of her.

Time sped up during this transition. The desperation of finding names, the avoidance of the columns by those who knew they wouldn't find their loved one's names, the despair and anguish of some of the mothers standing in front of their children's names, all overwhelmed the senses. It was like exiting a quiet room into a crowded bazaar. Being a helper during this period allowed me to witness the chaos without being in the way or merely spectating from the edges. What occurs next exemplifies an organizational failure of emotional management.

> Now seated and calm after the memorial chaos, we listen to speakers, listen to a musical performance, and settle into the chairs. The president approaches the microphone and reads the names of attendees' fallen children. After finishing the list, another mother stood. Her son's name was missing. She approached the microphone, sobbing, and said his name. Another mother followed suit. Some in the audience gasped and shook their heads at the omission. The president reminded the audience that people were supposed to send in names. More mothers stood. The president asked if she had the correct list. They said their children's names. A couple of mothers were not able to speak through their tears and the president's husband spoke their names clearly for them. It was evident by the shock and embarrassment that this was not intentional. The slippage did cause an emotional disturbance to the typically manicured and managed events attendees were accustomed to. It communicated a sense of forgottenness and challenged the authenticity of the organization that promotes remembrance, honor, and emphasizes "say their names" as a means of promoting legacy and keeping the social memory alive even after the physical body is gone. For the organization and

> its members, forgetting names equates to a social death or "second death" of their loved one. Tension was thick as we all boarded the busses. Silence permeated the majority of the ride back.

This was not the only convention or only time that a name was forgotten or that the order was disrupted, and the aftermath became uncomfortable. Part of a researcher's adaptability includes the capacity to sit with the awkward and to wait for events to play out.

Resilience Is a Marathon

The constant adherence to emotional codes, awareness of shifting tones, and emotional performance are tough for all involved, including the researcher. There were moments where participants became overcome with emotions and where others policed them informally. Not only is the experience of researching emotionally expressive sites consuming mentally but it also impacts the senses and can have a physical effect on the body, especially when combined with travel. The organization uses techniques to help manage the emotional expression and performativity of each event. Slide shows, monuments, ceremony, and music evoke sadness, remembrance, reverence, and grief. Loud music, live entertainment, close seating, and bright colors suppress grief and politics while evoking more joy. The formality and exclusion of business meetings and installation meetings cultivate an environment of politics and business. Throughout are moments when emotional expression merge, erupt, or become disorganized. Even for veteran mothers, keeping up with the emotional pacing can be tiresome and at times too much. A few times, mothers would recuse themselves from certain events by leaving early or skipping all together. Some verbally expressed the emotionality weighing on them.

Researching emotional sites can be confusing, overwhelming, and wear on a researcher. It is a marathon for all involved. Going in, one may not realize the extent to which a site is going to be emotionally expressive. This work has denoted some of the techniques that worked for me.

1. Be adaptable. The codes and expectations may shift rapidly and in unexpected ways especially if you are immersed in the environment and learning as you go. This can be tricky. There were times I was speaking to a mother about her son and the mother was crying. Another mother would approach to compliment me on something or to chat. The adaptability is crucial on macro- and micro-levels.
2. Acknowledging and feeling, not just performing is important. Emotions can help with connections and even be a way of giving back through vulnerability. One should be conscious of their emotional involvement though and how that may affect interpretation, recognizing their own positionality.

3. Be a helper when possible and appropriate. Being approachable helps one become integrated in the community without being in the way. It is also a way to give back to participants.
4. Though not mentioned in the sections earlier, a researcher should carve out time to decompress when able. For me, this might be during a bathroom break, a lull between events, or generally after writing field notes at the end of the day. It is a time to process what you have experienced and to recenter yourself so that you have the stamina needed for the next day. Your decompression will be different than mine but set aside the time.

As I have shown, the gold star conventions served as a field of opportunity for learning about the craft of ethnography, wherein, through the "working presence" of participant observation, ethnographic fieldwork is set apart methodologically, not understood through fixed and codified procedural terms, but imperatively viewed and operationalized as analytic craft that skims relatively close to its subject matter. Ethnographic fieldwork relies on lived immersion, wherein the researcher experiences the subject matter and related subjectivities at a physical, cognitive, social, and emotional level; they must respond at the moment to shifts in contexts and codes, undergo continuous vetting processes, and actively work toward recurrent rapport. This acts against "method" to some degree but concurrently is essentially and strategically methodical in practice.

References

Bettie, J. (2003). *Women without class: Girls, race, and identity, with a new introduction*. University of California Press.

Bruton, B. (2016). Gold star families attack trump over comments about Ghazala Khan. *NBC News*. https://www.nbcnews.com/politics/2016-election/gold-star-families-attack-trump-over-comments-about-ghazala-khan-n620671

Budreau, L. M. (2010). *Bodies of war: World war I and the politics of commemoration in America, 1919–1933*. New York University Press.

Budreau, L. M. (2021). Mothers, suffragettes, and gold stars. *Tennessee Museums*. Retrieved October 1, 2021, from https://tnmuseum.org/Stories/posts/mothers-suffragists-and-gold-stars

Cerwonka, A., & Malkki, L. H. (2008). *Improvising theory*. University of Chicago Press.

Fenelon, H. S. (2010). *American gold star mothers INC*. Winans Kuenstler Publishing; Collector's Edition.

Gadamer, H. G. (1999). *Truth and method* (J. Weinsheimer & D. G. Marshall, Trans.). Continuum.

Grader, D. A. (2005). Political communication faces the 21st century. *Journal of Communication*, 479–507.

Gubrium, J. F. (1975). *Living and dying at Murray Manor*. University of Virginia Press.

Gubrium, J. F., & Holstein, J. A. (2000). The self in a world of going concerns. *Symbolic Interaction*, *23*(2), 95–115.

Helmes-Hayes, R. (2010). Studying 'going concerns': Everett Hughes on method. *Sociologica*, *4*(2).

Hochschild, A. R. (1979). Emotion work, feeling rules, and social structure. *American Journal of Sociology*, *85*(3), 551–575.

Holstein, J. A., & Gubrium, J. F. (2000). *The self we live by. Narrative identity in a postmodern world*. Oxford University Press.

Hughes, E. C. (1984). *The sociological eye*. Transaction Books.

Jefferson, A. M. (2015). Performing ethnography: Infiltrating prison spaces. In *The Palgrave handbook of prison ethnography* (pp. 169–186). Palgrave Macmillan.

Loseke, D. R. (2017). Formula stories and support groups for battered women. *Social Problems: Constructionist Readings*, 241–247.

Lyng, S. (1990). Edgework: A social psychological analysis of voluntary risk taking. *American Journal of Sociology*, *95*(4), 851–886.

The National League of POW/MIA. (2017). *Missing man table and honors ceremony*. Retrieved December 31, 2017, from www.pow-miafamilies.org/missing-man-table-and-honors-ceremony.html

Passaro, J. (1997). 'You can't take the subway to the field!' 'Village' epistemologies in the global village. *Anthropological Locations: Boundaries and Grounds of a Field Science*, 147–162.

Roser, C., & Thompson, M. (1995). Fear appeals and the formation of active publics. *Journal of Communication, 45*(1), 103–122.

Vietnam Veterans Memorial Fund. (2019). *Emogene Cupp, gold star mother, celebrates 99th Birthday*. Vietnam Veterans Memorial Fund Blog. Retrieved September 2, 2021, from https://vvmf.wordpress.com/2019/01/20/emogene-cupp-gold-star-mother-celebrates-99th-birthday/

Vietnam Veterans Memorial Fund. (2021). *History of the Vietnam veterans memorial*. Vietnam Veterans Memorial Fund. Retrieved on September 2, 2021, from www.vvmf.org/About-The-Wall/history-of-the-vietnam-veterans-memorial/Wasterfors 2011

Wästerfors, D. (2011). Disputes and going concerns in an institution for 'troublesome' boys. *Journal of Contemporary Ethnography*, *40*(1), 39–70.

Wilson, W., Link, A. S., Davidson, J. W., & Hirst, D. W. (1966). *The papers of Woodrow Wilson* (Vol. 2). University Press.

8

CREATING ETHNOGRAPHIC SPACE FOR "FOREIGN BRIDES" TO TALK BACK

Hsiao-Chuan Hsia

> "I see! So you are actually a second-generation immigrant too! Just like our children!" This comment from Mangi,[1] a marriage migrant originally from Vietnam, suddenly made my subjectivity shift from a native citizen/researcher working on marriage migrants' issues for nearly thirty years to a daughter of marriage migrant in Taiwan.

This happened in a casual conversation with a group of marriage migrants about my experience accompanying my father to revisit his hometown in China. My father was uprooted from his village in China because of the Sino-Japanese War and forced to migrate to Taiwan with the troops of Chiang Kai-shek in 1949. My mother was a native citizen from a rural village and met my father while working in Taipei, the capital city. Since I was born and raised in Taiwan and had never met my father's family in China until our visits in recent years, I had never perceived myself as a daughter of immigrants, let alone that of marriage migrants.

While doing my dissertation on the emerging phenomenon of the so-called foreign brides in mid-1990s, I had an "epiphany" (Hsia, 1997; see also Denzin, 1989). I suddenly realized the connection between my family and the research subjects, the poorer Southeast Asian women migrating to Taiwan through their marriages with working-class or peasant Taiwanese men. It dawned on me that my interest in migration and cross-border marriages was rooted in my personal experiences as a little girl playing with the interracial child of my mother's best friend and her American husband. Nearly 30 years later, I have another epiphany: I myself am the product of a cross-border marriage!

Mangi, like other "foreign brides" in my research, used to be very restrained, not confident enough to share her opinions, in a Taiwanese society that perceived such migrants as social problems and labeled them as "foreign brides." Mangi's

DOI: 10.4324/9781003275121-11

insightful conceptualization of my subjectivity as a second-generation immigrant signifies the transformation of my field relations with the marriage migrants that I have worked with. In this long process, I have strived to make the asymmetric power relations between myself, an elite Taiwanese citizen/US-trained scholar, and those severely isolated and discriminated "foreign brides" in Taiwan, more balanced. I did this partly through my praxis-oriented research since the mid-1990s until the present. My goal has been to try to better the lives of my research participants rather than just studying them, the byproduct being a reconceived ethnographic self.

In this chapter, I focus on how the ways I related to them have changed. By highlighting the ethnographic details of several incidents, I argue that facilitating a space for marginalized researched subjects to feel confident to "talk back" is essential for creating equitable field relations. Moreover, these incidents will illustrate that the moments of "conflicts," or when I decided to "confront" my participants instead of merely establishing rapport with them, as most ethnographers are instructed to do, mark the tilting of the power relationship toward balance and symmetry. Of course, by leaning into disagreements and confrontations, I risked damaging my rapport, potentially leading to the collapse of the marriage migrants' organization that I had helped create through my praxis-oriented research. I will describe my self-reflection during these conflicting moments, why I decided to become confrontational, and the consequences of the confrontations.

Researcher–Participant Intersubjectivity and Social Change

Intersubjectivity between researchers and the researched has been an issue, particularly for ethnographers whose knowledge production relies on the depth of their involvements in the lives of their research participants. However, as Pels (2014) points out, intersubjectivity is more than the dyad of the researchers and the people they studied, since their relationships are embedded in broader sociocultural arrangements and inequalities in various forms.

Being fully aware of my own social status and critical of the asymmetrical power relationships between myself and those "foreign brides" in Taiwan, I began my research with the perception that research subjects should be treated as active participants rather than merely investigated objects. Many researchers concerned with intersubjectivity emphasize collaboration with the research subjects (e.g., Lassiter, 2004; Rappaport, 2008). However, for me, the emphasis on collaboration and democratic participation was not enough. I wanted my research to help change the structures of inequalities in which the researcher–researched dyads are embedded. Therefore, my research also became political with the specific goal of empowering the marginalized marriage migrants to speak for themselves and collectively change their social status.

This praxis-oriented research began in 1995 when I initiated Chinese classes in Meinung, a rural community in southern Taiwan. These classes laid the foundation for establishing the first grassroots organization for marriage migrants in Taiwan, thus spearheading a social movement that has helped reform and create policies and laws to protect marriage migrants' rights and welfare (Hsia, 2006, 2015, 2019). Along the way, new issues and challenges have arisen as lives of marriage migrants and the movement develop, and I have had to adapt my praxis-oriented research accordingly.

As a critical ethnographer with Marxist and feminist understanding of the political economic and social constraints imposed on my researched subjects and our relationships, I found it impractical or even pretentious to comply with the traditional doctrine for ethnographers to build rapport by approaching informants with frankness, honesty, and openly sharing their research agendas. As Charles Springwood and C. Richard King (2001) note, many critical ethnographers are uncertain about sharing with their research participants their own theoretical and practical vision of society, such as Marxist understanding of people, place, and power. In the beginning, I decided not to share such a view with the "foreign brides," who were isolated, discriminated, and could not even understand much of local language. I did not want to overwhelm them further with my sociological understanding of their transnational marriages and my long-term goal of empowering them to build a movement for marriage migrant's rights and welfare. Instead, I built my rapport with them by initiating a Chinese program for them to learn the native language of their new homes and become empowered to speak for themselves. As Springwood and King (2001, p. 411) argue, "Ethnographers literally construct (although not unilaterally) spaces of interaction with the informants in their inquiries as much as they construct the tellings of these spaces." My praxis-oriented research has been aimed at creating a rapport space for these marriage migrants to "talk back."

Elsewhere, I have described how a space for them to feel confident and comfortable to share and to speak their minds and feelings was created in the Chinese classes through artistic forms, such as theatrical performances (Hsia, 2006); and how they perceive the changes of their subjectivities in the process of empowerment initiated by my praxis-oriented research (Hsia, 2016). Here, I will further analyze how a space for them to "talk back" was created by my decision to explicitly discuss my goal of building a more equal relationship with them through my research. As the following examples indicate, these discussions, which at times became argumentative or confrontational encounters, evince the development of my rapport or intersubjective relationship with my participants. The process of empowering the migrant women unfolded over time, from informal Chinese classes to establishing a formal organization, participating in protest actions, and debating whether to dissolve the organization. In the following examples, the names have been fictionalized and the dialogue and comments were translated by the author from Chinese.

"The Chinese Classes Seem Unnecessary Now."

After a few years of providing "foreign brides" opportunities to break away from the "culture of silence" commonly observed among the oppressed people (Freire, 1970), the marriage migrants had become very outspoken in the Chinese classes. While a sense of sisterhood was emerging, it was still far from the goal of establishing their own organization. Sometimes, the volunteer Chinese teachers would propose to do something collectively after certain common issues came up in the classes, but they either showed no interests or did not put it into action after discussion. Some of them even lost the momentum of attending Chinese classes, since they had been more familiar with the language and the local environment. The volunteer teachers reflected on the development of the classes and felt that it was impossible to build up the energy for collective action depending merely on the classes that lasted only 2 hours. In 2001, the volunteer teachers and I decided to organize workshops with the hope that on two consecutive weekends, these marriage migrants could have extensive discussions about their common issues and came up with resolutions to solve problems collectively.

The beginning of the first weekend workshop went successfully as the marriage migrants shared experiences and analyzed their common problems, including their rights to work, social discrimination, and burdens of family care, with great enthusiasm. However, when they were asked what could be done to resolve the issues collectively, an aura of fatalism suddenly emerged and darkened the room: "It's no use." "I have only myself to count on." "It's fate." When a volunteer suggested that they could collectively lessen childcare burdens by forming a childcare program along with the Chinese classes and taking turns to care for children, they reacted almost in unison: "Impossible!!!" They burst out with reasons why this was impossible: "You could never scold children of others." "What should we do if something happens to other people's children?!" This workshop ended in considerable fatalism.

In the assessment meeting afterward, the volunteer teachers felt despaired and worried about the future of the marriage migrants, because after all, they could not rely on the Chinese classes for the rest of their lives in Taiwan. I tried my best to encourage the volunteers not to give up hope, but in vain. By the time I ran out of uplifting words, a flashing reflection came to my mind: Just like the volunteers could not accompany the marriage migrants forever, I could neither always be there guiding the volunteers nor always be there ensuring the Chinese classes to last. I then suggested to the volunteers that instead of worrying about the future of the marriage migrants, we had better present these issues to them and let them decide what to do. The volunteers agreed with my suggestion and we redesigned the workshop accordingly.

In the following weekends, the first session started with a "forum theater," a theatric technique pioneered by Augusto Boal (1979) that encourages audience interaction and explores options dealing with an issue. The theater composes two plays: the first one is performed by the acting group and stopped by a role named "joker," who will then ask the audience to discuss what happens in the first play and how they want the story to continue, which will become the second play performed by the audience themselves.

In this workshop, the story of the first play was about the volunteers of the Chinese classes, who were enthusiastically calling marriage migrants to remind them of the Chinese classes in the following day but became frustrated because none of the marriage migrants seemed excited about the upcoming classes. I acted as the "joker," who stopped the play while volunteers were all feeling down and sad. I asked why they looked so upset. After the volunteers expressed their worries about the fact that marriage migrants had lost interests in attending Chinese classes, I, the joker, turned to the marriage migrants and said, "It seems that all the volunteers are exhausted, and you are no longer interested in attending the classes. Why don't we just close the Chinese classes?" They immediately objected: "No! It can't be closed!" The joker asked, "But the Chinese classes seem unnecessary for you now?" They poured out meanings and emphasized importance of the Chinese classes to them, which they had never talked about before. I further challenged them, "If so, why did you seem apathetic to attend the classes?" With passion, they started discussing their difficulties, especially about one issue: The places where the Chinese classes were held did not give them a sense of belonging. I had not anticipated this to be the most crucial factor affecting the advancement of the empowerment process.

Since the Chinese programs did not have funding, we used free classrooms in elementary schools and had to move around schools depending on their availability. The volunteers explained that since we had kids playing in the classroom and some schools were upset that the kids messing with their equipment and would not allow us to use it again, so we had to change the places from time to time. I listed down on the board the issues they raised and later asked them how to solve the problems. One by one, they collectively came up with the list of resolutions: (1) Everyone contributes 300 NT (around 10 US dollars) as the collective fund; (2) Use this fund to rent a cheap house as "our own" (emphasis theirs); and (3) This new place will not only offer Chinese classes but also serve as a center for all marriage migrants to have all kinds of activities, from cooking Southeast Asian meals to discussing issues, or simply a temporary escape from the family matters. After this workshop, these marriage migrants started their collective action. As planned, we rent an old compound house, which became a space that had accumulated energy built up by various classes, discussion sessions, trainings, and social activities, which led to the plans for establishing an organization.

"Everyone is Tired"

Two years after we rented the old compound house, in 2003, the participants in these classes decided to establish an organization run and led by marriage migrants themselves, because they wanted to build their collective "maiden's home in Taiwan."

To lay the foundation for the organization and establish its mission and structure, the marriage migrants and local volunteers were divided into several working groups with specific tasks. Every other week, there was a large assembly for everyone to present the issues raised in their individual group discussions. Two weeks before the founding assembly, the primary agenda was to discuss the list of recommended officers for the election in the assembly.

I thought this would be a quick discussion because everyone had worked collectively for some time and our dream of establishing an organization was so close to realization. To my surprise, the active marriage migrants, whom I expected to be nominated as officers, began expressing reservations and complained about fatigue with statements such as "I am so tired," "I am already old and I wanna retire," and "I have had enough." The local volunteers, including myself, kept giving them pep talks like, "Don't give up. We will do it together!" "You can do it!" "We are almost there." However, the meeting continued to be clouded by their pessimism: "I am incompetent. Find someone else." At first, I remained cordial and tried hard to find more effective words to encourage my participants. Yet, in a split moment, I vividly imagined another me, critically looking at myself from the outside, questioning:

> Why do I always have to put up with their emotions? If I really, sincerely treat them as equals, how come we don't share the burden of my emotions? Why is it that it's always me unilaterally digesting their worries? Would this disempower rather than empower them? Is this really an equal relationship?

After these self-reflections and questions, I decided that I would not continue to unilaterally absorb their anxieties. I withdrew my smiles, looked at them with a straight face, and admonished:

> Everyone is tired. I even had to come all the way from Taipei to Meinung every other week just to have meetings with you. Speaking of tiredness, I definitely did not have less. If you all think it's all about being tired, and not at all worthwhile to establish an organization, we can call it off immediately. It does not matter to me if the organization will be formed or not.

And then, I dropped my notes on the table, stood up and walked out of the meeting room, and stayed in the courtyard. As soon as I walked out, I was so anxious because I was worried that I may break the group that I had been working hard to establish, along with its ethnographic opportunities. But at the same time, I knew I had to do this so that the marriage migrants would have the genuine ownership of this organization, if it would ever be formed. Otherwise, they would always depend on me to lead the organization and the asymmetric relationship would be reinforced. I tried to calm myself and stayed in the courtyard, determined to wait for them to make decision on their own.

After a while, one marriage migrant came to the courtyard to inform me of their decision: they still wanted to form an organization as planned. They explained to me that they were shocked and the air was frozen when I walked out, because they had never seen me upset with them. Someone broke the ice suggesting, "We should spit out all our hard feelings and talk about it!" So, they shared how each one of them felt while working together, resolved the hard feelings, and collectively decided to continue to prepare for the founding assembly, which to my surprise turned out to be a huge success. This successful founding assembly of TransAsia Sisters Association of Taiwan (TASAT) on December 7, 2003, is not the "live-happily-ever-after" end of a fairytale. Contrarily, as the subsequent examples show, many more challenges and organizational crises arose. In each crisis, it is a challenge for me as praxis-oriented critical ethnographer to reflect on roles and to continue to create a rapport space for them to "talk back."

"We Should Protest, But I Am Not Available Then"

A year before TASAT was formally established, in 2002, another Chinese learning program for marriage migrants was created in Taipei. I was originally invited to teach a class on feminism in a community school, but instead I offered to teach a Chinese learning program for marriage migrants in collaboration with female students in the school whom I would train to become volunteer teachers in the Chinese classes. This Chinese program became another space for marriage migrants' empowerment.

In 2003, as a board member responsible for the advocacy of marriage migrant women's issues in the Awakening Foundation (one of the leading feminist organizations in Taiwan), I was alerted that the Taiwanese government was planning to establish the National Immigration Agency (NIA). Many NGOs found the proposed NIA xenophobic because its main functions were to police, investigate, and deport migrants and immigrants whom NIA officials deemed illegal or dangerous. Moreover, the legal grounds for deportation—such as "threatening national security" and "violating the public interest"—were vaguely articulated and subject to manipulation. Human rights of immigrants and migrants would be vulnerable because this proposed agency did not provide any due process for prosecution or mechanism to which migrants and immigrants could make appeals before deportation. To promote the human rights of marriage migrants and migrant workers, in November 2003, Awakening Foundation initiated a consultation meeting with organizations, scholars and legal experts concerned about immigrants and migrants' issues to discuss the possibility for establishing an alliance. After two preparation meetings, a group of concerned organizations joined with lawyers and scholars formed the Alliance of Human Rights Legislation for Immigrants and Migrants (AHRLIM) on December 12, 2003. AHRLIM's first action was the protest in front of Legislative Yuan, the unicameral legislature of Taiwan, which propelled the movement for marriage migrants' rights and welfare (Hsia, 2009).

In the preparation meeting of AHRLIM's first protest action, I suggested that marriage migrants should be present speaking up their views on the proposed

NIA, since they would be the ones directly affected by such establishment and our protest action would not be legitimate without them. Since TASAT was newly established and was the only member organization that had active marriage migrant members, I was tasked by the alliance to invite marriage migrants to join the protest.

Since the Legislative Yuan is in Taipei, it was more practical to invite marriage migrants from Taipei. These marriage migrants had not had many experiences working collectively for a common goal, nor were they familiar with public issues. I needed to provide them with basic understanding before they could genuinely participate in the discussion.

First, to simply inform them of how the Taiwanese governmental systems work, I had to exhaust all my creative ways of using plain Chinese expression with references to stories in the movies, along with body languages. For instance, to tell them the legislative procedure that the establishment of a governmental agency must be approved by the Legislative Yuan, I needed to teach them several Chinese terms they had not encountered in their daily lives in Taiwan, including the courts, laws, and the Legislative Yuan. Since I did not speak their mother tongues (and they were from different Southeast Asian countries), I could not simply translate these Chinese terms to their languages (see the chapter in this volume by Hilde Fiva Busungu). Instead, I said:

> Have you seen in the foreign movies that when someone committed a crime, they would be sentenced by someone wearing black robe and white curly wig? (Along with my funny hand gestures demonstrating curly wig around my head). . . . This person wearing white curly wig is called the "judge" (and I wrote down the term in Chinese on the blackboard). . . . And how do the judges decide what kind of sentence they would send to the person committed a crime? There are rules, which are called the "laws" (more Chinese learning moments). . . . And who makes the laws? The members of the "Legislative Yuan."

After explaining the basics, I shared with them government's plan of establishing the NIA and the proposed structure and functions of such agency. They started questioning, "What if we are innocent? Can they still deport us?" "We are already part of the Taiwanese families. How can they separate us from our families?" "How come we are not even given fair trials in the courts?" "It's not fair!" Their active participation in the discussion led me to naively assume that they would be eager to join the protest action to speak out. I asked, "Who could join the protest?" To my dismay, they became very quiet. Standing alone in front of the class, I absorbed the awkward silence. I understood their fear of speaking in front of the government building and the possibility of being interviewed by news crews. So, I encouraged them: "You don't need to speak in public. It's OK if you just stand there along with members of AHRLIM. The local advocates will speak." Still nothing.

In an apparent attempt to ease my embarrassment, some of the marriage migrants offered reasons for not joining the protest: "I believe we should protest, but I am not available then." "My husband will take me to visit a friend." "I need to take care of my baby." "I have to work on weekdays." Their efforts to "comfort" me made me reflect, "This protest is supposed to protect their rights, not mine. Isn't it odd that it's me being comforted?" I thought to myself, "If they don't feel the urge to stop the establishment of the proposed NIA, as the locals, we should not speak on their behalf." With a mental preparation that AHRLIM may need to cancel the plan of action, I said to them,

> It's OK. Since the NIA would not affect the locals, and we could not have any marriage migrants to be present at the protest, the action would not be effective at all. I will inform AHRLIM that none of you are available and we will call off the protest action.

One or two seconds after my remarks, Yen, a Vietnamese marriage migrant, cried out, "It can't be!! If we don't stand up to speak for ourselves, no one can speak for us and to protect our own rights! I will be there!!!" An older marriage migrant from Myanmar said to her classmates, "Yen is right. We should go. If you are busy, just free up twenty minutes to join the protest, and then you can go wherever you are supposed to go." Following Yen's pleas, others committed to join the protest. The discussion continued with regard to how to make their voices heard more effectively in the protest.

Eventually, a group of almost ten marriage migrants from the Chinese classes in Taipei joined the first protest initiated by AHRLIM. Though their Chinese was not very fluent then, they garnered a good deal of attention from the media and the public. This was the first time ever in Taiwan for the "foreign brides" to protest in public, which paved the way for future demonstrations, press conferences, and dialogues with government officials (Hsia, 2009).

We regrouped at a café right after the protest to assess how things went. One migrant reflected: "I was afraid and almost decided not to cross the street to join the group. But then I saw you (the author) and other volunteer teachers, I felt relieved." "I was so surprised to see so many local people I have never met before to accompany and support us. I felt safe with them standing behind us." Another Cambodian migrant said enthusiastically, "It's so exciting, so much fun! I want to join again. Please let me know when there will be protests next time."

For the migrants, speaking against those in power is particularly daunting. To "talk back," they needed a safe space, which was created through the Chinese classes. In the class interactions, as an ethnographer and an activist, I was observing, learning, and advancing social change in collaboration with my students. As a marriage migrant told me,

> It's safe to talk about things in our Chinese classes. We can complain about our families and the societies. But it's very different outside of the classes.

> People outside are not like the volunteer teachers. We are afraid to say how we really feel and think outside of the classes.

This sentiment was echoed by other students. The space was not just a physical setting but an ongoing collaboration with emergent priorities and norms for how we related to one another. By extension, the ethnographic rapport at this site was always in the making.

"I Just Want to be a Participant"

In time, TASAT started to develop more programs and campaigns. For instance, we had a program for training marriage migrants to become multicultural speakers and arranged activities for them to share their multicultural experiences in Taiwan, or to teach Taiwanese citizens their Southeast Asian cultures and languages. After a series of training sessions, we formed a team of multicultural speakers and elected a core group to help coordinate various advanced trainings and activities. However, the elected coordinators did not always follow through with their assigned tasks.

The local volunteers, including myself, felt it was important to make more marriage migrants realize the importance of taking responsibilities. After some discussion, we decided to offer a workshop in which participants would share and discuss their experiences of being engaged in different modes of interaction: adults versus adults; parents versus children; and children versus children. The aim of this discussion was for them to realize that in the organization, we were all equals, and our interactions should be like in the mode of "adults versus adults," meaning that everyone should share responsibilities of ensuring the advancement of our goals.

After the short skits which the volunteers dramatized three modes of interaction, I asked participants to discuss characteristics and context of the three roles: adults, parents, and children. Following a lively discussion, Pei, a Cambodian marriage migrant, looked perplexed and asked, "What can I do?!I don't seem to have any experiences acting like an adult?!" Her groveling tone and swinging arms gave her a child-like appearance. As the youngest marriage migrant in TASAT, then Pei often presented herself in an ignorant and obsequious manner.

Instead of offering her straightforward explanation, I asked Pei why she could not find any experience acting like an adult when she actually had a son. She said, "Even though I have a son, my behavior and attitudes are still childish." I asked others how they observed Pei's behaviors, and they all gave feedback to her. I then turned the discussion to the importance of "adults versus adults" mode of interaction in an organization; and what should be done to act like an adult when working together. After a series of discussions, the resolution was that this team of multicultural speakers should be a team of adults, who should not merely "take" from others but should also "give" to others. In the last session of the workshop, Pei decided she would join and even volunteered to be one of the coordinators of the team. Everyone was glad to see Pei's commitment to becoming a more matured leader.

After the formal closing of the workshop, most participants stayed around the venue chitchatting. Pei quietly approached me and asked, "I just want to learn, just want to be a participant. Can I still join the team without taking responsibilities?" I was disappointed but attempted to say yes to Pei. Instead, I responded to her with a serious tone of voice,

> No, Pei, we talked about it. This team is different from Chinese classes. Everyone in this team must be a responsible adult. If you don't want to take the responsibility, you cannot join the team. But you can still attend Chinese learning or other classes to learn.

She welled up and nodded. I had to suppress my urge to grant her wish, because of her tears and sorrow. I remained firm, however, knowing that it is crucial for everyone to learn to be a responsible adult in an organization.

A few hours later, around midnight, I received an email from Pei sent to the group. I was worried that she was going to inform us of her leaving TASAT. I was delighted to find otherwise. Pei wrote:

> I have done a lot of self-reflection since I arrived home. I felt it's very irresponsible of me to simply give things up. It's also very immature behavior. So I want to take responsibilities. But would it be too late now? Can you all give me another chance to practice and transform myself to becoming mature and responsible? I feel very sorry and want to apologize to teachers and all of you.

We agreed to let Pei rejoin the group and were subsequently thrilled with her growth. As the youngest during that time, Pei used to overly depend on other marriage migrants. However, in the annual retreat the following year, when sharing our expectations for the coming year, Pei impressed us all with these words, "I want to grow up like a big tree so that my shade can make people feel cool and help them take a good rest."

A few months later, I organized an exposure trip for representatives of grassroots organizations to visit the Indigenous communities in the Philippines. Pei joined this exposure as one of TASAT's representatives. One evening, we were chatting in our shared hotel room. I said to Pei,

> I have been wanting to tell you something. I was saddened when I told you that you could not join the team unless you took responsibilities. I had a lump in my throat because I knew I had hurt your feelings. But I had to do it. I had to control my tears.

Before I could complete my sentence, Pei interrupted me and burst into crying, "I knew! I knew! I knew you meant to help me grow. I was not upset with you. I was disappointed by myself." With many more ups and downs, the once immature Pei had gradually become one of the leaders of TASAT, who served as a full-time staff for several years and later the elected chairperson.

As this example shows, in the context of my activist ethnographic work, rapport was not intended to "get to the truth" or a strategy for gaining greater access. My rapport with the migrant workers was purposeful in a different sense. I wanted them to become actively involved in an organization that aimed to empower them and elevate their status in the Taiwanese society. At times, this meant inviting my research participants, and students in some cases, to address the impediments to their full and effective involvement in the organization.

"We Won't Give Up!"

This example shows how rapport can be conceived as an ongoing dialogue and process that unfolds over time. As seen here, in the context of activism, the single-minded pursuit of better-quality data gives way to ongoing negotiations and emergent outcomes. In some ways, the ethnographer/researchers become another participant whose actions are guided by site-specific contingencies and preferences of other members in the field.

Since its establishment, TASAT has gone through countless highs and lows, like a rollercoaster ride. Many of these issues had to do with interpersonal disputes, fueled by allegations of favoritism, prejudice, and selfishness, to name a few. As an ethnographer and activist, I myself was implicated in these interpersonal dynamics. For instance, if a marriage migrant became the target of criticism, instead of siding with the majority, I would try to reason with those strongly condemning her and remind them of her strength and past contributions. In doing so, I risked losing rapport with the majority. Indeed, some gossiped about me showing favoritism toward the people who were the targets of criticism. Eventually, the internal disputes escalated to the point where some marriage migrants in Meinung decided that the best way to solve all the problems was to dissolve TASAT.

Before they proposed to disband TASAT, several officers based in Meinung called to explain their intentions to table this agenda at the next assembly and wish to acquire my approval. I told them,

> TASAT is not mine to decide its fate. It's up to all members to vote at the assembly if it should be dissolved. For me, it is OK to dissolve TASAT as long as it's been thoroughly discussed and assessed in the assembly. Don't worry that I would be saddened by this, because I am not.

The staff in the Taipei office did not agree with the proposal to disband the organization. They pleaded with me to intervene: "You have spent more than twenty years building it up. It would be a shame if TASAT would be dissolved. If you could take a stand against this proposal, I am sure everyone would follow because you are the most respected." Again, I responded,

> It's true that I have spent more than twenty years building TASAT, but it's not my personal property, since it's created by collective efforts of countless participants and supporters. If the majority feel it's time to let go, I'm fine with it.

I had stated this position many times before, especially when conflicts within the organization occurred and they expected me to "fix" problems. I even had to resign from being an officer in 2005 and again in 2017, when the internal conflicts became chaotic, and I felt they had to figure out ways to sort out problems without me. However, the migrants did not take my withdrawal very seriously. As one officer in Taipei, once told others, "Hsiao-Chuan was just upset with us for now. She will not let go of TASAT."

When the assembly met to discuss disbanding of the organization, I was not present because of my travel abroad. According to those present, Pei was quite emotional and objected to the proposal. Though fully aware of the long list of difficulties (e.g., running out of funds to pay staff salaries and rental fees for offices), Pei remained determined to keep TASAT intact. She shouted, "We won't give up!" Other marriage migrants were inspired by Pei's determination and agreed that TASAT should not be dissolved. The majority voted against the proposed dissolution. After some internal shakeups, Pei became the chair-elect followed by Mangi.

Recently, I came across an academic article (Momesso & Cheng, 2017) written in English, which, among other things, reviewed my work on the empowerment of marriage migrants. The author criticized my underlying assumption that marriage migrants would not be able to stand up to protect their own rights without a formal organization and the sense of "empowerment" it promoted and engendered among the migrants. This critique made me seriously question my life's work and its contributions to the betterment of the lives of marriage migrants. I raised the issue with Mangi, a marriage migrant and the president of TASAT at the time. She responded,

> It is simply impossible for marriage migrants alone to become activists daring to initiate campaigns for our rights and welfare. In our home countries, we were not educated at schools or in societies that it's our civil right to protest and to demand to the governments, not to mention language and cultural barriers.

Mangi also pointed out the changes of the environments. As the governments shifted policies and discourses toward valuing Southeast Asian marriage migrants and their children as part of their geopolitical strategies countering increasing threat of China (Hsia, 2021), many marriage migrants have space to speak in public, but they do not necessarily "talk back."

> It's true that there are a lot of marriage migrants active in various public space now, like serving as committee members in the governmental agencies, teaching Southeast Asian languages and cultures, performing at big events like on the National Days. Many marriage migrants are outspoken now. But from my observation, they only say what they are expected to say, to please the media, the researchers, the government officials, those people who have power and resources.

Mangi continued to share her criticism of some researchers, "They don't spend much time working with us. They just read some papers. Who was it that questioned the importance of empowerment? How come I never met her?" Our conversation went on and Mangi brought up an idea,

> It's better for us to speak out what we have actually experienced, instead of just waiting for researchers to study us. . . . I have been observing the impacts of YouTubers. I have been thinking TASAT can have our own YouTube channel and speak whatever we want to speak to the public.

Pei was excited about Mangi's proposal and agreed that we could also use podcast as a cheap and effective means of speaking out. This idea was brought to TASAT's board meeting and approved unanimously. Without funding resources and paid staff, a team was formed to discuss and implement TASAT's new project of podcast/YouTube channels, with active involvement of marriage migrants. As Mangi brilliantly put it, "Many marriage migrants can speak up now. But the key is the contents of the speaking."

Discussion

As Alaine Touraine (1988) explains, subjectivation refers to a process through which social actors (subjects) reflect on cultural dominance and are transformed from "personal subjects" to "historical subjects." This means that actors make their mark on history by remaking the social relations and the cultural models that shape identities. Moreover, Touraine (1995) stresses that the process of subjectivation is a type of social action that challenges the status quo (see also Beckford, 1998). Neither personal nor historical subjects evolve "naturally." Rather, they are developed through the struggle against the existing values and structures.

I consider myself a critical praxis-oriented ethnographer concerned with intersubjectivity between researcher and the researched and their asymmetric relations Therefore, through my research and activism, I have endeavored to help advance the subjectivation of marriage migrants. Specifically, I have encouraged marriage migrants to "talk back" by reconfiguring and adapting the ethnographer–participant, rather than merely establishing rapport for the purpose gathering better data. Through my participant observations at various sites, particularly TASAT, I was able to create a space for the migrants to challenge the values and structures in Taiwanese society that adversely affected their lives.

As illustrated in the examples earlier, "talking back" works on different levels. As actors (subjects), talking back for my students and research participants meant feeling confident enough to express their desires, aspirations, and disagreements first as individuals and later as a collective. The people they talked back to, or against, ranged from individuals in their networks (such as the volunteer teachers and researchers) to those outside of their supportive networks, especially those in power (such as the media and politicians).

In the long process of empowering marriage migrants through praxis-oriented research, the marriage migrants were encouraged to "talk back," initially as individuals expressing freely what they want to me and other volunteer Chinese teachers, and gradually to "talk back" as an organization to those in power, including the governmental officials and the media. This process can be understood as the transformation from "personal subjectivity" to "historical subjectivity" Touraine's terms (1988; see also Hsia, 2010).

Moreover, as an ethnographer and activist, I have also experienced a process of subjectivation, through which my historical subjectivity has been realized by constantly reflecting on and trying to reduce the marriage migrants' dependence on me. Essentially, I wanted them to "talk back" to me and advance toward greater autonomy, both as individuals and as members of an organization that continuously challenged their subjugation in Taiwanese society. My efforts to create this space of dialogue and potential confrontation were inspired by my self-reflections on my asymmetric relations with the marriage migrants. To avoid reinforcing or even widening the social divide between us, I had to rethink the traditional notion of ethnographic rapport. This meant ongoing work and involved the ups and downs that are part of any relationship. The process also meant being open and adapting to "surprises" that constantly challenged my imagined subjectivity in the field, or to discovering that I was not always who I thought I was.

Note

1 All names have been anonymized to protect the research participants' identities.

References

Beckford, J. A. (1998). Re-enchantment and demodernization: The recent writings of Alain Touraine. *European Journal of Social Theory*, *1*(2), 195.

Boal, A. (1979). *The theatre of the oppressed* (A. Jackson, Trans.). Pluto Press.

Denzin, N. (1989). *Interpretive biography*. Sage.

Freire, P. (1970). *Pedagogy of the oppressed*. Continuum.

Hsia, H.-C. (1997). *Selfing and othering in the "foreign bride" phenomenon—a study of class, gender and ethnicity in the transnational marriages between Taiwanese men and Indonesian women* (Dissertation). University of Florida.

Hsia, H.-C. (2006). Empowering "foreign brides" and community through praxis- oriented research. *Societies without Borders, 1*, 93–111.

Hsia, H.-C. (2009). Foreign brides, multiple citizenship and immigrant movement in Taiwan. *Asia and the Pacific Migration Journal, 18*(1), 17–46.

Hsia, H.-C. (2010). The subjectivation of marriage migrants in Taiwan: The insider's perspectives. In A. Choudry & D. Kapoor (Eds.), *Learning from the ground up: Global perspectives on social movement and knowledge production* (pp. 101–118). Palgrave Macmillan.

Hsia, H.-C. (2015). Action research with marginalized immigrants' coming to voice: Twenty years of social movement support in Taiwan and still going. In H. Brabury (Ed.), *The Sage handbook of action research* (3rd ed., pp. 315–324). Sage.

Hsia, H.-C. (2016). The making of multiculturalistic subjectivity: The case of marriage migrants' empowerment in Taiwan. In K. Iwabuchi, H. Mee Kim, & H.-C. Hsia (Eds.), *Multiculturalism in East Asia: A transnational exploration of Japan, South Korea and Taiwan* (pp. 141–161). Rowman and Littlefield.

Hsia, H.-C. (2019). Praxis-oriented research for the building of grounded transnational marriage migrant movements in Asia. In D. Kappor & S. Jordan (Eds.), *Research, peasant and urban poor activisms in the Americas and Asia* (pp. 248–269). ZED Books.

Hsia, H.-C. (2021). From 'social problems' to 'social assets': Geopolitics, discursive shifts in children of southeast Asian Marriage migrants, and mother-child dyadic citizenship in Taiwan. *Citizenship Studies, 25*(7), 955–974.

Lassiter, L. E. (2004). Collaborative ethnography. *Anthronotes, 25*(1), 1–9.

Momesso, L., & Cheng, I. (2017). A team player pursuing its own dreams: Rights- claim campaign of Chinese migrant spouses in the migrant movement before and after 2008. In D. Fell (Ed.), *Taiwan's social movements under Ma Ying-jeou: From the wild strawberries to the sunflowers* (pp. 219–235). Routledge.

Pels, P. (2014). After objectivity: An historical approach to the intersubjective in ethnography. *Hau: Journal of Ethnographic Theory, 4*(1), 211–236.

Rappaport, J. (2008). Beyond participant observation: Collaborative ethnography as theoretical innovation. *Collaborative Anthropologies, 1*, 1–31.

Springwood, C. F., & King, C. R. (2001). Unsettling engagements: On the ends of rapport in critical ethnography. *Qualitative Inquiry, 7*(4), 403–417.

Touraine, A. (1988). *Return of the actor*. University of Minnesota Press.

Touraine, A. (1995). Birth of the subject. In *Critique of modernity*. Blackwell.

PART III

Social Worlds

9

PRESCHOOL SOCIAL WORLDS IN INTERACTIONAL CONTEXT

John C. Pruit

The crafting of ethnographic fieldwork does not end with site identification and the subsequent collection of field data, but extends well beyond concrete participant observation. The craft of ethnographic discovery, as Malin Åkerström and David Wästerfors (2021) argue, continually evolves in hindsight with the rereading and reanalysis of field material and the reframing of ethnographic understanding.

Nine years ago, I completed ethnographic fieldwork in a Montessori preschool, focusing on how contrasting social worlds organize interaction. In this chapter, allowing for additional discovery, I reverse this to gain perspective on how social worlds, in turn, are brought to life in interactional context. As I hope to show, what 9 years ago was viewed as artifacts of members' social worlds is—through a shift in analytic standpoint—rediscovered as jointly constructed interactionally in practice.

Social Worlds

Social worlds (Shibutani, 1955; Strauss, 1978, 1982, 1984) were originally conceived as "sets of common or joint activities or concerns, bound together by a network of communication" (Kling & Gerson, 1978, p. 21). Sport and leisure (Bogardus, 2012), criminal justice (Ulmer, 1997), and human services (Gubrium, 1997; Jacobsson & Gubrium, 2021) are social worlds "built up by people in their interaction with one another; hence, each communication channel gives rise to a separate world" (Shibutani, 1955, p. 566). Writ large, social worlds may be divided into "specialized concerns and interests within the larger community of common activities" (Kling & Gerson, 1978, p. 26). Baseball, for instance, has specific lingos and concerns for pitching, fielding, batting, and analytics within the sports world.

DOI: 10.4324/9781003275121-13

The social worlds under consideration in this chapter were sited in the preschool, the joint activities and common concerns of which dealt with the general rubric "early childhood education" (ECE). The rubric is telling, as it suggests that what is worded as joint and common is understood in the contrasting and often conflicting terms of nurturing and schooling. Individually sensible and derivable from different social worlds, the one operates conceptually as a world of caring, centered in the preschool the everyday roles and relations of childhood. The other social world, schooling, is understood to be centered in the everyday roles and relations of teaching and learning.

While separate and distinct, these social worlds are peopled in the preschool by a common set of actors including administrators, preschool children, preschool teachers, parents, and, on rare occasion, preschool ethnographers, myself in this case. The preschool ethnographer's role is that of a participant observer of the social worlds in place, the interactional contexts of which are suffused with their differential understandings and related tensions and contradictions. The associated interactions in which tension and contradiction arise are understood to stem from the different social worlds in place.

Rereading Fieldnotes

Upon rereading my fieldnotes, I found that during my presence at the preschool field site, besides members' interactions, I had recorded several instances of what it was like interactionally to manage my role as participant observer. I previously had used these data to understand preschool teachers' experiences, not my own. In the following sections, using extended extracts from the fieldnotes, I return to the fieldnotes to argue that there is considerable contrast in practice with the view that social worlds articulate, if not formulate related interactions. In practice, the reverse is equally indicated that field members proper and the participant observer bring social worlds to life in interactional context. For purposes of illustration, I focus on the particular interactional contexts of classroom management, emotions, and organizational rules.

Classroom Management in Interactional Context

In educational understanding, classroom management emphasizes organization and order. Teachers organize classroom activities to establish a routine while also monitoring preschoolers to ensure they are behaving within the bounds of that routine. When teachers believe preschoolers are "out of bounds," they make decisions about how to proceed with that particular preschooler. Sometimes disciplinary decisions are made without sufficient empirical evidence. While the preschooler bears the brunt of the associated interaction, it can be troubling for researchers, such as participant observers, who are witness to the dynamics of practice in place, in which schooling and nurturing conflict.

The interactions considered later involve instances in which preschool teachers lacked sufficient knowledge about an event and instead relied on something other than empirical evidence to address perceived transgressions. In each instance, I witnessed the event in full and made a decision about if, when, and how to intervene as an active participant. I identify three strategies for managing these situations: checking in with the preschooler, intervening immediately, and discussing the event with the preschool teacher. My attempts to influence interactions relating to preschool teachers' disciplinary practices aimed at reducing the conflict between nurturing and schooling. In each instance, I had to strategically manage my role and relations as an ethnographer with the contrasting understandings of the attendant social worlds in mind (Pruit, 2014; Reyes, 2020; Soyer, 2014). As a matter of practice, the social worlds in tow wended their way through the interaction in play.

Checking in With the Preschooler

The following interaction involves teacher Bob,[1] an early thirties, White man and full-time staff member. Without witnessing the precipitating event, I observe Bob reprimanding preschooler Aaron, a 4-year-old Hispanic boy with a tendency toward excitability. Reprimanding preschoolers illustrates the contrasting worlds of schooling and nurturance. It restores classroom order, but it comes into conflict with nurturing in ECE. After the interaction, I checked on Aaron to try to establish a sense of nurturing.

> Bob is talking to me with his back turned to the peace octagon. Ironically, we are discussing the importance of letting children experience the world around them without intervening. Aaron, a preschooler, is in the peace octagon working with the broad stairs (Montessori work consisting of ten brown wooden prisms used to differentiate size on two dimensions). I can clearly see what all of the friends are doing in the peace octagon, including Aaron.
>
> A dispute arises between Aaron and another friend. The friend wants to work with Aaron, but did not ask. Aaron wants to work alone and voices this by shouting at the other friend. Bob turns and sees that it was Aaron and says, "Hang on a minute. I'm gonna nip this in the bud." Bob walks over to Aaron and begins discussing something with him. Bob makes a point to tell Aaron to "pay attention," which does not sit well with me because it shows a lack of mutual respect. I cannot hear whatever else is said, but I can see that Aaron is upset.
>
> I wait a couple of minutes to ensure the hierarchical order remains intact and then approach Aaron. He is sullen. Rather than explain to him what I saw, I decide to use a different strategy. I get down on my knees and say, "Aaron, I could use a hug." Without hesitation he lunges forward and wraps his arms around my neck. I then say, "Thank you. I feel much better now." He replies, "Me too" and resumes working with the broad stairs without incident.
>
> *September 6, 2012*

I first interpreted this interaction as Bob being too heavy-handed with Aaron and the entire incident as a misguided form of social control that represents a point at which participant observers must make the decision to become active participants. While this remains a valid interpretation, reframing the interaction using the preschool social worlds provides rationale as to why I felt unsettled witnessing this interaction. The contradiction between nurturing and schooling that emerges from reprimanding preschoolers defies the logic of the preschool. It establishes order, but it simultaneously sacrifices the child's well-being. Rather than teaching preschoolers to work through frustrating situations, children learn that frustration is not an acceptable emotion in educational settings and to not get caught by a teacher if they become frustrated with another person.

Intervening Immediately

The next extract details interaction associated with classroom management in the context of serving and eating lunch. Ceana is a 20-year-old woman of color and college student working part time in a primary classroom (ages 3–6). Mikayla, an active and energetic White, 4-year-old preschool girl, is eating lunch and accidentally knocks her plate to the floor.

> The lights are dim, and the friends are talking quietly as they finish their lunch. Ceana is sitting at a table with her back to the friends, while I am sitting in a position that allows me to see all of the friends. Ceana gets up to help two friends serve more food. Mikayla is the first. While Ceana is serving the second friend, Mikayla walks back to her seat. She sets her plate down first and then begins to sit down when her hand slips and hits her plate. The plate spins off the table sending her food crashing to the floor as her cup of milk spreads across the table.
>
> Ceana's reaction is quick, saying, "Mikayla!" I immediately intervene on Mikayla's behalf. I say, "It was an accident. Mikayla, what do you think we should do?" Mikayla replies, "Clean it up?" I agree by shaking my head up and down. Mikayla walks over to the bin with clean up rags and takes two out. She soaks her milk up and then takes the wet rags to the dirty rag bin. She then retrieves a broom and dustpan and begins sweeping the area. After this, she serves more food and finishes lunch seemingly unbothered.

In this interaction, I potentially threatened Ceana's status and the classroom hierarchy by intervening. However, my intervention taught Mikayla how to resolve the problem and spared her from potential emotional distress. My willingness to intervene prompted me to question my role in the preschool and how I managed it. In particular, I was concerned with why I intervened immediately in this situation, but not immediately with Bob previously. The fieldnote continues:

> I am not sure why I responded to Ceana the way I did when Mikayla spilt her food, especially when I didn't immediately intervene on Aaron's behalf

> with Bob. I believe it stems from at least four possibilities. First, I had seen the event directly and knew that it was an accident (and an opportunity to learn). The second possibility is overconfidence. I have been in the room long enough to feel comfortable saying something. The lead teacher has been letting me move about freely and work with the friends as I choose, although she is always careful to remind other teachers that "John does not count toward ratio." Similarly, the head of school remarked, "John is always welcome. He is like one of the teachers and always welcome." The third possibility is status relating to experience. I have been in the room longer than Ceana. Bob was a fulltime employee, while Ceana was a part time employee. Fourth, and as much as I dislike considering it as a possibility, race and gender. I did not intervene with Bob, but I did with Ceana indicating a linkage with race and gender. Because of the nature of the interactive moment, I did not fully consider the possibilities during the interaction. However, after considering the interaction, I have decided to temper my responses to teachers so as not to threaten the hierarchical order.
>
> *September 6, 2012*

My early interpretations involved grappling with my positionality as well as several related factors associated with immediate intervention. This was important to understanding my role in the preschool. Moreover, immediate intervention mattered for the good of field relations with teachers and children. It potentially helped the preschoolers, but could also put me at odds with the preschool teachers by overstepping boundaries. However, thinking through the interaction in terms of nurturing and schooling demonstrates how I tried to avoid the interactional contrast altogether only to find myself contrastingly center stage. For Mikayla, immediate intervention taught her how to troubleshoot and problem-solve her spill. In doing so, she remained within the established classroom order and routine. It also avoided what could be an emotionally distressing situation brought on by being chastised for an accident.

Discussing the Event With the Preschool Teacher

Zahra, an early twenties staffer of Middle Eastern descent using they/them pronouns, was interim lead and later assistant lead in a primary classroom (ages 3–6). The situation in place involved interaction with Mikayla, the preschooler from the preceding extract, in which the preschooler wanted to put her outermost shirt back on. This was not being presently allowed. Zahra did not know that earlier Mikayla was allowed to remove her outermost shirt to cool off.

> Lunch has just ended, and it is almost naptime. The friends are milling about preparing for their rest period. Mikayla had gotten hot earlier and decided to take off her outermost shirt to cool off. I had taken it and placed it in her cubby. Mikayla, by the way, was also notorious for wardrobe changes. Now Mikayla is ready to put her outermost shirt back on, but is

> not communicating it to the interim lead teacher, Zahra, in a way that makes sense. There is a bit of a power struggle at this point as the two go back and forth.
>
> Mikayla, pleading, "I want my shirt!"
>
> Zahra, in a gentle voice, says "I'm sorry friend, but you do not need to change clothes." This goes on for a minute and I try to politely intervene, but Zahra does not hear me. After a moment Mikayla continues to insist on putting her shirt on, with Zahra again replying that she does not need to change her clothes. Mikayla temporarily walks away, and I take this opportunity to gain Zahra's attention. I apologize and tell her, "Mikayla was wearing the shirt she wants earlier. I tried to tell you, but you didn't hear me. I apologize. I took her shirt and placed it on top of her stuff in her cubby." They look temporarily miffed, but recover quickly saying, "Oh, okay." They then call Mikayla over and allow her to put her outermost shirt back on.
>
> *September 7, 2012*

Zahra's actions upheld the classroom order and the demeanor with which they did so did not emotionally harm Mikayla. In this sense, Zahra's actions affirmed the social worlds of both nurturing and schooling. However, the incident was not fully immune to disruption since Zahra did not have a key piece of information about Mikayla previously being allowed to remove her outermost shirt. This information caused me and Zahra to have different understandings of the situation. Although Zahra was balanced in their approach, it was still punitive because it effectively changed the rules previously established for Mikayla.

Discussing an event with the preschool teacher afterward is beneficial because it gives the teacher an opportunity to reestablish classroom and emotional norms by amending decisions. Having recently considered that it would be best not to "step on the toes" of the preschool teachers, I was trying to be cautious and judicious. Zahra was interim lead teacher at the time and hence the main gatekeeper in the classroom, so I was selfishly being careful not to disrupt their status and perhaps selfishly trying to preserve mine. In any case, being unable to get Zahra's attention worked out well, because I approached them without Mikayla being present, creating less potential for conflict. I went on to write about the uneven nature of field relations:

> What this tells me is that participant observation in the preschool is a situated practice in which the researcher must weigh the pros and cons of any given decision, especially if it involves "stepping on the toes" of those being researched. This is, admittedly, selfish in that it considers my needs above the needs of others. This is part of the problem with being a participant observer. Sometimes we step in while other times we observe acts to see how they will play out. This is not a problem I will solve, but one I'll learn to manage throughout my research.
>
> *September 7, 2012*

At the time of my physical presence in the field, my concern was with documenting and analyzing interactions between preschool teachers and preschoolers, not my role in classroom management interactions in relation to social worlds. My previous framing of classroom management was as a form of social control (Pruit, 2019). Upon rereading and reframing the data, ethnographic patterns relating to my role as a participant observer took on new meaning from such interactions revealing the contradiction in early childhood education between nurturing and schooling as it relates to classroom management. Using this perspective, when classroom management is punitive it comes into conflict with common understandings of how to nurture children. In particular, regarding patterns relating to if, when, and how to address disciplinary situations that were overlooked at the time, now extend understanding of ethnographic role management.

Emotions in Interactional Context

Emotions are an important facet of schooling and nurturing. This is particularly true because of the preschool's cultural and local emotion rules (Hochschild, 2003). As the contrasting social worlds in place would have it, there are two sides to emotions in the preschool: those that preschool teachers and ethnographers are able to display for educational purposes and those that they must conceal for purposes of nurturing. Emotions for display include positive and neutral emotions such as being happy and calm. Negative emotions such as frustration and anger are those preschool teachers are expected to conceal. I knew it was imperative that I performed my roles in a certain manner, especially with the children. Learning the emotion rules in short order was vital to demonstrating competency. Honestly, it is not as if I never felt frustrated with a teacher or preschooler, because I most certainly did, but it was important that I never display negative emotions because it could jeopardize my standing in the preschool.

The events of the following extended extract from fieldnotes took place during morning line time (group learning) between me, a participant observer losing sight of his researcher role, and Cameron, a 3-year-old boy disinterested in this day's group learning. The note indicates that Cameron is disrupting line time and because I am the adult that is closest to him in proximity it is up to me to manage his behavior and my emotions.

> Claire, the lead teacher, was out sick and Cameron, a three-year-old, was driving me crazy today. He was having, well, a Cameron type of day. He was a bit rambunctious. At times distracting other friends from their work by talking at them, walking between them and their work, taking the work out of their hands, and so on. Each time he was met with a gentle redirection from a teacher or myself.
>
> At line time Marissa, the assistant lead, performed the morning message and lesson. A lesson on body space and the letter "o" were the topics for the day. The friends sat on their carpet squares, giving each other plenty

> of room, and did their best to learn about the sounds an "o" makes, and so forth. Cameron was "sitting" back with me near the end of the stage. He wasn't really sitting. He was rolling, wiggling, crawling, touching, talking loudly, and being generally distracting.
>
> For my part, I am not doing ethnographic fieldwork at this point. I am, for all practical purposes, a preschool teacher. I am not thinking about writing this down and analyzing it for my emotion work. Instead, I am thinking about Cameron and how I am going to reach him, literally and figuratively. I am one hundred percent in this moment with Cameron.
>
> I reach out to touch Cameron and succeed. "Stop!" he moans, half shouting and half respecting the social order of line time. "Cameron," I say as soothingly as possible, "you may sit next to me." Cameron temporarily gives up his goal of, well, whatever it is a three-year-old tries to accomplish. It is a short-lived victory. Cameron lifts his carpet square above his head and is about to club Dianna with it. Luckily, I catch it before he brings it down saying, "Cameron, that is not a safe choice, friend. I will take your carpet square now." With a slightly disappointed look he relents and sits on the floor while I take his carpet square and place it on my opposite side.
>
> I can feel myself getting frustrated with Cameron and know I have to let it go. Sometimes I have bad days, or days when I'm more distracting than helping. This is the type of day Cameron is having. The other teachers are either teaching, doing side work, or dealing with similar issues . . . "What would Claire do?" I think to myself.
>
> Cameron is on his hands and knees, which is pretty good considering he was going to waylay a friend only moments ago. I ask him to sit back closer to me. "Crisscross, applesauce, spoons in your bowl" I whisper. Although it takes a moment, Cameron recovers and sits up. I place my hand on his back and gently rub between his shoulder blades, something that relaxes my son. I lean over and whisper, "Look at Theresa. She looks like she is learning. Who else looks like they are learning?" He seems interested for a moment and points toward Laken. "That's right. Laken is sitting up straight with his hands in his lap and his eyes on Marissa. Who else?"
>
> Cameron doesn't care "who else." He is off to the races trying to get into the puppet house sitting stage right. Still, none of the other teachers are showing concern. My sense is that it is because they think I can handle the situation. What are they thinking?!?! I'm starting to feel like I'm the only teacher in the room and it's a battle to the death with Cameron. Three-year-olds never lose!! How long could it possibly take to discuss the letter "o"? And why do these people trust me?

At this point I was arguably close to being in over my head. I had been trying to keep up an emotionally-nurturing front, but there was a voice in my head shouting "get away from this kid," even though I believed I had to manage his distracting behavior. It felt like the other teachers had made a collective decision to offload Cameron on me, making me the last line of defense, so to speak, between "early childhood" and "education." As the next part of the extract indicates, I was struggling with my feelings not matching the site's feeling rules, but also trying to make it through the interaction displaying a calm demeanor so as not to sully the world of schooling. Eventually I came to terms with the situation as it was and my relative lack of control in it.

> Clearly, I am frustrated by this situation, but do not want to show it. I am not able to walk away because I do not want to abandon the other teachers. Besides, where would I go? This type of emotion work is internal and external. I, the preschool teacher, begin regulating my emotions. I know that a preschool is not an appropriate venue for the airing of anger, frustration, and resentment. Although I feel these rising in me, I have the external constraints of the institution weighing down on me. This includes the risks associated with losing my research site, getting kicked out of grad school, and becoming a manual laborer again. Preschools are happy and safe places. Preschool teachers are happy, gentle, loving, and nurturing people. I know I must perform this to the best of my ability because my audience, twenty plus three-to-six-year-old preschoolers, is quite adept at reading emotional cues.
>
> I recover and think to myself, "It's not a big deal." I do not want Cameron or any of the other friends to pick up on my negative emotions, so I take a deep breath and let it out slowly. I realize I must keep Cameron and the other friends safe by simply managing the situation as best I can. Managing the situation, in this case, involves minimization of distraction, as opposed to resolving it. Once deciding to manage Cameron's behavior and not worry about "fixing" it I begin to relax. I let Cameron be Cameron and I became Mr. John again (I despise being called "Mr." John), but still not researcher John.
>
> Looking around, I notice I'm the only person being bothered, which is probably a result of internalizing the rules of line time to such an extent that I became preoccupied with it. In becoming a preschool teacher, losing my researcher self in a sense, I was able to experience what it was like to get piled on emotionally and have my frustration level rise high enough to cause me distress. In this case, trying to correct undesirable behavior was pointless. Instead, contextualizing the situation in broader contours helped me deal with my emotions. No one was hurt and line time proceeded without incident.
>
> Cameron did not destroy the puppet house. As a matter of fact, without an oppositional force (me) he began exploring it quietly. So much so, that he ceased distracting the other friends. Over the course of this brief encounter, I learned I cannot solve every problem and sometimes it is best to just let go and see what happens.
>
> Line time is over, and the friends are stacking their carpet squares. Cameron looks at me and I ask, "Cameron, will you please stack your carpet square?" He takes the square and places it on top of the pile and then wanders off.
>
> *January 17, 2013*

My previous analysis of emotionally difficult interactions focused mainly on how preschool teachers managed their emotions (Pruit, 2019, p. 96), but in hindsight overlooked certain aspects of why they conform emotionally. During the interaction, for instance, I called on the idea of preschools being happy and safe and preschool teachers being nurturing to remind me to manage my emotions. Rereading fieldnotes about how I managed my roles illustrates the usefulness of ethnographic review for reframing these interactions as giving rise to tension and contradiction between schooling and nurturing. Early childhood education is constructed under the assumption those involved have similar goals. However, this overlooks the tension between "early childhood" and "education." Young children are not always concerned with learning. Instead, at times educators impose unwelcome goals on children. This creates tension between schooling and nurturing that is sometimes visited upon preschool teachers (and ethnographers) when preschoolers disrupt a learning activity and preschool teachers try to manage the situation. A teacher displaying negative emotions while teaching creates an unsafe atmosphere for learning, which constitutes emotional deviance (Thoits, 1985). In short, preschool teachers display positive emotions for the purposes of schooling and conceal negative emotions for the purposes of nurturing.

Organizational Rules in Interactional Context

Preschools are replete with formal and unwritten rules for both children (Stockstill, 2021) and adults. Formal and unwritten rules for teachers address who can perform practices relating to nurturing and schooling. In connection with schooling, the preschool's employee handbook instructs teachers on how to interact with children, what to do when children need help or misbehave, and how to address their needs. The preschool's unwritten rules often relate to perceptions of safety and suspicion regarding nurturing (Pruit, 2014, 2015, 2019). I learned some unwritten rules were for men preschool teachers (and ethnographers) not to be alone with preschoolers, change diapers, enter restrooms with the preschoolers (especially girls), or take preschoolers from the playground into the building. As I put it in my October 16, 2012, fieldnotes,

> I do not say all of this to negate the importance of a site's rules or the necessity of keeping it as a research site, but instead to show the abundance of social control targeting men that preschool sites use to emphasize the safety and wellbeing of the children.

These unwritten rules, however, also gave men a "patriarchal dividend" (Connell, 1995) because they did not have to do the preschool's dirty work.

The interactions in the following sections show how formal and unwritten rules are enforced or temporarily suspended depending on interpretations of the situation, which brings context to bear on the articulation of social worlds.

Enforcing the Rules

There was almost always a teacher in each room when the preschoolers were on the playgrounds. It was usually a lead teacher completing work in preparation for the next activity (teaching, meals, snacks, art projects, and so on). In the early months of fieldwork, I thought of taking a child into the building as nothing other than just that, but I soon learned about some formal and unwritten rules. In the following extract, Ceana, a staff member, gave me approval to take a preschooler into the building to get a bandage. Once I entered the classroom I encountered Mindy, a lead teacher who took issue with me walking the preschooler into the building because I was not an employee.

> At this time, all three of the primary rooms were on the playground. So, after pushing Carly on the swing there were plenty of friends to hug and tell about my knee [injury]. One of which was Sandra from P1. On her way to me, however, she fell. I let her pick herself up and asked her if she was okay. She said her knee hurt. I told her "Let's give it a few minutes and then look at it if it still bothering you." She agreed. A minute later she called me over to look at her knee. There was a small scratch on it. Rather than call an ambulance, I offered to take her in to get a bandage. She thought this was a good idea. I told Ceana that we were going in the building to get a bandage and up to P1 we went.
>
> I walked past Ben (the head of school) and Zahra (the assistant lead) into the primary classroom where Mindy (a new lead teacher) was in the room. She asked, "What's wrong?" I replied, "Sandra had a fall and we decided to get a bandage for her knee." This was apparently problematic for Mindy. "John, I appreciate your help, but you can't bring the friends into or out of the building since you're not on staff." I replied, "Okay, no problem." I knew it was better to keep a research site than to argue a bureaucratic point. I turned to walk out, and she pointed out "There's also bandages in the shed outside." I shook my head in understanding and told her that I had not known about them before now. She went on, "I didn't mean to offend you, but . . ." I cut her off because I could see that she was feeling awkward about the situation. "It's okay, Mindy, you have to do your job." This seemingly neutralized the situation, and she thanked me and told me "You're always welcome up here. We'd love to have you."

My hunch about this interaction during my physical presence in the field was that I was caught up in one of the unwritten rules about men in preschools. Reanalyzing this interaction reveals an additional set of circumstances at work in which contradiction emerged from the logic of the preschool's formal rules. On the one hand, preschool teachers must be present on the playground to teach children how to do things and to keep order. On the other hand, they are to nurture children by keeping them safe, including performing minor first aid (even when that first aid is mostly for emotional well-being). When I took Sandra into the school, the tension was between who could officially nurture and school preschoolers and who could not. In this case, if a woman employee took Sandra into the building, they would be in compliance and violation with the formal rules of the school. The child would be cared for, but there would be too few teachers on the playground to meet state and school ratio standards causing trouble in the social world of schooling.

Temporarily Suspending the Rules

I sometimes found myself in situations in which temporarily suspending the rules allowed teachers to accomplish the goals of the preschool (nurturing and schooling). A little over three and a half months after the previous interaction with Mindy, she temporarily suspended the rules by asking me to help on her side of the playground. In the following interaction, Mindy is short-staffed and asks me to help meet ratio (in an unofficial capacity) on the playground while she takes two preschoolers into the building.

> A few minutes after venturing onto the playground I hear "Hey, John" from across the fence. It is Mindy, a primary lead teacher. She asks me to come to the primary playground to help meet ratio while she takes a couple of friends inside to use the restroom. As she explains it to me and Bob she recants a bit, "Well, he isn't going to count toward ratio, but it's another adult on the playground." This is interesting because a couple of months ago Mindy made a point about me taking friends into the building because I was not an employee. However, it is equally important to note there is an unwritten rule about men not taking girls to the restroom, which I believe was part of the reason she did not want me to take the friend inside to get a bandage. In any case, I agree to come over and hang out on the primary playground for a few minutes. About ten minutes later Mindy returns and we make some small talk.
>
> *February 5, 2013*

My earlier interpretation of suspending the rules was in terms of the status of those involved and their situational needs, especially relating to gender. From this perspective, rules are malleable. However, in interactional context, the action of temporarily suspending the rules allows non-staff and/or men such as myself to act in the capacity of a preschool teacher. This temporarily sets aside the contradiction regarding formal and unwritten rules, but creates potential risks regarding outside interpretations of who can nurture and instruct young children.

Reframing situations of enforcing and suspending rules in interactional context adds layers to the decision-making context. Preschool teachers' interpretations of nurturing and schooling inform interpretations of formal and unwritten rules, and, moreover, create tension between nurturing and schooling. Namely, while some men are qualified to teach or do research in the preschool, they are not necessarily qualified to care for children. Disqualification is not solely based on employment status, but also based on the preschool teacher's interpretation of the situation. Thinking about rules in this context means there is consideration not only for who is capable and allowed to perform such tasks, but also for the accomplishment of nurturing and schooling as a practical matter. Organizational rules, then, can mask suspicion of men, but can also be bureaucratic barriers to accomplishing the goals of early childhood education. In these instances, preschool teachers must make decisions about their priorities in that situation. Ultimately, whether rules are enforced or suspended, tension remains between the social worlds of nurturing and schooling.

The Analytic Shift Summarized

Let me summarize. For this chapter, I reread all my ethnographic fieldnotes paying close attention to how I managed my role as a participant observer in this field site. Surprisingly, several fieldnote entries disclose various degrees of tension both internally and with field site members indicating I was "successively caught in situations in which conflicting demands were made" on me and preschool teachers (Shibutani, 1955, p. 567). Conflicting demands, which I had earlier construed as contrasting social worlds, were articulated through social interaction. In practice, social worlds are not just configurations of meaning but are separately activated in and through social interaction. The interactional contexts I encountered in relation to classroom management, emotions, and organizational rules served to articulate the social worlds in place.

But the argument presented in this chapter is that ethnographic fieldwork does not end with one's physical presence at a field site, but continues with the analysis of data. From this perspective, ethnographers can revisit their data and re-immerse themselves in a field, extending ethnographic fieldwork. Practically speaking, this means there is no expiration date on how ethnographers craft fieldwork. Rereading and reanalyzing my fieldnotes in light of the themes of this book (sites, interaction, and social worlds) produced new understandings about processes of ethnographic review as well as a reframing of the tensions and contradictions those in the field experience in relation to social worlds. Ethnographic review gives ethnographers the ability to continue crafting an understanding of the social organization of the site under consideration. As such, the interactions depicted in this chapter help clarify that the preschool is not just a site to be judged in terms of its excellence or degree of kindness, but in terms of the worlds in place (nurturing and schooling) that inevitably fuel what early childhood education is in everyday practice.

Ethnographic review involves the analytic processes of rereading, reanalyzing, and reframing data to make ethnographic discoveries after one's physical presence in the field (Åkerström & Wästerfors, 2021). Having completed my physical presence in the field site 9 years prior to this writing, I argue these practices extend ethnographic fieldwork's boundaries beyond what we typically think of as a time- and place-bound activity. This practice provides the grounds for gaining further ethnographic understanding beyond initial discoveries while in the field. From this perspective, the crafting of ethnographic fieldwork is always in the present, rather than being a time-contingent event in which participant observers go to a site for a period of time, document interactions, and then leave fieldwork behind. So, while ethnographic fieldwork does require presence in the acquisition of field data, the work is preceded by the pre-field framing process and continues into the post-field processes of ethnographic review. Fieldwork, then, does not end with field presence, but continues with the analysis of field material. One continues, in effect, being a participant observer before, during, and after one ethnographically orients to the site, its interactions, and its social worlds.

For this chapter, I also produced a set of new findings, one that stemmed from the rereading, reanalysis, and reframing in tow. I literally found that by reversing analytic attention to fieldnotes recorded 9 years ago, I came to understand an inherent shortcoming of the idea of social worlds bereft of a sense of real-world application of contextuality. I found that to be meaningful in practice, social worlds come to life in interactional context. And, equally important, it is context that brings on board their working conditions and their moral and physical consequences in practice.

Note

1 All names provided are pseudonyms.

References

Åkerström, M., & Wästerfors, D. (2021). Ethnographic discovery after fieldwork on troubled youth. In K. Jacobsson & J. F. Gubrium (Eds.), *Doing human service ethnography* (pp. 171–189). Policy Press.

Bogardus, L. M. (2012). Bolt wars: A social worlds perspective on rock climbing and intragroup conflict. *Journal of Contemporary Ethnography*, *41*(3), 283–308. doi:10.1177/0891241611426429

Connell, R. (1995). *Masculinities*. Polity Press.

Gubrium, J. F. (1997). *Living and dying at Murray Manor*. University Press of Virginia.

Hochschild, A. R. (2003). *The managed heart*. University of California Press.

Jacobsson, K., & Gubrium, J. F. (Eds.). (2021). *Doing human service ethnography*. Policy Press.

Kling, R., & Gerson, E. M. (1978). Patterns of segmentation in the computing world. *Symbolic Interaction*, *1*(2), 24–43.

Pruit, J. C. (2014). Preconstructing suspicion and the recasting of masculinity in preschool settings. *Qualitative Research in Education*, *3*(3), 320–344.

Pruit, J. C. (2015). Preschool teachers and the discourse of suspicion. *Journal of Contemporary Ethnography*, *44*(4), 510–534.

Pruit, J. C. (2019). *Between teaching and caring in the preschool*. Lexington.

Reyes, V. (2020). Ethnographic toolkit: Strategic positionality and researcher's visible and invisible tools in field research. *Ethnography, 21*(2), 220–240. doi:10.1177/1466138118805121

Shibutani, T. (1955). Reference groups as perspectives. *American Journal of Sociology, 60*(6), 562–569.

Soyer, M. (2014). Off the corner and into the kitchen: Entering a male-dominated research setting as a woman. *Qualitative Research, 14*(4), 459–472.

Stockstill, C. (2021). The "stuff" of class: How property rules in preschool reproduce class inequality. *Social Problems*, 1–21. doi:10.1093/socpro/spab019

Strauss, A. (1978). A social world perspective. *Studies in Symbolic Interaction, 1*, 119–128.

Strauss, A. (1982). Social worlds and legitimation processes. *Studies in Symbolic Interaction, 4*, 171–190.

Strauss, A. (1984). Social worlds and their segmentation processes. *Studies in Symbolic Interaction, 5*, 123–139.

Thoits, P. A. (1985). Self-labeling processes in mental illness: The role of emotional deviance. *American Journal of Sociology, 91*(2), 221–249.

Ulmer, J. (1997). *The social worlds of sentencing*. SUNY Press.

10

THE GOING CONCERNS OF ETHNOGRAPHIC MEMBERSHIP

James M. Thomas

Introduction

I arrived at Helter Skelter[1] and immediately went to the bar to grab a seat. There is one older man sitting at the bar. He appears pretty drunk, and is talking to the bar owner who also happens to be tending the bar tonight. Toward the back of the bar, I see two young comics I know—Ryan and Kyle. They're with another young person—perhaps a comic, too—shooting pool. There's about 30–45 minutes until the show is scheduled to start, so I assume they're here killing time and just hanging out . . . I have my notebook with me, and have taken a few notes already. But then it dawns on me—sitting at this mostly empty bar, conducting fieldwork here early on in my study, marks me as an obvious outsider. I decide to put my notebook away, and tuck it into the inside pocket of my jacket. Besides, my pen was starting to run out of ink anyway. I wait until after the show to head back to my office on campus, where I type up everything I can remember from this night.

(February 9, 2010)

I had a nice talk with Ryan before tonight's show. We started by discussing one of Mike's bits he's been working on the past few weeks. It's a routine about Hot Box Cookies, a late-night cookie shop that also delivers. I learn from Ryan that many of the other comics who perform at Helter Skelter don't care too much for Mike. Ryan says it's mostly because Mike comes off as unaware of his own performance. I get the sense that Ryan is making a comment about authenticity. Many of the other comics are now here, hanging out. No audience members just yet. Lots of what I am calling "shop talk"—comics talking about a joke they've been working on, what they think they need to do differently tonight for it to land better, etc . . . Ryan sits in the booth with me before the show starts. We continue to talk comedy in between the acts. He mentions, unprompted, that he thinks there are similarities between comedians and sociologists, an observation

DOI: 10.4324/9781003275121-14

> the sociologist Murray Davis also makes. Ryan mentions some of the comedians whose work he admires—Murphy, Pryor, Seinfeld, even Lenny Bruce. Ryan tells me he hopes he becomes a well-known comic one day, but more importantly he wants to be well respected. I get the sense in talking to him tonight that comedy is a craft for him, something he takes very seriously. I learned Ryan interned with The Daily Show this past summer. He talks about the internship as game-changing for him, both in terms of working on the popular television show and also the opportunity to live in New York City. As the show gets ready to start, Ryan brings over a young woman named Marina, and introduces her to me. Marina is Ryan's ex-girlfriend, and also a comic who plays here at Helter Skelter. Looking around the room, most of the audience members are comics, or close friends of the comics. I get the sense that there is an underground scene of standup comedy in this town, and much of it is here tonight.
>
> February 23, 2010

In 2010, I began conducting fieldwork across three urban nightlife scenes in the same medium-size Midwestern city: The Comedy Kitchen, a professional comedy club with a nightclub on its ground floor; La Maison De Soleil Levant (MDSL), an LGBTQ nightclub that hosted a popular drag revue each Thursday; and Helter Skelter a self-identified punk rock/horror/sci-fi bar that hosted an amateur comedy show each Tuesday. My original purpose was to better understand whether and how stand-up comedy contributes to the production of contentious politics.

The city in which I conducted my fieldwork has a rich history as a key stop for professional comics touring the Midwest. Moreover, at the time of my fieldwork Helter Skelter was a key site for the emergence of an active amateur scene. I had the benefit of having worked for several years at The Comedy Kitchen—the professional comedy club in town. First as a doorman, and then as a bartender. I knew most of the major acts who toured the Midwest, and some of them knew me. Yet I had almost no familiarity with the amateur scene, save for an existing relationship with Ryan, who also worked at The Comedy Kitchen. Through Ryan, I came to know the scene at Helter Skelter quite well, and those who played within it.

The previous epigraphs are drawn from my fieldnotes at Helter Skelter, fieldnotes which I still have saved to a hard drive. They're intended to reveal to you, the reader, those early trips to the field where I was still learning the "rules to the game," so to speak. Even so, as I look back upon those notes, my shift from an outsider's perspective to one increasingly on the inside is more obvious today than it was at the time I wrote those notes. In comparison to the first excerpt, the second shows that after just a few weeks I had begun to gain entry into the amateur stand-up comedy scene of Helter Skelter, meeting new comics like Marina, learning more about how comics like Ryan think about their craft, and getting a feel for the interaction order of the amateur stand-up scene (Duck & Keifer, 2019; Goffman, 1983).

As any seasoned ethnographer will tell you, this shift is an important one. Among at least one ethnographic tradition this shift is something like a rite of passage, taken as proof that not only have you come to know your site and subjects of study well but that those under study have begun to accept you as one of their own. You now have, in a word, membership (Adler & Adler, 1987). My aim in this essay is to trouble at least some parts of that perspective. I am not so interested in describing or explaining how an ethnographer-in-training makes this shift. There are several methodological texts and handbooks that explain this quite well (e.g., Becker, 1998; Emerson, 2011; Hammersley & Atkinson, 2019; Maanen, 2011). Rather, I'm interested in troubling the idea of the *shift*, itself. Put differently, I want to consider the following questions: What *is* the nature of the changing relationship of the ethnographer to the field? How does this relationship shift, and in response to what field-based conditions and concerns?

To answer these questions, I draw upon two different examples from my own fieldwork: my ethnographic study of urban nightlife venues (Thomas, 2015a, 2015b) and my ethnographic study of a public university's efforts to define, organize, and put into practice its campus-wide diversity initiative (Thomas, 2018, 2020). In reflecting back upon these two projects, and the orienting questions earlier, I scaffold Adler and Peter's (1987) typology of membership roles in ethnographic fieldwork with the sociological concept of *going concerns* (Hughes, 1962, 1971) as a way to better whether, why, and how we negotiate our membership roles in situ. My aim, then, is to draw our attention toward the more practical and contingent features of ethnographic fieldwork that, like a rocky terrain, we must traverse.

Membership Roles in Ethnographic Fieldwork

Students of the trade know well how far ethnography has come as both method and perspective. Henrika Kuklick (1997, p. 47), for example, shows that the tradition of fieldwork was, in the beginning, tethered to a Victorian-era set of beliefs that "personal growth (of an implicitly masculine sort) could be effected through pilgrimages to unfamiliar places, where the European traveler endured physical discomfort and (genuine or imagined) danger." Similarly, Lisa Wedeen (2009, p. 75) argues that ethnography has historically been considered a practice of suffering. The ethnographer, believing that culture is something that exists above and apart from where they reside, travels to some distant there to observe what they cannot possibly imagine as residing in the space they call here.

Yes, indeed, ethnography has come a long way. Today, there is general agreement that culture is not just *there*, but everywhere. And, there is if not consensus at least a strong belief that wherever and whatever *here* might be to the participant observer, it is as worthy of study as anywhere else. This shift in where the ethnographer turns their gaze has also resulted in a shift in how we, ethnographers, think about our membership within the field of study. By the 1940s, the distance between *here* and *there* shrank as the famed Chicago School had established its host city as a "backyard" for social scientific observation and analysis. And yet, Chicago School traditionalists remained deeply committed to a distant, so-called objective ethnographic gaze. Adler and Peter (1987) contrast the Chicago School's ethnographic tradition with what they understood at the time as the growing California School tradition of existentialist and ethnomethodological fieldwork. Unlike its Midwestern counterpart, the California School tradition viewed the researcher not as detached from the field under study but as deeply embedded, even co-constitutive of its cultural life (see Adler & Peter, 1987).

The Adlers, in an attempt to link the California and Chicago systems of thought without dismissing the latter for the former, put forward a useful framework through which to understand how the ethnographer's position within the field shifts, over time, as the conceptual (even if falsely conceived) distance between *here* and *there* shrinks if not altogether vanishes. Their framework is delightfully simple, consisting of three primary relationships to the field: peripheral, active, and complete membership. *Peripheral membership* involves frequent contact and may perhaps involve close relationships with some of the key actors within the setting under study. *Active membership* involves taking on a more central, even functional role, within the place under observation. The Adlers viewed active membership as one in which trust and acceptance are greater, but that this can prove challenging for the ethnographer who, they argue, must develop increasing reflexivity and awareness so as not to jeopardize their primary role as a researcher. Finally, and as the term implies *complete membership* entails full immersion, including the ethnographer themselves becoming the object of study.

View From the Field: Urban Nightlife

My own study of urban nightlife offers a unique way of viewing each of these membership roles independently, as well as in relationship to one another. My research, taking place from 2009 through 2011, was comparative by design. I set out to study three distinct nightlife venues in the same city, each offering a qualitatively different environment for the production of stand-up comedy.

When I first began my ethnographic study, my membership role varied between each venue. At the time I set out to conduct fieldwork, I had been employed at The Comedy Kitchen for some 8 years. Aside from the general manager and the head bartender, I was its longest tenured employee. I was well liked and well respected among the staff, had great rapport with many of the regulars who frequented the comedy show and downstairs nightclub on the weekends, and knew many of the comics who performed semi-regularly throughout the year. Moreover, I had institutional memory and direct knowledge of the rules, regulations, and organizational structure of the establishment. This afforded me a unique perspective on the goings-on of The Comedy Kitchen and allowed me even greater access to conversations among staff and management that I would not have had if I began my fieldwork with a more peripheral role.

Consider, for example, the following account from fieldwork at The Comedy Kitchen:

> Around 9:35pm, Ryan introduces John, a feature comedian from Saint Louis, Missouri. The first few bits in John's set focus on women and women's bodies. He talks about getting his girlfriend into "fun-size" shape, for example. He then segues into a bit about trying to get laid, and follows that up with a bit on basketball players trying to hook up with "White chicks". The crowd reacts a bit mixed to this joke—there is some laughter, but also audible groans. John draws attention to the mixed response, almost like he enjoys it. He decides to push the material further by telling the crowd, "Oh come on, you know it was White chicks who gave Magic Johnson HIV." I notice in this bit that the race of the basketball players is never stated, but clearly implied, by both John and the audience—if who basketball players are hooking up with are White chicks, the implication is that the players are Black. This is partly why the joke has an effect. Around 9:50 p.m., there's a problem with the microphone that breaks John's set up a bit. The energy of the room shifts, and there are more table conversations. One of the tables in front of me is beginning to speak really loudly. If I were working tonight, I'd say something. I consider letting some of the door staff know, but decide against it because I want to be a fly on the all and don't want to interfere directly with anything happening in the room.
>
> *February 4, 2010*

As I review my notes today, I am especially drawn to how they compare and contrast with those from Helter Skelter at the beginning of this essay. At Helter Skelter, I describe myself as very aware of my role as a field researcher at that moment. I even make the active decision to put away my field notebook so that I don't draw too much attention to myself. At the same time, I make a note to myself that I need to return to my office as soon as I leave Helter Skelter so that I can recall everything that happened.

At The Comedy Kitchen, I do not seem to have that same problem. I know the scene, and the people working within. I also know the rules and norms that govern behaviors during the comedy show. I'm not just ethnographically aware of the interaction order of The Comedy Kitchen—I'm a key part of it! When I notice a group of audience members talking loudly during a show, I have to remind myself to remain in my role as a researcher, rather than an employee or someone who knows the scene well enough to ask staff at The Comedy Kitchen to intervene. I'm able to describe what is happening, and why it is happening, because even upon entrée I already have a certain knowledge of the field.

Compare this to my role at Helter Skelter. Here, I had some knowledge of the bar and its staff from my time spent working in what many of us within referred to as "the industry"—the larger nightlife scene in this Midwestern city. I also knew some of the key actors responsible for organizing and producing the weekly amateur show. Ryan, as I mentioned earlier, also worked at The Comedy Kitchen. So did Kyle, who also performed at Helter Skelter and occasionally helped out with setting the schedule of performances on amateur night. My relationship with Ryan, Kyle, and a handful of others helped me get my foot in the door, so to speak. I did not have direct knowledge of the organization of the show, its aims and goals, and several of its key players. But I had what we might think of as weak ties to the amateur comedy show and its members (see Granovetter, 1973). More importantly, I understood how to pull on those ties as I remained in the field in order to learn more about the cultural order of Helter Skelter's amateur night. I was, even at the beginning, an active member in this setting.

Finally, my third fieldwork site of MDSL represented a setting to which I had few if any close connections at the onset. I had only been to one drag performance at MDSL prior to the beginning of my fieldwork, and that was some 5 years prior. I had no firsthand knowledge of any of the drag performers and knew very few of the staff who worked there. I had some familiarity with the owner, as he occasionally frequented both The Comedy Kitchen and another bar and nightclub where I was employed. This familiarity allowed me to gain initial permission to study MDSL as part of my dissertation, and thanks to the generosity of the owner I was usually reserved a seat at the show, near the bar to the side of the stage.

The Adlers understood that the more time an ethnographer spends in their setting getting to know the people and places within, the more likely those relationships change. Relationships become more intimate, ties become stronger, and cultural knowledge of the field and its actors deepens. So, having identified the types of membership I had at the onset of my fieldwork, it's worth asking, *when and whether should a researcher's membership role in the field change? And in response to what conditions?* The Adlers noted several factors that affect a researcher's membership role and its maintenance during fieldwork, including the initial conditions of the setting, and the individual abilities, perspectives, and characteristics of the researcher themselves.

To put this in sharp relief, consider Kathleen Blee's (2003) study of women within the white supremacist movement. Though Blee's primary source of data for this study was life history interviews with women who held some role, informal or formal, within the white supremacist movement, Blee does incorporate some ethnographic fieldwork including attending gatherings and events sponsored by racist groups (Blee, 2003, p. 204). Blee herself holds views that are in direct contrast to those espoused by the women she studied. You might imagine, then, that to gain access to these women, and to the events and gatherings Blee attended, she needed to minimize in some way her own personal politics. Moreover, Blee needed to convince those within the racist organizations and networks she was interested in studying that she was not "running game," so to speak; that she was not feeding the information provided by her participants to law enforcement, or criminal prosecutors (Blee, 2003, p. 200). We can say with some confidence, then, that Blee's relationship with the racist organizations and the women within them remained peripheral over the course of her study, though the interview data makes clear Blee gained a high degree of trust among these women despite their initial skepticism of her and her study.

Kathleen Blee's membership role is made even more complicated by the fact that her initial efforts to maintain confidentiality and safeguard her participants' identities so as not to run the risk of exposing them to criminal liability was actually a point of contention among the women she studied. As she writes,

> Rather than seeking assurances that their identities would be obscured, they argued that the interviewing consent form be changed to require me to use their actual names in any publication. (I declined to do so, fearing that this could provide additional recruits to organized racism) . . . In this case, confidentiality was imposed to support the academic and political goals of the researcher, against the expressed interest and desires of the informants.
>
> *(Blee, 1999, p. 995)*

What Blee's methodological reflections reveal are what we might refer to as some of the *going concerns* of ethnographic fieldwork that arise as our membership roles are actively negotiated, sometimes contested. It is to this particular matter that we now turn.

Going Concerns in Fieldwork

The late Everett Hughes coined the concept *going concerns* as a means of illuminating the dynamic, even contested, nature of organizational life. Hughes aimed to show us that, rather than static entities that exist above and beyond the actors within them, organizations are ongoing practical endeavors, shaped by an active core of people, and "the social definition of how and when they act" (Hughes, 1962, see also 1971). As Gubrium and Holstein (2000, p. 102) note, the concept points us toward the active, discursive quality of organizational life, "an ongoing commitment to a particular moral order, a way of being who and what we are in relation to the immediate scheme of things."

While Hughes's original concept refers to the scenes under which we turn our ethnographic attention, what I want us to consider here are the *going concerns* of ethnography-as-practice. For several decades, methodological debates have given great consideration to the fact that when an ethnographer enters into the field, they then become a part of that which they study. This shapes what happens in the field, and subsequently the kind of knowledge and understanding ethnographers produce from their engagement among actors within it. The Adlers' typology of membership roles, described earlier, is a useful way of thinking about the distinctions between the researcher's role in the field, and the relationships they create and maintain with the social actors under study. Elsewhere, feminist research and criticism have further interrogated those relationships by way of standpoint theory and cultural critique (e.g., Clough, 1998; Naples & Gurr, 2013). Indeed, my own positionality as a White man does, at minimum, provide initial access to the kinds of bars and clubs I studied where race, class, and gender are not only principal organizing features of the interaction order within but also themselves tightly managed for the purposes of reproducing particular raced, classed, and gendered experiences (see Thomas, 2015a, 2015b).

Nevertheless, how those membership roles themselves constitute a "going concern" during fieldwork remains an area ripe for further debate and discussion. From a practical perspective, it's worth considering what the "going concerns" of our membership roles are, in the field. How are these negotiated, how do they change, and in response to what particular set of conditions?

View From the Field: Diversity Regimes

In 2014, I began an ethnographic study of a large, southern university, and its ongoing efforts to define, organize, and implement a campus-wide diversity initiative. I referred to this university as Diversity University (DU), not necessarily because I was interested in cloaking my site of study in any secrecy but more so because I wanted to draw attention to how, at least in appearance, this particular university was making a public commitment to a particular kind of moral order about the kind of organization that it is, or trying to become at least.

In the beginning, I had a peripheral membership role to the field. I did not know much about the university's diversity initiative, only that the university talked about it all the time. I also did not know many of the actors involved in producing the university's public commitment to diversity, or what work in which they were engaged behind closed doors to put this commitment into practice.

To begin, I started by attending events on campus that were in some way aligned, at least through campus advertising, with the university's diversity efforts. As an audience member, I not only took notes but also participated by asking questions of panelists, staying afterward to engage speakers and other members of the audience, and trying to get a sense of who is involved, and how do they think about their events and activities within the larger campus-wide initiative. I have research interests in the study of race, racism, and inequality, and found that sharing my expertise in these events was welcomed by many. After attending several of these events and making a point to participate as an audience member, I received my first of several invitations to participate in an event as a panelist.

With regard to membership roles, mine was clearly changing! My being asked to participate in a diversity-related event on campus indicated that I was developing a more functional role within the very initiative I was studying. I was being shown greater trust and acceptance. All signs of an emergent *active* membership role in the field. At the same time, I was also becoming part—albeit, at least initially a, small part—of an active core of people shaping the social definition of diversity, contributing to its discursive quality within DU. Put differently, I was increasingly becoming part of the *going concerns* that I was interested in studying.

To some, this methodological dilemma simply indicates a greater level of immersion in the field, and ought to be met simply with increasing reflexivity and awareness so as not to jeopardize my primary responsibility as a researcher. This, however, is too vague. I certainly wrote memos about my shifting role, indicating reflexivity and awareness. Yet in the field, we have to negotiate these shifts in real time.

In my own work, I made the decision to participate in events and activities when asked. This allowed me greater access to the organizational processes I was most interested in understanding. It also gave me more opportunities to get to know the key actors involved and helped recruit people with whom I wanted to speak, in-depth. Importantly, I would argue my decision to shift my membership role within this research—to become more actively involved in the activities that structured the diversity initiative I was studying—helped me to better understand the kinds of negotiations that other actors were having to make as they worked through the *going concerns* of diversity work.

One of the women with whom I got to know and speak with during my fieldwork was Ella, a Black woman who had been employed at DU for over two decades, and at the time held an administrative position within the Office of Student Affairs. At the time of our interview, in 2014, Ella was the highest-ranking Black woman in Student Affairs. Having worked at DU for some time, Ella had seen multiple changes in leadership—not just in her own office but within the executive cabinet of the University. With each of these changes, there was a discursive shift in the kind of work she was asked to do. In the following, she explains:

Me: "So tell me, what do you do on campus, like what is your role and what does it involve?"

Ella: "Well my role has changed in the last, since April. Currently I am associate dean of students. It's a director's level position so I answer directly to the Vice Chancellor's office. And I supervise a staff for fraternity and sorority life, for leadership development, for civic engagement and for students of concern. So students who are dealing with crises whether that is substance abuse, homesickness, debt, it just. It runs a gamut. Prior to that I served as assistant dean of students for Multicultural Affairs and volunteer services for nearly 14 years, at one point, it was the coordinator, then I was promoted to the "assistant dean." In that role I was advisor to pretty much every African American student organization on campus along with the African Caribbean student association and the International Student Organization at one point. Mostly any under-represented group would find me first until I found them another home."

Notice how Ella identifies a whole host of responsibilities in her position, including crisis management. She also implies (and later clarifies) that in her previous position in multicultural affairs, she became the go-to person for any non-White student organization seeking guidance or an advisor. As we continued to talk, Ella spoke about how her position and responsibilities changed over time, and in response to the *going concerns* within her own office:

Me: "So it was a coordinator position before it was the assistant dean position?"

Ella: "It was actually a graduate assistant position that I was in prior to that. It was the coordinator's position and then it was assistant dean position, but there are two areas attached to the Assistant Dean's position. Before that, the person who had Multicultural Affairs on his title was over Student Conduct. So for several years prior to me, it was attached onto some position, but the position hasn't always been named the same. It might be assistant dean, sometimes it was graduate assistant it just kind of moved around. And when I took it, I stayed here too long maybe? So it stayed with my position as it changed through the years."

Me: "And as it changed, did it change in response to things that you were kind of pushing for in the role that you were in? Or was it about more general university changes?"

Ella: "I think a little bit of both, I think probably some of what I was doing was facilitating the change or at least . . . in the appearance that there was a need for a person to be present on a full-time basis. And also the students were pushing it. I don't know that it was me as much as students saying we need somebody. Because even as a GA I remember being here far longer than a full-time person would be here in terms of hours in a day. So I think that the individual who was my supervisor at that time recognized that position, that there needed to be a full time person. It may be too that he didn't want it back on his title. So we kind of went through a transition. A new dean of students came in. That was Clark. And the person who was my supervisor before Clark said, "We need to hire Ella full time." And that's how it became a full-time position. I think the assistant dean of student's title to it was certainly more so connected to the work that I had done. I do think there was a level of work after I was in that position for a while that was deserving of an Assistant Dean title. Our student body grew, so the time commitment was necessary. The other political piece was that there were three coordinators and there was an Assistant Dean's position open, and I was probably in line for the other Assistant Dean's position but just to keep things in a good space, the supervisor had promoted *everybody* to assistant dean of students. So, instead of moving me into an Assistant Dean's position in this area where there might have been some uncomfortableness—that's my personal opinion, I think people would agree with me—he just made everybody who was a coordinator an assistant dean."

As Ella indicates, her title in part shifted as she and some students advocated for a position within Student Affairs that would be responsible for non-White student groups and crisis management. I asked Ella if she could explain a bit more about what she meant when she indicated that everybody received a promotion so as to avoid discomfort in the office.

Ella: "I think traditionally that area has been run by a man, for one. And two, I think that—my personal opinion is that—my advocacy for African-American students contributed to the idea that I might not be trusted with that kind of work."

Notice the rub here. On the one hand, there is a growing recognition that *someone* needs to be responsible for Black student organizations on campus who are increasingly more visible due to both demographic shifts in the student body and the university's own public commitment to diversity and inclusion. Yet Ella perceived that in taking on this responsibility she became *less* trusted by her peers. What work, then, is the commitment to diversity actually doing in this context? How is Ella having to actively negotiate her own role not only within the university's campus-wide diversity initiative but also within the more local context of the unit in which she works? These questions became increasingly more salient for me as I, myself, began to negotiate the shifting conditions of my membership role in the field, and as a result began to better understand the conflicts and contingencies involved in defining diversity, and putting it into practice.

Elsewhere, Gubrium and Holstein (2000, pp. 103–104) use the term *discursive environments* to draw our attention toward the "interactional domains characterized by distinctive ways of interpreting and representing everyday realities." Discursive environments, they argue, set the "conditions of possibility" for ourselves and how we put ourselves into action with one another. Discursive environments are of course not static but dynamic. They are fraught with *going concerns*, so that the conditions of possibility are constantly expanding and contracting as actors wrestle with how to define and organize their everyday realities.

My interview with Ella helped put all of this in sharp relief for me. I had noticed in my fieldwork that the terms "diversity" and "inclusion" were increasingly coupled together, especially by senior leadership at DU. Anytime diversity was mentioned, so was inclusion, and without much explanation as to what was meant by either term. I asked Ella what she thought about all of this:

Ella: "You know, for the longest people used to tell me diversity was a bad word here. I've been told that in meetings with upper-level administration, "Don't say diversity, it makes people uncomfortable." I was told to use "bridge builders" one year instead of saying diversity. So, no. I don't think we have a good understanding of that word, or appreciation for that word on our campus. I don't want to say we fear it, but we are very uncomfortable with it and we work very hard to come up with something different. So the co-mingling happens because it is the word. We've got to use it somehow, so I think our way of coping with it as a campus is to co-mingle it

> with something that sounds better. More positive. Less controversial, less confrontational. No hierarchy in it. So inclusivity, you know, like kumbaya, flowers, balloons, whatever you feel. Like nice soft grass."

Ella's perspective, especially her identification of the active contestation over what kinds of words the university prefers when describing its diversity initiative, was clarifying for me as I continued with my fieldwork over the next few years. She helped me to better hone in on the conflicts and contingencies associated with diversity work, especially as I myself became more involved in that work at DU. I began to better recognize, understand, and even appreciate my own role in the conflicts and contingencies surrounding how diversity is defined, organized, and put into practice. For example, as I became a more active participant in DU's diversity-related programming, and in conversations about DU's diversity initiative, I noticed that I was becoming more skeptical, even cynical, of the work I and others were doing.

This observation presented me with a dilemma, or a set of questions that I needed to actively wrestle with: *is my skepticism a barrier to my researcher's role, or byproduct of that role? Could it be both?* The more immersed I became, and as my membership role shifted from that of a peripheral member to an active member in the field I studied, the *going concerns* of diversity work at DU became, in many ways, my own. This acknowledgment is not meant to be taken as normative. I do not view this development as good or bad. Rather, it is part and parcel of the ethnographic trade.

We are often trained, as ethnographers, to remain skeptical of our surroundings; to not accept what we see and hear at face value. At the same time, we are trained to build rapport and trust, to engage with the people and places we are studying, so that we can better understand how they make sense of themselves in situ. In my case, however, the skepticism Ella described and I began to experience seemed to be a kind of epistemological orientation that develops from engaging in diversity work. The aim is less to separate one kind of skepticism from another, but rather to recognize when and how they arise, and from what conditions.

Conclusion

In reading debates surrounding ethnographic methods and discussions I'm often left frustrated, longing for something more than simply a rote recommendation to remain reflexive; or to simply acknowledge ourselves in the research process. Is that really all that is required of us? A simple statement that we, too, are social actors, capable of self-reflection? This does little to dispel a popular, yet false, claim that ethnography is a vanity project. In this essay, then, I've tried to put more flesh to bone to these oft-given recommendations by reflecting upon my own experiences in conducting two distinct ethnographic projects: a study of urban nightlife venues and a study of a university's ongoing diversity initiative.

In reflecting upon these two ethnographic projects, I've drawn from my fieldwork in order to identify some of the more practical issues that rise when conducting ethnographic research, and also show how these issues are negotiated in real time within a given field setting. My emphasis has been on how the ethnographer's membership role, including the shifts to that role, produces a kind of *going concerns* that we must negotiate in real time. The aim here is not necessarily to generalize my negotiations in my fieldwork to all other settings, though I do not think the conflicts and contingencies I noted in my own previous work are at all unique or special cases. Rather, my aim has been, as I stated in the introduction, to trouble the notion of the *shift*, itself.

In a recent and deeply important critique of ethnographic methodology, Rebecca Hanson and Patricia Richards (2019) argue that traditional "ethnographic fixations" on solitude, intimacy, and even danger encourage practitioners to endure various forms of violence in the field. These fixations, they argue, not only put researchers at risk but also affect how ethnographic knowledge is constructed in the first place. Without minimizing or ignoring Hanson and Richards' larger point that traditional values around intimacy and danger can lead to various forms of harassment and violence in the field, I want to draw our attention for the moment toward the other significant point they make about the construction of ethnographic knowledge.

As Hanson and Richards (2019, p. 4) note, we often think of our fieldwork as an amorphous or dual workplace. Our *doing f*ieldwork is what makes us legible, to one another at least, as social scientists. At the same time, what we do in the field is shaped by scholarly norms, rules, values, and expectations. What we do in the field is also shaped by the norms, rules, values, and expectations of the social settings that we study. As you might imagine, these sets of norms, rules, values, and expectations are not at all congruent. Indeed, they often come into conflict with one another. As a result, we often feel pressured to resolve this pressure through how we produce ethnographic knowledge. We write ourselves out of our studies, because scholarly standards often demand the voice of a distant observer. We frame our fieldwork as a linear movement from naive but curious researcher to all-knowing cultural commentator. This, of course, obfuscates ethnography as practice; not just how we collect our data or what we do with it but also *what* that data even is in the first place (Hanson & Richards, 2019, p. 14).

By drawing our attention toward the *going concerns* of ethnographic membership, my hope here is to better position ourselves as ethnographers of our own trade. To better see and understand what we do in the field as a set of practical negotiations meant to, on the one hand, preserve a critical relationship between ourselves and the fields toward which we turn our gaze, while also not losing sight of the fact that whenever and how we enter into a field, and begin to interact with the people within it, we are indeed shaping its discursive environments. We do not just document the "conditions of possibility" among social actors; we help negotiate them as we seek to understand them. Our task is not to avoid this, or to treat it as an affront on the altar of objectivity. Rather, our task is to account for ourselves, our actions and interactions, as much and as well as we account for the places, people, and "goings-on" that draw us to fieldwork-as-practice in the first place.

Note

1 All names provided are pseudonyms.

References

Adler, P. A., & Peter, A. (1987). *Membership roles in field research*. Sage.

Becker, H. S. (1998). *Tricks of the trade: How to think about your research while you're doing it*. University of Chicago Press.

Blee, K. M. (1999). The perils of privilege. *Law & Social Inquiry*, *24*(4), 993–997.

Blee, K. M. (2003). *Inside organized racism: Women in the hate movement*. University of California Press.

Clough, P. T. (1998). *The end(s) of ethnography: From realism to social criticism* (2nd ed.). Peter Lang Inc.

Duck, W., & Keifer, M. (2019). Interaction order as cultural sociology within urban ethnography. In *Urban ethnography research in urban sociology* (Vol. 16, pp. 113–130). Emerald Publishing Limited.

Emerson, R. M. (2011). *Writing ethnographic fieldnotes* (2nd ed.). University of Chicago Press.

Goffman, E. (1983). The interaction order: American sociological association, 1982 presidential address. *American Sociological Review*, *48*(1), 1–17.

Granovetter, M. S. (1973). The strength of weak ties. *American Journal of Sociology*, *78*(6), 1360–1380.

Gubrium, J. F., & Holstein, J. A. (2000). The self in a world of going concerns. *Symbolic Interaction*, *23*(2), 95–115.

Hammersley, M., & Atkinson, P. (2019). *Ethnography: Principles in practice* (4th ed.). Routledge.

Hanson, R., & Richards, P. (2019). *Harassed*. University of California Press.

Hughes, E. C. (1962). Good people and dirty work. *Social Problems*, *10*, 3–11.

Hughes, E. C. (1971). Going concerns: The study of American institutions. In *The sociological eye: Selected papers on institution and race (Part I) and self and the study of society (Part II)* (pp. 52–64). Aldine Atherton.

Kuklick, H. (1997). After Ishmael: The fieldwork tradition and its future. In J. Ferguson & A. Gupta (Eds.), *Anthropological locations: Boundaries and grounds of a field science*. University of California Press.

Maanen, J. V. (2011). *Tales of the field: On writing ethnography* (2nd ed.). University of Chicago Press.

Naples, N. A., & Gurr, B. (2013). Feminist empiricism and standpoint theory: Approaches to understanding the social world. In S. N. Hesse-Biber (Ed.), *Feminist research practices: A primer* (pp. 14–41). Sage.

Thomas, J. M. (2015a). Laugh through it: Assembling difference in an American stand-up comedy club. *Ethnography*, *16*(2), 166–186.

Thomas, J. M. (2015b). *Working to laugh: Assembling difference in American stand-up comedy venues*. Lexington Books.

Thomas, J. M. (2018). Diversity regimes and racial inequality: A case study of diversity university. *Social Currents*, *5*(2), 140–156.

Thomas, J. M. (2020). *Diversity regimes: Why talk is not enough to fix racial inequality at universities*. Rutgers University Press.

Wedeen, L. (2009). Ethnography as interpretive enterprise. In E. Schatz (Ed.), *Political ethnography: What immersion contributes to the study of power*. University of Chicago Press.

11

WHEN FIELDWORK COMES HOME

Beatriz Reyes-Foster and Shannon K. Carter

Those who have never fed human milk to a baby may not know that it separates. Left standing, the creamy white fat rises to the top and a thin watery substance remains beneath. Many first-time parents have mistakenly thrown out perfectly good milk because they did not know this. Current breast milk science suggests the milk should be swirled, not shaken, to combine the fatty and liquid parts while not breaking down the nutrients. Some milk, when frozen, takes on the smell of soap. This milk has higher lipase and, though it is perfectly healthy for infants to drink, some do not prefer it. Breast milk comes in different colors, ranging from creamy white to a bluish hue to various shades of yellow. Some people produce fattier milk than others, and the same persons produce milk that varies in fat content, antibodies, and analgesic properties, depending on the needs of the child they are feeding. Milk is a surprising substance that is biologically and, as this chapter will show, socially complex.

Human breast milk is at the same time very organized and also very messy. Milk itself is organized, as indicated through scientific research, and the social practices surrounding milk are organized too. Routines are created around expressing and storing milk. It is placed in carefully labeled storage bags, and entire organizational systems are developed around producing, handling, and freezing it. Some users purchase freezers dedicated solely to the storage of human milk. Those who engage in sharing breast milk follow a set of strict spoken and unspoken rules that guide the practice. At the same time, milk is messy. It leaks from human bodies and from plastic storage bags. It spills. It stains. It makes users happy, and it makes them cry. Human milk is organized and messy in much the same way that ethnographic fieldwork is organized and messy.

This chapter explores an ethnographic engagement with peer human milk sharing communities. We define peer human milk sharing as the gifting of human milk from one person to another with the intent of feeding a child (Carter &

DOI: 10.4324/9781003275121-15

Reyes-Foster, 2020a). We studied human milk sharing practices through an ethnographic study that spanned at least 4 years. During that time, we organized and attended numerous breastfeeding and milk sharing community events, participated in breastfeeding support groups, talked with participants and their maternity care providers about breastfeeding and milk sharing, became members of online breastfeeding and milk sharing communities, and volunteered at numerous outreach events and the local milk bank. At the same time, we also were breastfeeding mothers ourselves, and we both engaged in sharing milk, Shannon as a donor, and Beatriz as a recipient.

Our ethnographic approach was framed by feminist actor-network ethnography (Carter & Reyes-Foster, 2020a, 2020b). Feminist actor-network ethnography (FANE) brings together the material-semiotic approach of actor-network theory (Law, 2009; Latour, 2005) with a feminist lens attentive to how intersectional systems of power manifest materially and symbolically in people's everyday lives (Davis & Craven, 2022). As feminist ethnographers, we combined research on breastfeeding and milk sharing with outreach work that advocated a pro-breastfeeding stance, providing support and empowerment to the participants we engaged with. While we recognize and critique the ways in which pro-breastfeeding discourse has been utilized to shame people who cannot feed their babies breastmilk, we also recognize the structural and institutional constraints that make breastfeeding inaccessible to many parents. We support every parent's right to make decisions about what they feed their infant. Our work aimed to understand and alleviate constraints for people who wished to feed their babies human milk without judging parents' preferences or circumstances. As feminist actor-network ethnographers (Carter & Reyes-Foster, 2020b), we went a step further to become embodied participants, engaged biologically with the communities we studied through our participation in the sharing of human milk. In what follows, we reflect on our fieldwork experiences through an analytic sense of ethnography as embodied practice and by examining the related problem of "extractivism" in ethnographic work.

From Malinowski to Home and Beyond

From the time of pioneering anthropologist Bronislaw Malinowski, ethnography has typically been understood to require rather stringent procedural distinctions: the ethnographer initially departs home for "the field" somewhere, remains there for a finite amount of time collecting data, and only writing up results upon returning home. Volumes have been written about the now rather naïve separation of ethnographic practice into steps of "separation," "rapport," "re-integration," and the like. With the publication of Malinowski's diary (1967), it became clear that some of the underlying assumptions about traditional ethnography, most notably the ideas of objectivity, dispassionate observation, and intellectual separation from the people we study, had always been based on an ideal more than a reality. Fieldwork was always messier than Malinowski's classic book *Argonauts of the*

Western Pacific would have us believe. Nevertheless, for us, part of the messiness of fieldwork in practice lay in the fact that we never left for the field. "The field" was our home community. Our professional and personal lives and responsibilities did not stop because we left for the field, but rather, the field—the human milk sharing communities with which we engaged for over 4 years—became integrated into our daily lives. Like other ethnographers, we became part of the community we were studying. However, in traditional ethnography, there is a clear boundary for when data collection begins and ends, demarcated geographically and temporally. For us, this boundary was unclear. We never arrived, and we never really left.

Today, the traditional Malinowskian view of ethnography is becoming a thing of the past as sociologists and anthropologists conduct research closer to home. The increasing diversity of those in PhD programs who are becoming sociologists and anthropologists has created a need to reimagine what fieldwork is and where people must go to do it. Increased diversity also means that new sociologists and anthropologists have a diverse set of resources and responsibilities that may make extended fieldwork abroad impossible. Ongoing conversations in both disciplines have also raised concerns over the disciplines' roles in perpetuating colonialism and being complicit in white supremacy (Smith, 2012; Simpson, 2014; Burman, 2018), when sending White researchers to work with Indigenous and other historically oppressed populations both in and out of the United States. Finally, in the context of the COVID-19 pandemic, increased restrictions on travel have created new barriers to research abroad. This led to new and innovative uses of technology and expanding notions of what constitutes ethnography. At the same time, the emergence of online social worlds has widened sociological and anthropological understandings of what constitutes "the field."

At the same time, debates have emerged over the boundaries and limits of autoethnography (Anderson, 2006), auto-anthropology (Strathern, 1987), and reflexive autobiographical ethnography (Delamont, 2009), all of which turned ethnographic fieldwork to itself. Sara Delamont argues that in autoethnography, "there is *no* object except the author herself to study" (p. 58, emphasis in original). Through our own fieldwork experience, we became members of the communities we studied; we also lived and continue to reside, geographically, in our research location. However, because the focus of our work was on the social world of breastmilk sharing, not exclusively on our own experiences, our work falls under what Delamont (2009) refers to as reflexive autobiographical ethnography: the ethnographic focus of our work has always been a particular social phenomenon, milk sharing, or a particular methodological question. In this particular chapter, our interest is in analyzing and understanding the blurred boundaries which made the research possible, and the scholarly and analytical implications of this blurring, particularly as it pertains to the crafting of fieldwork itself. In other words, in our research on breastmilk sharing, we didn't go to the field, the field came to us.

After the birth of co-author Shannon K. Carter's second child, Ella, Shannon began attending a breastfeeding group at the birth center where she had given birth. Seeking to establish a community of mothers with similar parenting styles, she participated in the weekly discussions with topics covering breastfeeding positions, challenges and solutions to milk supply issues, breastfeeding in public, and much more. She established friendships with other attendees, fostered through playdates, beach trips, and participation in online social networking groups. She continued participation in the breastfeeding groups for several years, co-founding a nonprofit organization with other members of the groups, The Breastfeeding Project, which distributed breastfeeding educational materials and supplies to expectant parents in local communities. Through this position, she helped organize many events, including a "nurse-in" at a local Target after an employee asked a mother to stop breastfeeding in the store, and several "Big Latch On" events, which are annual international celebrations of breastfeeding.

These events and the corresponding social networks eventually transformed into fieldwork. Later, when co-author Beatriz Reyes-Foster joined the project, Shannon and Beatriz would drive all over our home base in Central Florida, tabling events, and handing out our primary product: a reusable grocery shopping bag containing a rice-filled warming and cooling compress, a folder full of information including free, local breastfeeding support groups and other resources, a water bottle, and coupons for various baby products (infant formula not included). These bags were our organization's answer to the bags of infant formula found at every local pediatrician's office and distributed to mothers at discharge after giving birth in hospitals. Other members of The Breastfeeding Project were involved as well, and our presence in the community attracted others to become involved. We held monthly social events which featured speakers who provided breastfeeding support and information.

It was in building this social community and engaging in breastfeeding activism ("lactivism") that Shannon encountered peer breastmilk sharing. The first instance was a heartbreaking encounter where a new attendee came to the breastfeeding group in tears because her baby was diagnosed as "failing to thrive" due to her low breastmilk supply. The support group leader and all the members offered comfort and various tactics to help increase her supply, but they were ineffective. A member, Chelsea, who became a friend and co-founder of The Breastfeeding Project, offered breastmilk she had stored in her freezer due to her oversupply. After a quick blood test, promptly administered at the birth center, the two established a milk sharing relationship that lasted almost a year. In another early encounter, a friend and co-founding member of The Breastfeeding Project collected breastmilk from everyone who had extra to give to a baby who was suffering due to low breastmilk supply. Although Shannon struggled to pump enough milk to meet her own daughter's needs while she was at work, she gave the 40 ounces in her freezer and committed to pumping extra over the weekend to replace it. Over the years of engaging in online and in person breastfeeding communities, peer milk sharing kept coming up.

Shannon and Beatriz met at a coffee shop on campus one day to talk about mutual research interests in reproduction and reproductive health. Beatriz, an anthropologist, had just returned from fieldwork in Mexico. She was expecting her second child and was interested in pursuing research that did not pull her away from her family. The conversation eventually led to human milk sharing. Beatriz, having struggled to breastfeed her first child, was intrigued. "You can do that?" was her initial reaction. Beatriz had already been establishing connections with the natural childbirth and breastfeeding communities that overlapped with Shannon's network. We each had one foot in the field. When we met, we decided to step into it together as researchers.

When the "Field" Is Home

Ten months later—a hot, muggy Florida morning in August 2014—Beatriz wiped sweat from her brow, pulled her infant out of his car seat, wrapped him to her body, and took her 5-year-old's hand. She walked into a church gymnasium. The place was dingy. Shannon had moved some old couches to line the far side of the gymnasium and rows of vendor tables filled the floor. A food vendor was setting up in the kitchen. Beatriz found Shannon, and together with the rest of the board members of The Breastfeeding Project, we quickly worked to prepare for the main event: the 2014 Big Latch On. The Global Big Latch On is an annual event which takes place over a 24-hour period during World Breastfeeding Week. The goal each year is to break the world record for the most babies to simultaneously latch on and breastfeed for 1 minute. The "latch on" event takes place at 10:30 am local time in countries around the world. The events themselves often last several hours, during which people gather together to offer peer support and gain public recognition for breastfeeding. An event with origins in New Zealand in 2005, the Big Latch On was first introduced to the United States in Portland in 2010, and by 2018, had expanded to 778 different locations with nearly 60,000 participants in attendance (including 21,500 latched children and 22,592 breastfeeding people). 2014 was the first year Beatriz both participated in and helped organize a Big Latch On event. The event in Daytona was Shannon's third Big Latch On.

Soon enough, vendors and mothers with infants and young children in tow started arriving. The vendors set up, selling essential oils, Lularoe, Scentsy, and all other manner of multi-level marketing products—many of the vendors were breastfeeding mothers themselves making extra money with a multi-level marketing business on the side. Some were artists selling their handcrafted jewelry and pottery, and others were small business owners who sold baby-related items such as cloth diapers and babywearing wraps. The mothers walked around, admiring the wares. Toddlers and young children played with the games and coloring wall that had been set up. Shannon and Nichole performed a puppet show they had written. A woman dressed up as the princess Rapunzel led the children in singing some songs and another painted butterflies on their faces. At 10:28 am, Shannon made the announcement: we were only 2 minutes away. Everyone with an infant or child to latch—including Shannon and Beatriz—got settled into a space, and at 10:30 am, 38 women latched their babies to their breast at the same time. The event was a joyful celebration of breastfeeding. It was also a stressful, difficult event to pull off.

The Breastfeeding Project and our involvement with the breastfeeding communities in Central Florida illustrate the blurred boundaries of our ethnographic approach. We were both breastfeeding mothers with a commitment to supporting and promoting breastfeeding. When we engaged in ethnographic fieldwork around human milk sharing, we were part of the communities we were studying, including participating in human milk sharing. Beatriz came to milk sharing after she had begun milk sharing research. When her second child, Rowan, was born, she soon found that despite an environment that was supportive of breastfeeding, after numerous meetings with lactation consultants, hundreds of dollars spent on supplements, and many needless calories consumed from "lactation cookies," she simply couldn't produce sufficient milk. Around that time, a woman in our community had given birth to a surrogate baby and had decided to donate her milk through a local milk sharing organization, Get Pumped! Having already spent time in the community, getting to know others who had used donor milk, Beatriz reached out to the woman and asked if she would be willing to share some of her milk. She immediately agreed and began setting aside 10 ounces of milk each day for Beatriz' child. Thanks to her generosity, Beatriz was able to keep feeding her son exclusively human milk for his first year of life. It also motivated her to continue breastfeeding, and she went on to breastfeed him for nearly 3 years—her longest and most satisfying breastfeeding relationship. Shannon donated her milk a few times, twice to people in her extended network who she did not know personally but knew they were in need, and once to a lesbian couple who were friends and colleagues. In this sense, our research was also embodied: for 4 years, motherhood, breastfeeding, and research became "intertwined."

The concept of intertwining, in our case that of motherhood, breastfeeding, and research, meant there were no boundaries between home and fieldwork. Fieldwork became like other forms of reproductive labor (Oakley, 1974; Glenn, 1992), which is never complete. Be it through the work of procuring and feeding milk, spending time sharing thoughts and advice in online communities, or engaging in the organizational volunteer work of the Breastfeeding Project, "research" became part of the mental load (Dean et al., 2022) and embodied labor we managed in our daily lives. (The related quotation marks flagged the working contours of method, the collapse of home and field.) The only semblance of a boundary between fieldwork and not fieldwork occurred when we came to the university, our formal work site, to engage in the more traditional academic labor of teaching, writing, and service. However, the many writing sessions we engaged in with Beatriz' infant in the office, taking breaks in order to care for him, or for Shannon or Beatriz to pump milk, illustrate how, even in more traditional forms of labor, those boundaries were blurred. One may wonder about the boundary work involved in carrying out a project such as this one. Like mothering, there were no boundaries, so there was no boundary work to be done.

In addition to the lack of boundaries in the community and at the university, much of the work in the field literally took place in our own homes. We hosted small gatherings to prepare for fundraising events for the Breastfeeding Project. We assembled breastfeeding support bags. We stored supplies. We held board of directors' meetings. Because everyone involved was a breastfeeding mother, this meant our children were present at these events, and the work of mothering, including breastfeeding and otherwise caring for our children, happened simultaneously with work related to our research. We built a community at the same time we studied it. At times, the work outlasted our friends' children's stamina, and work was left to be completed by our families: Shannon's husband and older child, Joshua, spent hours preparing items for fundraisers. Our fieldwork in our homes also took place in the quieter moments of family life: Beatriz and her family stored and fed donor milk to her child—one day, her spouse was dismayed when he accidentally spilled some donated milk on his hands. Shannon continued to pump and store milk for donation, and her spouse at times helped her deliver it.

Another aspect of our fieldwork that blurred boundaries between the field and home was our engagement in online breastfeeding communities. In these communities, we were active participants. We shared articles and other information, engaged in lively discussions, provided emotional support and advice to others who were struggling, and organized face-to-face events. These were hybrid communities that used online social networking as a tool for establishing real-world connections. Participants were often members of overlapping groups that would organize meetings and events related to their particular interests (e.g., natural childbirth, babywearing, breastfeeding) and occasionally come together for a larger cause. Our engagement in these communities was organic rather than systematic. We did not join to collect data, but rather as mothers and participating members of the communities. However, these online communities became a resource that enabled us to establish and maintain our presence in the face-to-face community. This engagement took place at home on our computers or cell phones, often with a baby at the breast, further blurring boundaries and bringing our research home.

Our involvement in community events further illustrates the absence of boundaries between mothering, home, and fieldwork. Because our topic focused on breastfeeding, most events we attended were child-friendly, especially for nursing babies. This meant our children constantly accompanied us to myriad research-related events. We participated in fundraisers for nonprofit organizations related to our own, such as a stroller walk to raise money for the Mother's Milk Bank of Florida, annual family picnics for Get Pumped!, and the International Caesarean Awareness Network (ICAN) Mom Prom. We hosted fundraisers for our own organization, which included children's clothing sales, holiday events, and monthly social events. We also attended organizational events such as Improving Birth.org's Rally to Improve Birth, the Great Cloth Diaper Change, and Baby Expos. We attended these events as participants, as mothers, and as researchers.

The fieldwork was only possible because of this blurring. The presence of our children at these events gave us legitimacy, but we also would not have willingly left them behind during what one might consider our personal time in their formative years. Researching a field that we could participate in with our children meant that we could spend more time with them, even if our attention was at times divided. We were there when they needed us, and the intertwining fostered our breastfeeding relationships as we were able to breastfeed as needed. Our fieldwork also provided a social environment for our children. Their early peer socialization took place at these events and in breastfeeding groups, and it was here that they developed some of their earliest friendships. Shannon's daughter Ella recently reminisced about her playdates with the daughter of a Breastfeeding Project leader, and she recalled the puppet show and princess cookies from the Big Latch On as perhaps her earliest memory. Likewise, this fieldwork would also not have been as productive without our involvement in breastfeeding support and advocacy through the Breastfeeding Project.

Joys and Frustrations of Doing Fieldwork at Home

The intertwining of the field and home came with many joys and frustrations. Some of the separated elements commonly associated with fieldwork—gaining entry, establishing rapport, and identifying informants—were not concerns for us, as we were already established members of the field we studied. This integration as members allowed us to focus instead on building friendships within the community. The Big Latch On and other social events we organized were moments of camaraderie and interconnectedness. These relationships were not only socially and emotionally fulfilling for us but they facilitated our data collection processes because we had already developed trusting relationships in the community. Early in our ethnographic research, we developed an online survey in Qualtrics to gather data about the range of milk sharing practices people engaged in, and the ways these practices were patterned throughout the community. When we initially shared the survey within the breastfeeding communities of which we were a part, we were met with excitement and enthusiasm; people wanted to share their stories and they trusted us to convey them. Community members not only took the survey but they shared it widely within their own social networks. Based on this enthusiasm, we surpassed our goal to collect 200 completed surveys in 2 years, instead collecting nearly 400 completed surveys in 4 months. As members who contributed to the community we studied, our participants likewise became active members of our research team by facilitating data collection. Thus, in the same way that our status as researchers was blurred with our roles as mothers and community members, our participants' roles were blurred as well.

This blurring of boundaries continued throughout our research. Later, we were awarded a small research grant to conduct in-depth interviews and collect milk samples from milk sharing participants. This opportunity brought us into new participants' homes, where we were able to observe the spaces and routines where participants expressed, fed, and otherwise handled human milk. We set out to collect 30 interviews and milk samples over a semester. Due to the enthusiastic response from our breastfeeding community, we completed this aspect of our data collection in just 5 weeks. This aspect of our data collection happened later in the project, when many of the initial community members' children had already weaned. We already knew 3 of our 30 interviewees, and the rest were recruited through community members' enthusiastic support for our research, as they worked to recruit participants who were actively sharing milk at the time of the interview. Our position as trusted members of the community alleviated challenges with participant recruitment often associated with ethnographic research while blurring the boundaries between participant and research assistant as our participants actively recruited for our research.

Our position as trusted community members came not only from being active members of the field but also from our intimate knowledge of the research subject. Knowing and studying milk sharing in an informal way for years prior to the study and being connected with many others who engaged in the practice meant that we knew how to approach the subject through data collection processes including observation, surveys, and interviews. Many participants recommended our study to other participants *after* taking part in it. Thus, the design and implementation of data collection processes were viewed positively by members who participated, as they considered their experiences and practices accurately reflected in our questions and conversations. The interview encounters in particular were often emotional: participants always had their babies with them, setting a tone of intimacy and vulnerability, and further illustrating the interconnectedness of motherhood and research in our project. The topics discussed during the interviews could be difficult, and participants often shared stories of trauma and bodily disappointment. Participants told us about their milk sharing practices while simultaneously enacting them during the interviews. They did not have the luxury of stopping their practices for 2 hours to participate in an interview, but rather the ongoing, daily, embodied routines continued as we spoke. Through these experiences, and as milk sharing mothers ourselves, we often shared tears and found meaningful connection with each other.

Our position as members of the community also gave us intimate knowledge of the phenomenon we studied. The satisfaction derived from being able to feed children, in Shannon's case, someone else's child, and Beatriz's case, her own, was not only emotionally fulfilling but also gave us insight that eventually led to the use and development of key concepts in our work such as bio-intimacy (Shaw & Morgan, 2017), biosociality (Rabinow, 1996), and emotive value (Carter & Reyes-Foster, 2020a). We experienced firsthand the feelings of emotional connectedness facilitated through milk sharing and we felt in an embodied way the emotive value of human milk as we worked to produce it and watched it make our babies grow. This deep, embodied connection with our research topic and the communities we studied made certain insights possible that would be difficult for an outsider to access. It enhanced our work, while also providing social and emotional satisfaction. In addition, our engagement in the field and our academic writing about human milk sharing provided a space for us to process and theorize our own mothering identities as we engaged analytically with a range of mothering practices and ideologies. Conversely, this intertwining of motherhood, breastfeeding, and research also came with frustrations. Our regular work responsibilities as academics on the tenure track—teaching, writing, and service—did not abate during our time in the field. At the same time, many of the regular community events, including breastfeeding support groups, Breastfeeding Project volunteer days, and other community meet-ups, were held during weekdays. We did our best to arrange our teaching, writing, and department service schedules around these community events, which often resulted in shifting more work to the days we were on campus. Many of the larger community engagement events and Breastfeeding Project monthly socials and monthly board meetings took place in the evenings and on weekends. This meant that our responsibilities in the community took us away from our families regularly, particularly our spouses and older children, during times that could have been spent with them. Thus, while the intertwining of motherhood, breastfeeding, and fieldwork made it possible for us to achieve all three, it was often overwhelming and burdensome work that was hard not only on us but also on our families.

We also discovered the frustration and tribulations of running a nonprofit organization. With no regular source of revenue to sustain the organization, we relied solely on the volunteer work of ourselves, our board members, and community members who supported our efforts. This was almost exclusively mothers of young children, who, like us, engaged in multi-tasking at all of our work events. This meant that everyone's attention was divided between their own children's needs and the work of the organization, at every meeting, and at every volunteer event. We often spent more time feeding, soothing, and entertaining our children than we did attending to the business at hand. At some point, each of the children would become overly cranky and tired, and the group would slowly dissipate. Volunteers cycled in and out of The Breastfeeding Project as their capacity ebbed and waned, making it difficult to accomplish the goals of the organization. Eventually, the commitment became too much for us to sustain, and we left too.

Extractivism and Its Discontents

The dangers and possible pitfalls of conducting fieldwork "at home" have been the subject of associated political debate, especially in anthropology (Strathern, 1987; Voloder, 2008; Delamont, 2009). Some scholars (Strathern, 1987; Hastrup, 1992) argue that in order to carry out ethnographic research, it is necessary to identify an "other" as an object of study, and this inherent power asymmetry makes any ethnographic fieldwork inherently violent. As we discuss later, other critiques link ethnography to extractivism and colonialism (Smith, 2012; Simpson, 2014). This inherent violence is seen and pushed against in feminist ethnography, the tradition informing our work (Davis & Craven, 2022). Feminist ethnography is engaged, gendered, attentive to marginality and power differentials, and emotionally committed. We did not attempt to occupy a neutral or objective subject position, as we recognized the inherent problems with such an approach, particularly to the topic we were studying. We were active participants in the communities we studied, engaging in the day-to-day online and offline activities of the groups, and as embodied participants engaged in the exchange of human milk. As milk sharing participants ourselves, we could not be outside observers.

The communities we were studying were made up of people who were similar to us in many respects: they were not "others" in the tradition of Malinowskian ethnography. In that tradition, the ethnographer must maintain objectivity and distance from the object of study. Our positionality as ethnographers and members of the breastfeeding community did not negatively impact the quality of our work, but rather enhanced it. During the time we spent as part of this community, our identities as researchers, mothers, and lactivists merged in ways that produced 10 articles and an ethnographic monograph. We formed lasting relationships and contributed to building community. In so doing, we played an important role in shaping contemporary understandings of human milk sharing.

In recent years, critiques from within feminist and Indigenous ethnography have highlighted the ways in which ethnography has been used as a tool of extractivism. Ethnographers, they have argued, enter communities, study them, and build careers from the results of these studies, without a serious commitment to the communities they study. They extract from the communities, rarely giving back. In contrast, like feminist ethnographers, native ethnographers embody a different set of commitments to their communities. A decolonizing methodology seeks to avoid extractivism by working with communities to identify research priorities and identify ways of giving back. Rather than imposing a research question on a community, decolonizing ethnography works with communities to develop research priorities and produce knowledge useful to the community (Smith, 2012; Simpson, 2014; Davis & Craven, 2022).

In our ethnographic work with milk sharing communities, we aimed to avoid extractivism. We were conscientious about how we represented the community and the people we worked with in both our research products and our engagement with the media. In November 2013, the Sunday edition of *The New York Times* published a cover story about the so-called dangers of milk sharing, which was conflated with the online purchase of human milk. This caused indignation in our community over the way in which their practices were being misrepresented in the national news. Blog posts and memes quickly circulated the internet, pointing out the problematic assumptions about peer milk sharing inherent in the research methodology of the publicized study. However, at the time there were no scientific publications describing common milk sharing practices. We identified this dearth of information and prioritized it for research not because of a detached scholarly interest but because the community wanted accurate representation of their practices. We published articles in *Breastfeeding Medicine* and *Journal of Human Lactation* which served as counter-stories to the dominant narrative taking place. When our first article describing milk sharing practices (Reyes-Foster et al., 2015) was published, it garnered media recognition. This allowed us to amplify the voices of our research participants by inviting them to participate in media interviews, including a live television appearance at our local Fox 35 news station. We worked together with our participants to push back against dominant narratives that painted milk sharing as ill-informed and even dangerous (Bakalar, 2013), and our participants eagerly shared news coverage of our research with their own social networks. We eventually wrote an article exploring our participants' responses to the research study that conflated milk sharing with milk selling (Reyes-Foster & Carter, 2018), and we sent it to the principal investigator of the study.

Our engagement through The Breastfeeding Project and the services and support we provided were other mechanisms by which we avoided extractivism in our work. Shannon co-founded The Breastfeeding Project as a way of engaging with the breastfeeding community and to support breastfeeding. Beatriz joined the Project when she began collaborating with Shannon. While we participated in many events which were happening already, we also helped create and sustain them. We were not just extracting knowledge from the community; we were helping people who wanted to feed their babies human milk.

Despite these efforts to avoid extractivism in our ethnographic work, The Breastfeeding Project eventually ended. After several years, the volunteer work became taxing on our family and professional lives. Breastfeeding communities tend to attract people from opposite sides of the political spectrum. This created wonderful opportunities for finding common ground, but political divisions between members of the Board of Directors also made participation with the group more emotionally difficult, particularly in the wake of the 2016 election. We stepped away from the Breastfeeding Project in 2017, but the organization remained active until shortly before the COVID-19 pandemic began.

The Field Transformed

Eventually our babies grew up. Like many breastfeeding mothers who become involved in their local breastfeeding support communities, once our children were weaned our lives were overtaken by new, different demands. Similarly, faces that had once been familiar in our communities started disappearing, as these mothers, too, weaned their babies and found other paths. Some moved away, and others moved on. Breastfeeding support communities have a life cycle, as most of their members eventually age out. Birth professionals such as lactation consultants and midwives remain, but the people they serve change over time. Although we maintain many of the relationships with people we met in the communities, the people who are now active in breastfeeding support communities are part of a new cohort. The community, as we knew it during our fieldwork, is no more.

At the same time that we outgrew the field, the field itself shifted and changed. The onset of the COVID-19 pandemic exacerbated political and ideological divisions within many breastfeeding and natural parenting communities. These communities are often made up of people on opposite ends of the political spectrum, who set their political differences aside to unite around parenting practices and infant health. In Florida, as in other parts of the United States and around the world, divisions between people who supported government-issued quarantines to suppress the spread of COVID-19 and those who advocated "natural immunity" through open practices like those in Sweden created tensions. Some who had become moderators of the social media groups we had once been so integrated in used their platforms to organize anti-vaxxing and anti-masking rallies and share related stories and information. New concerns emerged among people seeking to engage in milk sharing regarding exposure to COVID-19 by meeting up to exchange milk, or exposure to the COVID-19 vaccine through the milk itself. In very recent events, the infant formula shortage in the United States has prompted caregivers who ordinarily would not consider human milk sharing to turn to it as an alternative (Pearson, 2022). Thus, the field that we studied now exists in a different form, with a new set of people navigating different social and health environments.

As we reflect on our ethnographic work, we look back fondly at the time we shared within the breastfeeding and milk sharing community, the memories we created, and the knowledge we collectively worked to produce. We continue to maintain some of the relationships we formed, connecting through social media and through family social events. The field—in all its messiness and interconnections with home life and childrearing—will always be a special place where we were able to navigate motherhood, breastfeeding, and research.

References

Anderson, L. (2006). Analytic autoethnography. *Journal of Contemporary Ethnography, 35*(4), 373–395.

Bakalar, N. (2013, October 21). Breast milk donated or sold online is often tainted, study says. *New York Times.*

Burman, A. (2018). Are anthropologists monsters? An Andean dystopian critique of extractivist ethnography and anglophone-centric anthropology. *Hau Journal of Ethnographic Theory, 18*(1–2), 48–64.

Carter, S. K., & Reyes-Foster, B. M. (2020a). *Sharing milk: Intimacy, materiality and bio-communities of practice.* Bristol University Press.

Carter, S. K., & Reyes-Foster, B. M. (2020b). Considering materiality: The utility of actor-network theory to study social problems. In A. Marvasti & A. J. Traviño (Eds.), *Researching social problems* (pp. 139–155). Routledge.

Davis, D.-A., & Craven, C. (2022). *Feminist ethnography: Thinking through methodologies, challenges, and possibilities* (2nd ed.). Rowman & Littlefield.

Dean, L., Churchill, B., & Ruppaner, M. (2022). The mental load: Building a deeper theoretical understanding of how cognitive and emotional labor over*load* women and mothers. *Community, Work & Family, 25*(1), 13–29.

Delamont, S. (2009). The only honest thing: Autoethnography, reflexivity and small crises in fieldwork. *Ethnography and Education, 4*(1), 51–63.

Glenn, E. N. (1992). From servitude to service work: Historical continuities in the racial division of paid reproductive labor. *Signs: Journal of Women in Culture and Society*, *18*(1), 1–43.

Hastrup, K. (1992). Writing ethnography: State of the art. In J. Okeley & H. Callaway (Eds.), *Anthropology and ethnography* (pp. 115–132). Routledge.

Latour, B. (2005). *Reassembling the social: An introduction to actor-network-theory*. Oxford University Press.

Law, J. (2009). Actor network theory and material semiotics. In B. S. Turner (Ed.), *The new Blackwell companion to social theory* (pp. 141–158). Blackwell Publishing.

Malinowski, B. (1967). *A diary in the strict sense of the term*. Stanford University Press.

Oakley, A. (1974). *The sociology of housework*. Robertson.

Pearson, C. (2022, May 22). What parents need to know about sharing breast milk. *The New York Times*. Retrieved May 26, 2022, from www.nytimes.com/2022/05/20/well/family/breast-milk-sharing-formula-shortage.html

Rabinow, P. (1996). Artificiality and enlightenment: From sociobiology to biosociality. In *Essays on the anthropology of reason* (pp. 234–252). Princeton University Press.

Reyes-Foster, B. M., & Carter, S. K. (2018). That's not the milk sharing I'm doing': Responses to a *Pediatrics* article from women who milk share. *Human Organization*, *77*(3), 262–272.

Reyes-Foster, B. M., Carter, S. K., & Hinojosa, M. S. (2015). Milk sharing in practice: A descriptive analysis of peer breast milk sharing. *Breastfeeding Medicine*, *10*(5), 263–269.

Shaw, R. M., & Morgan, M. (2017). Bio-intimate economies of breastmilk exchange: Peer-milk sharing and donor breastmilk in the NICU. In R. M. Shaw (Ed.), *Bioethics beyond altruism: Donating and transforming human biological materials* (pp. 319–342). Palgrave Macmillan.

Simpson, A. (2014). *Mohawk interruptus: Political life across the borders of settler states*. Duke University Press.

Smith, L. T. (2012). *Decolonizing methodologies: Research and Indigenous peoples* (2nd ed.). Zed Books.

Strathern, M. (1987). The limits of auto-anthropology. In A. Jackson (Ed.), *Anthropology at home* (pp. 16–37). ASA monographs 25. Routledge.

Voloder, L. (2008). Autoethnographic challenges: Confronting self, field, and home. *TAJA: The Australian Journal of Anthropology*, *19*(1), 27–40.

12

INTERPRETIVE COMPLEXITY IN LANGUAGE-DISCORDANT FIELDWORK

Hilde Fiva Buzungu

I enter a meeting room of a Norwegian social welfare office with a social worker, a woman and a man. The woman is a service user at the social welfare office; the man is an interpreter. I am there to observe a meeting between the social worker and the woman as a part of my ethnographic research on social work with linguistic minorities in Norway (Buzungu, 2021, 2023). For the duration of the meeting, the social worker speaks Norwegian, and except for a few Norwegian words now and then, the service user speaks Somali. The interpreter renders utterances in both languages, but as I am only proficient in one of the languages, I understand only the Norwegian half of what is being said. Am I getting the full picture of what is transpiring in the meeting I am observing, when I understand only the Norwegian bits of the conversation? Would I not be better served by limiting my research to ethnographic observations of encounters in languages in which I am proficient? These are the questions I aim to address and explore throughout this chapter.[1]

Language-Discordant Research

When research is carried out without a shared language with the research participants, it can be termed "language discordant." Language discordance occurs when two people lack proficiency in the same language(s) (Rossi et al., 2019, p. 2; Sears et al., 2013, p. 535). Ethnographic research in linguistically diverse settings, where the researcher is not fully proficient in the languages that are used is not uncommon. Since the birth of the discipline, anthropologists have carried out research among people whose language they did not share (Malinowski, 1922; Mead, 1928/1961). When researchers and research participants differ in minority/majority status, this adds complexity to the research process (Gunaratnam, 2003). This complexity is further exacerbated by language discordance, increasing the

DOI: 10.4324/9781003275121-16

risk of misunderstandings and misconceptions (Berreman, 1962; Borchgrevink, 2003). Borrowing from my PhD dissertation on language-discordant social work (Buzungu, 2021), in this chapter I consider the benefits and risks of language-discordant ethnography.

With some notable exceptions focusing particularly on the impact of interpreters in settings where the researcher is not proficient in the community language (Berreman, 1962; Obeyeskere, 1981; Borchgrevink, 2003), limited attention has previously been paid to the overall impact of language discordance on the process and usefulness of ethnographic research. Language discordance and language competence are not necessarily either/or determinations, as people may be more or less proficient in various languages. Furthermore, someone may be proficient enough in a language to carry out some tasks but not others. For example, a Norwegian doctor may be proficient enough in English to be in London as a tourist, but not consider himself proficient enough in English to give a patient her terminal diagnosis. Similarly, a researcher may be proficient enough in Arabic to exchange greetings, but not necessarily proficient enough to understand fully a court case she is observing. Thus, language discordance is particular to the situation or activity that is to be carried out. In this chapter, I use the concept of "language discordance" for situations where ethnographers and field members lack sufficient proficiency in a shared language *for the research task at hand.* Some encounters described here as "language discordant" involve no shared language while in others our limited proficiency of a shared language was insufficient for the research task at hand.

The foundation of all ethically responsible research is informed consent. Language discordance offers specific challenges to this area of our work as researchers. Ensuring informed consent in the absence of a shared language requires planning and preparation, in addition to access to interpreters or translated materials. In the project that this data is from, all potential research participants were invited to information meetings at the social welfare office. At these meetings, there were interpreters present when the potential participant had limited proficiency in Norwegian. The information about the research project was presented in Norwegian and interpreted into a language the service user understood. The potential participant then had the opportunity to ask questions and request more information before deciding whether to participate or not. In addition, subsequent oral consent was requested for observations of meetings and for interviews directly before the observation/interview was to take place. All those service users who were observed and interviewed had thus given their explicit consent on two occasions.

Listening to Mariam and Anna

In the meeting with which I started this chapter, I sat for an hour listening to Mariam and Anna[2] trying to talk to each other. This chapter is based on observations of this meeting and 25 other meetings between social workers and service users. Twenty-four of these meetings were language discordant, and of these, 15 were interpreter mediated. In addition, I carried out interviews with 36 social workers and 8 service users (Buzungu, 2021, p. 25). The meetings and interviews were not audio-recorded, but rather observed, sensed, made notes of, and made sense of. The reason for observing rather than recording was first and foremost the sensitive nature of the contents of these talks. Moreover, observations invite a different kind of sense-making than that which is based on audiotapes. The focus of my research was on language-discordant social work as a communicative activity, my aim being to capture the nuances and intricacies of this through participant observation in the social sites where this communication goes on.

When listening to Mariam and Anna, I could only understand what was being said by Anna in Norwegian, and the interpreter's renditions in Norwegian of what Mariam had said in Somali. From my notes, I could later represent their talk as fragmented dialogues with only the Norwegian utterances visible to the reader. An example is from the end of the meeting between Mariam and Anna, when Anna had just asked whether there was anything else Mariam would like to talk about. The time for the meeting was up, the room was booked for another meeting, people were waiting outside the glass wall of the room, and the interpreter had already said that he must go because his parking was already 10 minutes over time. Instead of saying no and goodbye, the woman started to cry. She said that she had a daughter who was alone with relatives in a country neighboring her country of origin (Buzungu, 2021, p. 144):

Mariam: ". . ."

Interpreter: "Nine years I have not seen her. You people only care about those children who are in Norway. I cannot bring her here because our permits are only one year one year, and they say we don't have that kind of permit."

Anna: "For us, me and Nina [Anna's colleague], the most important thing is that things get better for people we work with. We are social workers, and we have also taken further education to help people, and now we only have twenty families."

Interpreter: ". . ."

Mariam: ". . ."

Interpreter: "I understand that you cannot make magic, but when you don't have your child with you, then everything is just grim. Here in Norway, you only care about those children who are in Norway."

Anna: "OK, but I think we really have to round off there, because now my colleague needs the room."

Observing this meeting between Mariam and Anna meeting made it possible for me to learn something about how they interacted, and about how language-discordant social work can transpire. In this case, Mariam said some excruciatingly painful things, culminating in her final words, "When you don't have your child with you then everything is just grim. Here in Norway, you only care about those children who are in Norway." This came after a conversation in which the social worker had been asking a lot of questions about her and her children in Norway, plans for school and work, activities the children might like to participate in, what they enjoy doing, etc. When the woman said this, her pain was not communicatively recognized or responded to by the social worker. There may have been several reasons for this, such as the time constraints of the meeting or the people waiting for the room. It may also have been related to the somewhat cumbersome form of communication that interpreter-mediated talk can take, in that everything must be said twice, and utterances and responses have this translation space between them and are thereby less immediate. Finally, there may have been other reasons, such as the social worker not knowing how to respond or not grasping the severity of what the service user had said. However, the interactional dynamics of their talk, and the distance of their subjectivities, was quite different from language concordant meetings I have observed.

Excluding language-discordant encounters from our observations of professional practice may result in us not discovering the particular complexities and challenges for professionals in these settings. If there are phenomena that occur more frequently or need to be addressed differently in language-discordant settings, our research may not give practitioners insight into that if we do not include these in our observations. However, that is not to say that observing language-discordant meetings left me with a clear picture of what had transpired and why. I was often left with unanswered questions regarding what had transpired, how misunderstandings had arisen, and why participation attempts had failed. One of the unique features of ethnographic research is the opportunity to sit with, and to learn from, the experience of such voids.

Observing Failed Attempts at Participation

The meeting between Mariam and Anna was interpreter-mediated, and Mariam spoke Somali throughout the meeting. However, that was not the case in all the language-discordant meetings I observed. In nine of them, the meetings were carried out in Norwegian despite substantial language discordance with service users who had very limited proficiency in Norwegian. I refer to these nine meetings also as language discordant. Specifically, I take the position that if we observe people trying to participate in a meeting that is taking place in a language they are not proficient in, we are in fact observing a language-discordant encounter. In such meetings, although every word is spoken in a language I understand, the encounter is still marked by the language discordance between the social worker and the service user.

One example of such a meeting was a home visit by two social workers, Cathrine and Lisa, to Karwan's house (Buzungu, 2021, pp. 161–162). The focus of the meeting was to give information about a project Karwan had been invited to participate in. At one point in the meeting, Karwan raised concerns about his application for Norwegian citizenship. In connection with this, he needed to involve social services, as travel abroad complicates issues of financial support and benefits from the welfare office:

Karwan: "As well I have a case in home country, must I apply for one that ID-card there. And what I have apply for Norwegian citizenship. As I have heard about from UDI [the Norwegian Directorate of Immigration], they asking for this new documentation from home country."
Cathrine: "Mm."
Karwan: "Must I say, must I travel. And it taking time, maybe I stay there one month, two months."
Cathrine: "Because you have to travel there to get the documentation?"
Karwan: "Yes, yes."
Cathrine: "Yes."
Lisa: "You have to document that you are you there as well."
Karwan: "No, I giving documentation from there to Norway."
Lisa: "OK, I understand."
Cathrine: "Maybe we should say more about the project?"
Lisa: "Yes."

Following this exchange, the social workers went back to talking about what they had planned for this meeting to be about, "the project," as Cathrine says toward the end of the exchange. In this exchange, the contributions from Karwan were seemingly recognized first ("OK, I understand"). Nevertheless, his participation attempts were subsequently treated as communicatively irrelevant and ignored, though this was neither explicitly stated nor explained to him. One could have imagined the social workers saying something to the extent of "I understand you're concerned about this, but now we need to talk about the project, we can talk about the citizenship application next time." Given his insufficient proficiency in Norwegian, Karwan's attempts at actively participating in the meeting failed and accomplished little. In effect, he was no more successful than minority language speakers with no proficiency and who made no such participation attempts at all. When Karwan's queries are ignored without explanation, he is discouraged from further participation. In this meeting, Karwan became completely passive after the first 10 minutes.

Toward the end of the meeting, the social workers had provided a lot of information about the project, and asked Karwan some open-ended questions (Buzungu, 2021, p. 184). At this point, his limited language proficiency in Norwegian made it difficult for him to respond:

Cathrine: "So, does she [a health care worker] come here some days a week?"
Karwan: "But if . . . I calling her, I needing, I have her number job, telephone, ehm, his private."
Cathrine: "Oh yeah, that's great."

In this utterance, his lexicon and vocabulary are clearly limited, and his syntax and morphology are not proficient, all of which leads to fragmented speech. His substantial shortcomings in speaking proficiency indicates challenges in comprehension as well. Cathrine, however, does not probe, but rather pretends to have understood by saying "oh yeah, that's great" and moves on to something else. In fact, substantial effort here is going into sustaining interaction, mutually saving face when the language discordance becomes too visible. This work includes glossing over misunderstandings and miscommunications to sustain the task at hand—to carry on with the meeting. In all of my observations of language-discordant meetings, I never once saw anyone give up on this and say something to the extent of "honestly, I think we just don't understand each other, we need to find another solution."

A methodological advantage of ethnographic fieldwork in comparison to more isolated instances of observation is the emphasis on social context, which sometimes expands into social worlds beyond the interaction under immediate observation. After the meeting between Karwan and the two social workers, I went back to the office together with them. As soon as we got into the car outside Karwan's house, the two social workers commented on how they had perceived the communication in the meeting:

Cathrine: "He didn't understand much of that."
Lisa: "No, but at least we got through everything."
Cathrine: "Next time we need to meet with the wife, or to have an interpreter if we're meeting with him again."

From this exchange, it is clear that social workers are not oblivious to issues of language discordance and communication difficulties. However, it is somewhat mind-boggling that they downplay the importance of this to the extent that they do not see the need for important information to be repeated, as when Lisa here says "at least we got through everything" referring to all the information they had planned to give him in the meeting. We can see this as a reflection of the meeting having two goals: an informational goal which was clearly not met (as "he didn't understand much of that") and in that sense the meeting failed. However, the meeting also had a procedural or organizationally mandated goal of "getting through everything," at which they did succeed.

What can this teach us about the usefulness of language-discordant ethnographic research? My lack of a shared language with Karwan did not prevent me from gaining important insights from observing this meeting. If I had chosen to exclude research participants I lacked a shared language with, my data would not have included meetings where service users' participation attempts failed. Moreover, I would not have had the opportunity to hear social workers reflect on such encounters and their experiences of language discordance and the consequences of this phenomenon.

Experiencing Unresolved Language Discordance

Most of the language-discordant meetings I observed were interpreter mediated. Unfortunately, the interpreters I observed were without the necessary qualifications for their assigned tasks (Buzungu, 2021, pp. 112–113). Being present to observe these meetings frequently left me as confused as the primary participants in the encounters. As an ethnographer attempting to make sense of the unfolding interactions, I too was at a loss for meaning when interpreters lacked basic skills. One such occasion was the following meeting. I was already in the room with a social worker as her colleague Mona entered with Fadumo (Buzungu, 2021, pp. 195–196). Mona and Fadumo both sat down at the table with us, Mona called an interpreter and put her on speakerphone. Then, the following dialogue transpired:

Mona: "Hi, good to see you."
Interpreter: ". . ."
Fadumo: ". . ."
Interpreter: "Yes welcome she says."
Mona: "Have you been in school today?"
Interpreter: ". . ."
Fadumo: ". . ."
Interpreter: "Yes, I have been in school today, she says."
Fadumo: ". . ."
Interpreter: "Who are you?"
Mona: "Hm?"
Fadumo: ". . ."
Interpreter: "First, I will ask, who are you?"
Fadumo: ". . ."
Interpreter: "The reason I ask, are you NAV, or you are not? Caseworker or not? Are you from NAV or you are from other department?"

As this happened, I was sitting there thinking, did Mona bring in the wrong lady? Or had the social workers forgotten to have an information meeting about the project? Or did they have such substantial communication problems in the information meeting that the lady did not understand anything at all about what was going on? Trine, the other social worker in the room, looked startled. Mona, however, looked completely relaxed. She explained in a few words that they worked in NAV, and that they were family coordinators, as she had explained last time. I was still not sure that they had the right lady, but I thought to myself, I guess we'll find out.

The meeting went on, and it became clear it was the right woman. After the meeting ended and we went back upstairs to the social workers' office, the three of us burst out laughing. Trine started by saying "When she was like 'who are you?' I was just like, oh lord, what is this?" I then chipped in saying I thought they had brought in the wrong woman from the waiting room. Both of them laughed. Mona said "no, no, no" and explained that they had previously had an information meeting and also a session where they filled in the questionnaire. In addition, both social workers had been to her house for a home visit, and Mona had even gotten a hug from the woman when they arrived at her house that time.

This whole situation made me question whether the interpreter could have contributed to the fact that the situation became so strange. Was it possible that Fadumo had in fact invoked another dimension of the task at hand, not accessible to the other participants in the room? Had she asked in Somali something along the lines of "What is your role, in relation to the case worker, I don't quite understand the difference between you and the case worker?" Or was she at least trying to say something like this? But since the interpreter was on the phone, it was not easy for the interpreter to see that these were people who knew each other relatively well. If the interpreter had been there when they met, her rendition might have been something like, "Could you say something more about who you are and what your job is?" instead of "Who are you and what is your job?" When the interpreter is not able to understand the interaction between those taking part in the talk, chaos ensues, and the interaction order collapses. This is not unlike what Garfinkel (1967) described as a "breaching experiment." The lack of physical and visual contact may have contributed to misunderstandings and to certain ancillary acts, such as requests for clarification. However, interestingly, the language-discordant interaction between Mona and Fadumo is still somehow sustained using supplemental material from past shared encounters. These are insights into the intricacies and insecurities about interpreter-mediated communication that I see few other methodological approaches could have given.

Understanding the Consequences of Unqualified Interpreters

Observing meetings where people without the necessary qualifications were trying to carry out interpreting also gave insight into the communicative consequences when government services do not secure access to sufficiently qualified interpreters for their staff and service users. One such meeting was in a NAV office, between Camilla and Jin. This meeting, in contrast to the previous one, had an interpreter present in the same room as all of us (Buzungu, 2021, p. 164). At one point in the meeting, Camilla attempts to help Jin complete an application online, but to do that Camilla needs for Jin to log in with her bank chip:

Camilla: "Did you bring your bank chip?"
Interpreter: ". . ."
Jin: ". . ."
Interpreter: ". . ."
Jin: ". . ."

Interpreter: "..."
Interpreter: "You told her last time that she had to bring it, right?"
Camilla: [smiles with a little laugh]
Interpreter: "..."
Interpreter: "I told her she must bring it. She is wasting the time of you and me when she is always forgetting and not doing what she must be doing."
Camilla: "It's OK, it's easy to forget. We can do the application next time."
[A little pause, no one says anything]
Camilla: "But what we can do is talk about insurance."
Interpreter: "..."

Here, the interpreter took it upon herself to reprimand the woman for not having brought the bank chip. In this passage, none of what Jin said is interpreted into Norwegian by the interpreter, and as such, Jin's voice is not heard even if she is attempting to participate. Moreover, the interpreter in effect prevented Camilla from dealing with the forgotten chip as she preferred, by first reprimanding Jin on her own initiative and thereafter not interpreting when Camilla said, "it's OK, it's easy to forget." In this way, the interpreter potentially alters the relationship between the social worker and the service user. Camilla did not comment on either of these issues during the meeting, but her comments to me after the meeting made it clear that she was aware of these problems and concerned by them.

The problems of how the interpreter carried out her job persisted throughout the meeting. Toward the end, one of the most detrimental exchanges occurred (Buzungu, 2021, p. 168):

Camilla: "Have you heard something from Child Welfare, when the meeting will be?"
Interpreter: "..."
Jin: "..."
Interpreter: "She says no, but I have it here [the interpreter starts to leaf through the pages of her own calendar]."
Camilla: "No, no, it's OK, you don't need to look for it."
Interpreter: "I have it here."
Camilla: "Yes, but it is possible there will be a change, so you don't need to look for it now. Don't do it. Don't look for it."
Interpreter: "..."
Interpreter: "I told her the meeting is on the 25th at 12."
Jin: "..."
Interpreter: "..."
Jin: "..."
Interpreter: "..."
Interpreter: "She is just asking more about the meeting, she didn't know."

Camilla:	"Right, but I think we have to round off now. Today we have talked about how things are going with your health, the problem with the bills and the bank, we tried to do the application, but we'll do that next time, and the home insurance." [silence, no one says anything]
Camilla:	"Right, so what did you think about the meeting?"
Interpreter:	". . ."
Jin:	". . ."
Interpreter:	"Very good, you have helped me a lot."

Here, Camilla asks Jin about a meeting with child welfare services, and Jin either does not know about it or does not want to tell Camilla. The interpreter is aware of the meeting, though, and tells both Camilla and Jin the date and time for the meeting. This is followed by an exchange between Jin and the interpreter, which the interpreter summarized for Camilla as having answered questions about the meeting.

In this meeting, the interpreter did not see herself as restricted by the common communicative conventions for interpreter-mediated talk, in which the interpreter is expected to remain uninvolved in the matter being discussed. This interpreter took part and interjected with her own initiatives and comments in both languages, and frequently omitted entire utterances. Because several of these omissions pertained to utterances made by the minority-language-speaking client, the service user's voice was often silenced. In addition, the interpreter silenced the voice of the social worker by ignoring several of her requests and not interpreting a number of her utterances. The interpreter used her communicative power to dominate both the service user and the social worker, and the social worker's attempts to prevent her from doing this were futile. In this way, the practice of the interpreter led to communicative ruptures that impacted the relationship between the social worker and the service user, and that left the service user effectively muted.

Both before and after the meeting, Camilla told me that she was concerned and frustrated about how the interpreter-mediated meetings with this service user usually transpired. Prior to the meeting, Camilla told me that she had tried to get another interpreter for the meeting that I was going to observe, because "this one carries out her job in a manner that is far outside of the boundaries of how interpreters are to interpret." However, the interpreting agency denied her request. Camilla then commented that it was just as well, because then I could see "how it really is" for my research. Throughout the meeting, Camilla did make some attempts to influence the practice of the interpreter, such as when she tried to tell the interpreter not to say anything more to Jin about the child welfare services meeting. Even so, the interpreter consistently ignored Camilla's attempts, and Camilla did not persist or interrupt the meeting to address the issue with the interpreter. This type of interpreting practice significantly hampers the service user's ability to participate in her own social work meeting. The actions of the interpreter silence the service user rather than enable her to participate. In most of the meetings I observed, the interpreters did not display such dominant participation. However, once again I would argue that few other research methods would enable us to get insight into how social order is maintained, and at times disrupted, than ethnographic observations.

Language-Discordant Participant Observation

When observing language-discordant encounters in professional settings, a researcher who does not understand the minority language has a status similar to the service providers. In this sense, the researcher's experiences can provide insights into being in a linguistically dominant position. Being unable to understand half of what was being said forced me to direct my attention to other aspects of the communication than the fidelity of interpreted renditions. Instead of accuracy of translations, I became interested in other dimensions of interpreter-mediated interaction, such as how people relate to each other, how service providers and interpreters negotiate responsibilities, and how interpreters cope with communicative challenges. It was through participant observation and ethnographic interviews that I was able to explore these topics related to language in use.

In most ethnographic research, interviews are carried out in addition to participant observation. For researchers, the question becomes whether they should interview only respondents with whom they share a language. Interviewing people outside one's own linguistic group presents many challenges, most important of which is whether the interview should be conducted in a language the respondent is proficient in with the aid of an interpreter or in a second language in which they are less proficient. Acquiring proficiency in a new language is a difficult task, requiring substantial commitment as well as physical, intellectual, and emotional effort (Brown, 1987, p. 1). Listening to someone talking in a language one has limited proficiency of is tiring and requires a great deal of concentration (Skutnabb-Kangas, 1986, pp. 82–83). With constant pressure to try to understand the words and sentences that are uttered, there is less capacity available to focus on contents, which may cause stress, loss of confidence, disengagement, disaffection, and alienation (Baker, 2001, p. 213). If researchers interview people in a language they are not sufficiently proficient in, these issues pose a risk to the quality of our research data. To avoid such problems, all my interviews with non-Norwegian-speaking participants were conducted through an interpreter. In all of my interviews, I had certified interpreters with university-level interpreter training. The interpreting was carried out over the telephone, and the interpreters were briefed in advance about the project and the interview guide (Buzungu, 2021, p. 59). One of the topics I was interested in was how minority language speakers experienced their previous interpreter-mediated meetings with social workers. For this reason, I would have chosen to have a different interpreter for my research interview than the one who had interpreted in the meeting with the social worker, even if the interpreter in the meeting had been sufficiently qualified. With a different interpreter, the people I interviewed could hopefully speak more freely about their previous encounter with social workers.

Conclusion

I am not suggesting that language discordance is inherently beneficial for qualitative research. Being proficient in the language(s) of encounters we observe will always give the richest data. However, all researchers have limited language proficiency; the question is what we should do in the face of the interpretive complexity of language discordance. Should we attempt to include those situations and those people as well, or are the interpretive risks too great for us to do so? Exploring the complexities and risks of language-discordant research may lead us to conclude that we should limit our ethnographic observations to settings where we understand the languages that are used, and limit our interviews to people we have a shared language with. However, making such choices limits our research to an incomplete picture of the contexts and phenomena we aim to study and understand. Had I limited my research in the Norwegian social welfare offices to observing encounters in languages I understand, it would not have been possible for me to see how linguistic minorities encounter our welfare services.

In the face of language discordance, it is essential not to underestimate the complexities of linguistic domination and subordination. The choice of language for a meeting or an interview will significantly influence the process and contents of that encounter. Understanding linguistic domination as something that can mark multilingual communication beyond the intentions of individuals is essential. Gerald Roche discusses "language oppression" as a form of domination that works like other forms of oppression based on race, skin color, ethnicity, and nationality (2019, p. 2). He suggests that language oppression, or *linguicism* (Skutnabb-Kangas, 2000), should be analyzed in dialogue with these other forms of oppression (Roche, 2019, p. 27). Moreover, he argues that we as researchers need to explore how language oppression transpires in various contexts (Roche, 2019, p. 27). When planning and carrying out ethnographic research projects, these are essential issues for us as researchers to take into account.

The benefits of including language-discordant meetings in our observations, and including people we do not have a shared language with, is that our research more truthfully and comprehensively reflects the realities of contemporary ethnographic research of bureaucratic systems. Moreover, our research mirrors the communities we live in and the lives lived in our communities better when minority language speakers are also among those whose lives we seek to understand. These are the complex and chaotic realities of people who either at work or in life experience the lack of a shared language. If ethnographic research does not aim to discover and document these social worlds, I fear that we as researchers lose out on them entirely as we certainly do not reach them with surveys and questionnaires. Language-discordant ethnographic fieldwork enables us not only to hear and report on the experiences of people experiencing lack of linguistic access to each other but also to perceive and feel the effects of this on ourselves. Through this reflexivity as both participants and observers, we may aspire to gain understanding and insight from ourselves as well as from what our research participants so generously share with us.

Notes

1 My deepest gratitude to my PhD supervisors Marianne Rugkåsa and Hilde Haualand for all your guidance throughout my fieldwork and beyond, and to Amir B. Marvasti and Jaber F. Gubrium for their feedback on all my drafts of this chapter.
2 All names provided are pseudonyms.

References

Baker, C. (2001). *Foundations of bilingual education and bilingualism* (3rd ed., Vol. 27). Multilingual Matters.

Berreman, G. D. (1962). *Behind many masks: Ethnography and impression management in a Himalayan village*. Bobbs-Merrill.

Borchgrevink, A. (2003). Silencing language: Of anthropologists and interpreters. *Ethnography*, *4*(1), 95–121. www.jstor.org/stable/24047803

Brown, H. D. (1987). *Principles of language learning and teaching* (2nd ed.). Prentice-Hall.

Buzungu, H. (2021). *The space between: Language discordant social work in Norway* (PhD Thesis). Oslo Metropolitan University.

Buzungu, H. F. (2023). *Language discordant social work in a multilingual world: The space between*. Routledge.

Garfinkel, H. (1967). *Studies in ethnomethodology*. Prentice-Hall.

Gunaratnam, Y. (2003). *Researching race and ethnicity: Methods, knowledge and power*. Sage.

Malinowski, B. (1922). *Argonauts of the Western Pacific: An account of native enterprise and adventure in the archipelagoes of Melanesian new guinea*. G. Routledge & Sons.

Mead, M. (1928/1961). *Coming of age in Samoa: A psychological study of primitive youth for Western civilization*. Morrow.

Obeyesekere, G. (1981). *Medusa's hair: An essay on personal symbols and religious experience*. University of Chicago Press.

Roche, G. (2019). Articulating language oppression: Colonialism, coloniality and the erasure of Tibet's minority languages. *Patterns of Prejudice*, 1–28. https://doi.org/10.1080/0031322X.2019.1662074

Rossi, C., Grenier, S., & Vaillancourt, R. (2019). Literature review: Strategies for addressing language barriers during humanitarian relief operations. *Disaster Medicine and Public Health Preparedness*, 1–9. https://doi.org/10.1017/dmp.2019.90

Sears, J., Khan, K., Ardern, C. I., & Tamim, H. (2013). Potential for patient-physician language discordance in Ontario. *BMC Health Services Research*, *13*(1), 535. https://doi.org/10.1186/1472-6963-13-535

Skutnabb-Kangas, T. (1986). *Minoritet, språk och rasism [Minority, language and racism]*. Liber.

Skutnabb-Kangas, T. (2000). *Linguistic genocide in education, or worldwide diversity and human rights?* Lawrence Earlbaum Associates.

PART IV
Afterword

AFTERWORD

Elaborating Contours of the Craft

James A. Holstein

Crafting Ethnographic Fieldwork explores diverse contours of field research and analysis. In the "Introduction," Jaber F. Gubrium offers a set of crucial insights into the practical, site-specific work of describing social worlds and social interaction. The top-notch ethnographers assembled for this volume provide myriad valuable demonstrations of ethnographic practice that they've used to capture the dynamic contingencies of everyday life and the complex substances of ethnographic discovery. The book's goal—which is masterfully achieved—is an imaginative "pedagogy of exemplification."

The craft of ethnographic fieldwork, the editors argue, develops in relation to three enduring concerns: site-specificity, imagined subjectivity, and social worlds. Each is mediated by social interaction. But make no mistake: the concerns don't stand in isolation. Ethnography's challenge is to adroitly balance and shift focus, keeping each interest in mind even as primary emphasis necessarily converges on a single concern as the others are temporarily consigned to the background. The *craft* of ethnography requires flexibility and inventiveness to maintain this balance. "Procedural tolerance," Gubrium argues, is crucial to the balancing act.

Ethnography's craft isn't constrained by strict procedural regimen or standardized techniques and recipes. No system of analytic rules or guidelines can adequately address the dynamic contingencies of everyday life. Instead, Marvasti and Gubrium view method as ways of knowing, seeing, and understanding which implicate perception, understanding, and representation (Gubrium & Holstein, 1997). "Analytic inspiration," they suggest, resonates with method, offering the provocations and possibilities that come with distinctive ways of knowing (Gubrium & Holstein, 2014). Most importantly, the editors recognize that method and its empirical artifacts are themselves mutually implicative. To capture the

DOI: 10.4324/9781003275121-18

manner through which method *produces* knowledge, they borrow an important concept from Emilie Whitaker and Paul Atkinson (2021): "methodological reflexivity." Their description of the concept bears repeating because many versions of "reflexivity" populate the social science literature (Lynch, 2000): "Methods create the possibility of research. . . . Issues of method are, therefore, productive in the creation of knowledge, as well as implicitly constraining what knowledge is thinkable" (Whitaker & Atkinson, 2021, pp. 38–39).

While ethnography produces diverse variants of knowledge, it is also accountable to the demands of the realities it presumes merely to observe. This is where Gubrium's "procedural tolerance" enters the picture. Methods of observation change in response to the demands of field realities. Those realities simultaneously are made possible and observable by the methods used ostensibly to observe them. Field realities and research methods are thus intertwined: mutually constitutive.

Crucially, this observation insists that the three focal points of the book do not operate apart from one another, even as they are separated in the text and table of contents. As Marvasti and Gubrium remind us, the concepts of variable ethnographic sites, ethnographic selves—that is, imagined subjectivities—and descriptively emergent social worlds are themselves reflexively related. Thus, as one methodological or procedural gambit proceeds, it is likely to effect variation in the object under study. This, in turn, may prompt an adjustment of prior perspectives and procedures. The consequent ever-changing ethnographic landscape thus demands procedural tolerance—methodological flexibility and innovation. And, once again, this sets the stage for further "analytic inspiration" (Gubrium, this volume; Gubrium & Holstein, 2014).

The linear, partitioned format of an academic book limits the editors' and authors' ability to fully demonstrate the intertwined complexities of methodological reflexivity. Charged with addressing one of the three key topics, the authors consign alternate concerns to the background as they highlight their designated topics—as diverse as everyday life in prisons in India, aging selves in a senior activist organization, and stand-up comedy venues. They produce a superb collection of analyses of ethnographic practices that underscore the emergent and contingent nature of the research process. Nevertheless, the authors can't fully capture the convergent, intersecting, reflexive dynamics of the *craft* of ethnography across the textual divides.

This afterword re-engages the editors' vision of the contours of the ethnographic craft from a meta-analytic platform. It's a more distanced, free-floating commentary on the dynamic and emergent character of the craft than might be possible in the individual chapters. Pursuing the editors' penchant for analysis by way of exemplification, the following sections highlight two crucial aspects of doing ethnography that the editors subtly interweave throughout the fabric of the book's diverse sections and chapters. "Methodological reflexivity" and "analytic inspiration" don't appear in the book's table of contents, nor do they appear in chapter titles. While their importance is implicit in the chapters, the terms appear infrequently. Nevertheless, this low profile doesn't temper the significance of the concepts, nor does it temper their prominence in the editors' scheme of things. Here, I offer illustrations from my first and from my most recent ethnographic projects—which are rife with examples of procedural tolerance—to highlight aspects of the book's central premises that may fly beneath the radar.

Analytic Inspiration

The term "analytic inspiration" places conceptual and methodological imagination at the center of the research process, significantly shaping empirical findings and analysis. While it may provide the initial impulse or strategy for field research, analytic inspiration also implicates transformative conceptual, empirical, and interpretive moves throughout the research project, which may, themselves, reconfigure ethnographic research. Elsewhere (Gubrium & Holstein, 2014), we have characterized analytic inspiration as the impetus that comes with a distinctive way of seeing—a type of momentum that exists during, as well as before or after, research begins. Analytic inspiration not only provides perceptual insight—tentative or otherwise—but also supplies a game plan for how to conduct research both conceptually and procedurally. Analytic inspiration and methodology thus go hand in hand, implicating conceptual understandings, technical procedure, empirical sensibilities, and analytic results, conclusions, or generalizations.

My first major ethnographic project illustrates some of these interrelated themes. As I began my incipient study of a courtroom where mental health-related cases were conducted (see Holstein, 1993), I was essentially unaware of the roles played by analytic inspiration and methodological reflexivity. To be honest, I'd hardly considered the concepts, let alone used the terms. Upon reflection, however, analytic inspiration and methodological self-consciousness were working reflexively to designate, and then reconfigure, the very site, objects of research, and social reality that I thought I was studying, working assiduously, though discreetly, behind my back, so to speak.

Approaching the study of involuntary mental hospitalization proceedings, I was captivated by high-profile sociological discussions of the labeling theory of deviance (Kitsuse, 1962). The essence of the labeling argument was that "residual deviance" such as mental illness was identified and stabilized by societal reaction (Scheff, 1966). Accordingly, mental illness was an artifact of labeling, not an objective, organic condition. One controversial tenet was that non-psychiatric variables—social contingencies and structural factors such as race, gender, age, and social class—influenced the likelihood of being identified and treated as mentally ill, and ultimately, involuntarily hospitalized. (See Holstein, 1993 for a brief summary of the labeling controversy.)

Fortuitously, I was working in the sociology department at UCLA as I began my project, and Robert Emerson pointed me to a courtroom in Los Angeles (which I call Metropolitan Court) that handled only mental health-related cases, including involuntary commitment hearings. My first visits to the courtroom revealed myriad displays that resonated with the labeling process posited in the literature. Florid psychiatric conditions were on full display, as were occasions of labeling symptoms and persons. Reading Erving Goffman (1961), Harold Garfinkel (1967), and Robert Emerson (1969) primed me to see the courtroom as a stage for the ceremonial moral degradation and denunciation of candidate mental patients as they were involuntarily committed. At the same time, I was poised to see social forces and extrinsic variables operating "behind the scene" (and beyond the vision) of courtroom actors. In effect, the labeling literature of the day served as both implicit and acknowledged analytic inspiration for my research.

The labeling debate highlighted an explanatory "competition" between psychiatric and non-psychiatric variables: put simply, which variables could best account for labeling outcomes. The challenges of the controversy encouraged researchers—myself included—to virtually *see* issues in relation to the landscape of variables, prompting them to ask *why* labels were applied, which variables were most significant, and *what* consequences resulted. In Metropolitan Court, the *why* initially seemed obvious. A raft of social contingencies seemed to go hand-in-hand with involuntary commitment. These non-psychiatric variables—race, gender, age, and socioeconomic status—seemed to work against candidate patients, even if this work was unacknowledged, seemingly done imperceptibly while in plain sight.

But there were empirical complications. Almost *all* candidate patients in Metropolitan Court were troubled, socially and economically disadvantaged, and appeared to be at the mercy of social forces and exogenous factors that incited labeling, yet only about half of them were being committed. Moreover, the seeming capriciousness and complexities of the labeling process were confounding, if not inexplicable, if analyzed in terms of the variables presumed to be at play. Myriad factors appeared to matter, but a search for correlation came up empty. It was far from clear how either psychiatric or non-psychiatric factors were implicated in actual commitment decisions.

Coincidentally and fortuitously, new analytic inspiration eventually helped me sort through these matters, transforming my research focus, and ultimately changing my fundamental research questions and methods. As I watched court proceedings, it gradually dawned on me that I was not asking an important (perhaps even prior) question: *How* were involuntary commitment proceedings and decisions socially organized? It's not surprising that I should eventually ask this question, given that I was working at UCLA—ethnomethodology's hallowed ground. From the beginning, ethnomethodology has been preoccupied with the *hows* of social organization (see Heritage, 1984). The inspiration to concentrate on the *hows* of court processes, rather than on the *whys* of court outcomes, was close at hand. Being at the center of discussions of ethnomethodology, conversation analysis, phenomenology, and ethnography, it was almost preordained to look into how commitment hearings and their outcomes were "done"—socially produced or accomplished. To do so would require me to set aside my anticipated field of causally related variables and look instead at a field of locally accountable social processes through which commitment hearing actors and outcomes were fashioned.

Examples from my fieldnotes and subsequent analyses reveal crucial differences this transformation would make. At the beginning of my study, I carefully recorded fieldnotes—brief narratives that Robert Emerson et al. (1995) call "jottings"—about what was going on in the hearings. These jottings tended to focus on the variables I figured would be central to the commitment process. I also recorded jottings of casual conversations or informal interviews I had with court personnel. At the end of each day, I would clean up my notes and write analytic memos regarding what I observed. The jottings and memos were substantive and organized narratives describing relations I observed between variables, as well as larger patterns of labeling in the courtroom. The *whats* and *whys* of the moment took precedence over the detail of the *hows* that brought matters into view. But I still didn't have an analytic handle on how commitment decisions were made. I wasn't alone. The labeling literature was replete with contradictory or equivocal findings (see Holstein, 1993; Warren, 1982).

As I grappled with my inability to come to analytic terms with the commitment process, I was simultaneously learning some of the fundamentals and subtleties of ethnomethodologically informed fieldwork from colleagues at UCLA—most prominently Robert Emerson, Melvin Pollner, and Michael Lynch. I was also developing a rudimentary, primitive facility with the empirical apparatus of conversation analysis—most importantly an appreciation for recording and analyzing the fine-grained, real-time detail of talk in interaction. Being in the same departmental hallways with Harold Garfinkel and Emanuel Schegloff didn't hurt.

The upshot of my exposure to these new sources of insight and inspiration was clearly manifest in the ways I began to conceive of and record happenings in the field. In order to grasp how courtroom talk transpired, I began to pay much closer attention to the turn-by-turn dynamics of talk during the hearings, instead of presumed relations between variables. This wasn't a doctrinaire shift to a conversation-analytic agenda, but it did involve greater appreciation for the sequential environment of courtroom talk.

Jottings and summary fieldnotes didn't lend themselves to this sort of approach, so I began to produce close-to-verbatim "do-it-yourself" transcripts of the commitment hearings (Gubrium & Holstein, 2009; West, 1996). The procedural shift is evident from a simple glance at my fieldnotes before and after my conceptual and analytic shift. Narrative jottings and summaries gave way to notepad pages divided into columns labeled by categories of routine commitment hearings participants (e.g., judge, public defender, assistant district attorney, psychiatric professional, candidate patient). My scribbled recordings of the turn-by-turn hearing talk eventually took the form of imperfect utterance-by-utterance "transcripts" of courtroom talk, which hardly resembled my previous fieldnotes (see Holstein, 1993). These transcripts could then be closely scrutinized and analyzed for their socially organized and socially organized components.

A series of analytic inspirations started my courtroom study on one conceptual track, and then switched it to another. And as my fieldnotes and transcripts graphically show, my observational procedures changed accordingly. My methodological concerns shifted from attempts to capture correlations between variables into methods for seeing in close detail how salient courtroom matters were "talked into being" during commitment hearings. Inspiration transformed both the conceptual and empirical fields and the methods used to apprehend them.

But the methodological transformation wasn't the end of the story. My do-it-yourself transcripts of talk-in-interaction now made it possible to see the field (i.e., commitment hearings) in a different light. Detailed, sequenced records of courtroom talk now became the field, replacing relations between causal variables. Detailed records of the reconfigured empirical field made it possible to pursue ethnomethodology's concern for the practical accomplishment of accountable social realities—the *hows* of commitment hearings. Accordingly, changes in data collection procedures made it possible to *conceptualize* and *analyze* the interactional, discursive work of "doing" commitment proceedings, accountably constructing the situated meanings of what had previously been seen as fixed variables, and accomplishing accountable hearing outcomes.

Analytic inspiration thus provoked procedural change, which, in turn, made it possible to ask new analytic questions and devise new analytic strategies. This was methodological reflexivity in action—conceptual inspiration inciting procedural change which provoked further conceptual and analytic innovation—with procedural tolerance always in tow. The analyses that emerged along the way hardly resembled the fixed-variable studies of the labeling debate; they involved far more than specifying new variables with greater explanatory power. Instead, the analyses radically reconsidered what a "variable" might be and concentrated on the local, discursive *production* of variables, their situated meanings, and their effects on hearing proceedings and outcomes. Taking further inspiration from new variations on ethnographic analysis—for example, Gubrium's (1988) "ethnography of practice" or Hugh Mehan's (1979) "constitutive ethnography"—methodological reflexivity constantly reflected and refracted analytic inspiration.

Methodological Reflexivity

It is tempting to suggest that the false starts and reconceptualizations of my courtroom research resulted from the practical demands encountered by a neophyte researcher who was a newcomer to the particular field site. There's some truth to this. But the fact remains that more than simple procedural adjustments marked the evolution of the fieldwork and analysis. Procedural tolerance worked hand-in-hand with analytic inspiration to transform the very parameters of *the field*, which in turn prompted new fieldwork procedures. The practical and reflexive evolution of ethnographic methods is not just visible in the mistakes, missteps, and false starts of the novice. Methodological flexibility and reflexivity are part of the ethnographic craft a*cross the board*. Consider some observations regarding my most recent field project.

Colleagues Richard Jones, George Koonce, and I were in the early stages of expanding Koonce's doctoral research on American football players' "transition" out of the National Football League (NFL)—their version of "retirement." Koonce, a former NFL player, had established the groundwork with a biographical account of his transition, augmented by a set of semi-structured interviews with other former NFL players. The more extensive project aimed to expand, confirm, deepen, and/or reject the explanatory power derived from Koonce's personal experience. The research team decided it was advantageous for Koonce to conduct additional interviews with key informants—former players with transition experiences of their own. Factors such as his presumed rapport and access were key.

Reviewing Koonce's previously collected interview data, two methodological challenges developed. First, the structured interview guidelines were inadequate for capturing the narrative realities that emerged in and around the interview situation itself, but that were not technically or procedurally part of the interview. Koonce knew there were important stories left untold, and all three team members realized from viewing interview transcripts or listening to recordings of interviews that more might be gleaned than the formal interviews were eliciting. It became clear that themes or threads of insight and experience not only wended their way through the interview narrative but also infused the surrounding conversations between research team members (especially Koonce) and informants that opened up entirely unexpected realms of experience for consideration.

Accordingly, we needed to modify our research strategy and procedures. The emergent plan implicated practical demands, procedural tolerance, and analytic inspiration. We didn't simply revamp the interview guide—a common, straightforward procedural move. Rather, we reconceptualized the interview itself, and the selves and social worlds that we were attempting to study. Analytic inspiration wasn't far off, given that I had been exploring a more "active" understanding of the interview process for over two decades (see Holstein & Gubrium, 1995, 2021). The procedural upshot of viewing the interview itself as "active" meaning-making practice was to sequester many traditional tenets of scientific interviewing, most notably setting aside the use of formal interview questions, abandoning if not subverting "standardization." The more active vision of the interview process let us imagine the interview subject (as well as the interviewer) in terms of far greater narrative agency and scope. Our analytic stance vis-à-vis the interview material changed from a vision of tapping the more-or-less passive respondent's vessel of answers into engaging a more interpretively active subject who might collaboratively generate project-relevant information within the interview interaction. The interview—now more actively construed—became a distinctly collaborative venture.

Informal conversations between research team members—mainly Koonce, but occasionally Jones and Holstein—and informants now became occasions for information gathering. Casual talk, reminiscences, interview preliminaries, and disengagements became "data," not simply the "niceties" that surrounded formal data collection. Participants in conceptually reconstituted interviews provided mutual provocation and elaboration for recollections of NFL transition experiences. This vastly expanded our field of information to include myriad encounters with former players where they spoke of their careers, start to finish.

By most counts, such interviewer participation is "bad form," methodologically speaking. It certainly destabilizes the standardization which underpins survey research's interest in generalization. But situations in which researchers are interested in exploring uncharted horizons of meaning often challenge methodological dogma and formal data collection procedures. As Gubrium (1993) has shown, biographical particulars, narrative linkages, and horizons of meaning mutually incite and inform one another (also see Gubrium & Holstein, 1998; Marvasti, 2003). Moreover, occasions for "speaking of life" are ubiquitous and emergent; collecting discursive data in only formal information-gathering settings is likely to forfeit opportunities to hear how experience is given voice on myriad other occasions. Conversations involving more than a single speaker and/or listener frequently implicate more than one teller of life's tales, so to speak. Gubrium's rich examination of how stories of the lives of nursing home residents came in many forms and circumstances—often involving multiple tellers of the tales—serves as an exemplar for how experiences can be collaboratively and authentically constructed—a bit of analytic inspiration in its own.

Interestingly, as we reconceptualized how we might gather information, Koonce situationally became both researcher and research subject on various occasions as ostensible respondents took the opportunity to interrogate Koonce for his own reflections on the transition process. This, of course, involved a rather dramatic reconfiguration of selves, subjects, and subjectivity in our research. As Marvasti and Gubrium suggest, researchers hold and constantly revise images of who research participants are—including the researchers themselves—and what roles they occupy in the field of study. This, by reflexive turn, often results in reformulations of how a research situation is construed, observed, and analyzed. As Gubrium notes, ethnographers are constantly asking: "Who are these subjects we are observing?"

This happened often in our NFL project, particularly around the issue of who was an informant and who was the object of inquiry. Such questions brought into focus the pervasiveness of methodological reflexivity. Not only did we constantly grapple with the place and role Koonce held in the research, but we often discovered that persons we had a priori designated as "informants" were also key practitioners in unanticipated social worlds we had heretofore not considered. Subjects became objects, and vice versa, in a continually unfolding process.

For example, at one point in our research, Jones and I attended a "reunion" of former NFL players. Koonce not only attended as a participant but also used the occasion to schedule formal interviews with a number of former players. As part of the "festivities," Jones and I accompanied Koonce to an autograph signing at a popular sports bar where a group of former players were "selling" their autographs to avid fans. The setting for the signing was modest—an adjoining room where folding tables were set up. Players took seats at the tables and autograph seeks lined up and, having paid appropriate fees, proceeded to get the autographs they sought. Jones and I were joined on the periphery of these close quarters by perhaps a half dozen other onlookers. As time passed, I found myself standing for a couple of hours next to a woman—I'll call her Nicole—who I came to discover was attending the reunion in the company of her long-time boyfriend, one of the former NFL players. Having introduced myself and made my researcher identity clear, I casually inquired about the post-NFL-life of her boyfriend (assuring her of confidentiality). At that moment, I took Nicole to be an interesting informant—a source of information about the former NFL player's life after he retired. Nicole—like me—was killing time so she gladly responded to my questions and offered observations about the challenges her boyfriend faced, providing stock answers about his loss of fame, his reduced financial status, and lingering effects of his many past on-the-field injuries.

As the conversation progressed, however, it became increasingly clear that Nicole had stories to tell that went beyond the present state of affairs of her boyfriend's now-mundane post-football life. Rather, her stories became both more personal and more general as she began to talk about her own shared experiences with former players. She placed *herself* prominently in the stories of the post-NFL transition and began to speak of "women" in the lives of NFL players—how they held significant and prominent roles in the players' everyday lives, both pre- and post-retirement. She spoke of how roles and relationships changed as players retired. In ways that I hadn't anticipated, the conversation transformed Nicole from merely an informant about former players' lives into an integral part of the social worlds of players, both before and after retirement. Whereas I had approached Nicole to get an "up close" description of the challenges of her boyfriend's transition, I came away viewing her (and others in roles like hers) as prominent features of the social worlds I was trying to describe. Viewing Nicole as an agentic subject with a pivotal role in an NFL player's life resulted in my rethinking important dimensions of NFL lives that needed to be analyzed. After the conversation with Nicole, who I had considered a "mere informant," I now thought about the lives of NFL wives, girlfriends, and families, and their places in the stories and social worlds of post-NFL transitions. Nicole was now a significant actor in her own right—a person whose life warranted study. Using Nicole's stories as points of departure, I began to piece together a frequently ignored dimension of pre- and post-NFL life in which significant others—usually wives or girlfriends, but also other family members, friends, posse members, etc.—had constituted major aspects of pre- and post-NFL social worlds. This transformation of selves, subjects, and objects eventually resulted in significant sections of several chapters of the subsequent book, *Is There Life After Football?* (Holstein et al., 2015).

Returning to the issue of methodological reflexivity in Whitaker's and Atkinson's terms, reframing our view of the interview—that is, reconceptualizing a research method—reoriented our project regarding the object of study as well as how it should be studied. Our way of seeing in effect produced what we saw; method produced knowledge. And so did the reconfiguration of subjectivities, which pointed our project in new directions. This, in turn, led us to tweak our research procedures.

Crafting Ethnography

Reflexivity is a slippery concept, promising a whirlwind of reflection, taunting us with the possibility of infinite regress (see Lynch, 2000). In the version emphasized here, methods of observation produce that which is observed. At the same time, that which is ostensibly observed encourages particular methodological choices. This, of course, suggests a conundrum: An empirical field itself may apparently mandate particular methods of observation, but observational procedures create the phenomena that are subsequently observed to be the field. This realization may incite ontological debates regarding the absolute nature of objects, being, and existence (see Gubrium & Holstein, 2009). Acknowledging methodological reflexivity, however, doesn't require the researcher to resolve ontological matters regarding the primacy of observational methods versus the objects of observation. The craft of ethnography doesn't demand particular points of analytic or procedural departure, only an awareness of the reflexivity of research methodology. Nor is awareness of the various incarnations of reflexivity license for procedural carelessness. Despite the challenges, ethnography still aspires to the systematic, empirically centered understanding of social lives and worlds. The complexities of doing ethnography challenge methods but don't subvert them.

This afterword highlights some of these complexities, displaying the enigmatic character of reflexivity in the chapter's inability to clearly separate the phenomena it describes into the analytic categories it specifies for those descriptions. Ostensibly about "analytic inspiration," one section ends up highlighting the ways research methods reflexively constitute the research field. A second section, putatively about methodological reflexivity, inescapably calls upon "analytic inspiration" as the point of departure for the reflexive transformation of the field of study.

Fortunately, the key to *Crafting Ethnographic Fieldwork* is not to belabor the daunting complexities or philosophical paradoxes of reflexivity. Rather it is to approach ethnography as *practice*. This is evident across the substantive contributions to the book. These chapters deftly showcase everyday ethnographic practices centered on the book's three areas of emphasis: concrete ethnographic field sites, everyday conceptions of ethnographic selves, and the challenges of engaging social worlds. The chapters present in close detail what it means to "be there" ethnographically. In situ practice is the very heart of each ethnographic project. The chapter lineup—from the boxing ring and youth detention homes to migrant camps, preschools, and breastfeeding communities—takes readers to "where it's at," so to speak. The practical challenges of site-specificity, imagined subjectivity, procedural tolerance, analytic inspiration, and methodological reflexivity constitute the practical contours of the ethnographer's craft.

Accordingly, engaging these contours alerts ethnographers to myriad formidable methodological, analytic, and empirical challenges. But it also encourages them to confidently proceed, even while facing the potentially daunting prospect of not knowing what will emerge in and as "the field." One can't anticipate all contingencies, even when the terrain has been sketched beforehand. Strategy and procedure are both principled and practical matters that can't be fully specified in advance. As they proceed, ethnographers must understand and appreciate that the field itself may change based on encounters with empirical discoveries as well as conceptual and procedural decisions researchers make. There's no formula for doing good ethnography, just good craft.

References

Emerson, R. M. (1969). *Judging delinquents*. Aldine.

Emerson, R. M., Fretz, R., & Shaw, L. L. (1995). *Writing ethnographic fieldnotes*. University of Chicago Press.

Garfinkel, H. (1967). *Studies in ethnomethodology*. Prentice-Hall.

Goffman, E. (1961). *Asylums*. Doubleday.

Gubrium, J. F. (1988). *Analyzing field reality*. Sage.

Gubrium, J. F. (1993). *Speaking of life: Horizons of meaning for nursing home residents*. Aldine de Gruyter.

Gubrium, J. F., & Holstein, J. A. (1997). *The new language of qualitative method*. Oxford University Press.

Gubrium, J. F., & Holstein, J. A. (1998). Narrative practice and the coherence of personal stories. *The Sociological Quarterly*, *39*, 24–50.

Gubrium, J. F., & Holstein, J. A. (2009). *Analyzing narrative reality*. Sage.

Gubrium, J. F., & Holstein, J. A. (2014). Analytic inspiration in ethnographic fieldwork. In U. Flick (Ed.), *Sage handbook of qualitative data analysis* (pp. 35–48). Sage.

Heritage, J. A. (1984). *Garfinkel and ethnomethodology*. Polity.

Holstein, J. A. (1993). *Court-ordered insanity: Interpretive practice and involuntary commitment*. Aldine de Gruyter.

Holstein, J. A., & Gubrium, J. F. (1995). *The active interview*. Sage.

Holstein, J. A., & Gubrium, J. F. (2021). Interviewing as a form of narrative practice. In D. Silverman (Ed.), *Qualitative research* (5th ed., pp. 70–85). Sage.

Holstein, J. A., Jones, R. S., & Koonce, G. E., Jr. (2015). *Is there life after football? Surviving the NFL*. New York University Press.

Kitsuse, J. I. (1962). Societal reactions to deviant behavior. *Social Problems*, *9*, 247–256.

Lynch, M. (2000). Against reflexivity as an academic virtue and source of privileged knowledge. *Theory, Culture & Society*, *17*(3), 26–54.

Marvasti, A. B. (2003). *Being homeless: Textual and narrative constructions*. Lexington Books.

Mehan, H. (1979). *Learning lessons*. Harvard University Press.

Scheff, T. J. (1966). *Being mentally ill*. Aldine.

Warren, C. A. B. (1982). *The court of last resort*. University of Chicago Press.

West, C. (1996). Ethnography and orthography: A (modest) methodological proposal. *Journal of Contemporary Ethnography*, *25*, 327–352.

Whitaker, E. M., & Atkinson, P. (2021). *Reflexivity in social research*. Palgrave Macmillan.

INDEX

Printed in Great Britain
by Amazon